EMPIRICAL MUSICOLOGY

D0841171

Empirical Musicology
Aims, Methods, Prospects

EDITED BY

Eric Clarke and Nicholas Cook

OXFORD
UNIVERSITY PRESS

2004

OXFORD
UNIVERSITY PRESS

Oxford New York

Auckland Bangkok Buenos Aires Cape Town Chennai
Dar es Salaam Delhi Hong Kong Istanbul Karachi Kolkata
Kuala Lumpur Madrid Melbourne Mexico City Mumbai Nairobi
São Paulo Shanghai Taipei Tokyo Toronto

Copyright © 2004 by Oxford University Press, Inc.

Published by Oxford University Press, Inc.
198 Madison Avenue, New York, New York 10016

www.oup.com

Oxford is a registered trademark of Oxford University Press

All rights reserved. No part of this publication may be reproduced,
stored in a retrieval system, or transmitted, in any form or by any means,
electronic, mechanical, photocopying, recording, or otherwise,
without the prior permission of Oxford University Press.

Two figures from F. Lerdahl and R. Jackendoff, *A Generative Theory
of Tonal Music* (Cambridge, Mass.: MIT Press, 1983), pp. 259, 260, are
reprinted with permission from MIT Press.

Figure 8 (Pitch/contour schemata recognised in early Mozart by
Robert O. Gjerdingen's ART pour l'art neural network, p. 360) from
R. Gjerdingen, "Categorization of musical patterns by self-organizing
neuronlike networks," *Music Perception* 7 (1990): 339–369, is reprinted
with permission from Blackwell Publishing Ltd.

The segmentation graph of Berg, "Warm die Lufte," bars 19–21 (p. 199),
from J. Doerksen, "Set-class salience and Forte's theory of genera," *Music
Analysis* 17 (1998): 195–205, is reprinted with permission from Blackwell Publishing Ltd.

Quotations from pp. 49–54 and figure 18 (Harmonic analysis of "Yankee
Doodle," p. 63) from D. Temperley, "An algorithm for harmonic analysis," *Music Perception* 15 (1997): 31–68, are reprinted with permission
from the University of California Press.

Library of Congress Cataloging-in-Publication Data
Empirical musicology : aims, methods, prospects / edited by Eric Clarke
and Nicholas Cook.
  p. cm.
Includes bibliographical references.
ISBN 0-19-516749-X (hardcover); ISBN 0-19-516750-3 (pbk.)
ISBN-13 978-0-19-516750-4 (pbk.)

1. Musicology. 2. Empiricism. I. Clarke, Eric F. II. Cook, Nicholas, 1950–
ML3797.1.E47 2004
780'.72—dc22   2004012210

9 8 7 6 5 4 3

Printed in the United States of America
on acid-free paper

CONTENTS

CONTRIBUTORS

Eric Clarke, Professor of Music at the University of Sheffield, has published on the psychology of performance, the study of rhythm, and musical meaning. Recent publications have focused on motion in music, artificial modeling of expressive performance, meaning in pop music by Pulp, Frank Zappa, and P. J. Harvey, and the relationship between music, psychology, and cultural studies. He was Chair of the Society for Research in Psychology of Music and Music Education from 1994 to 2000 and is on the editorial boards of *Psychology of Music*, *Music Perception*, *Musicae Scientiae*, and *Music Analysis*.

Nicholas Cook, Professor of Music at Royal Holloway, University of London, has published journal articles on a wide range of musical topics from aesthetics and analysis to psychology and pop. A Fellow of the British Academy and former Editor of the *Journal of the Royal Musical Association*, his books include *A Guide to Musical Analysis*; *Music, Imagination, and Culture*; *Beethoven: Symphony No. 9*; *Analysis through Composition*; *Analysing Musical Multimedia*; and *Music: A Very Short Introduction*. He is Director of the AHRB Research Centre for the History and Analysis of Musical Recordings (CHARM).

Jane W. Davidson, Reader in Music at the University of Sheffield, completed M.A. and Ph.D. degrees in Music at City University while working as an opera singer. After jobs at Keele University and City University, she took up her current post at Sheffield in 1995, where she lectures and researches on psychological issues related to performance. She has published very widely on this and other topics, and was Editor of the journal *Psychology of Music* from 1997 to 2001. She maintains an active career in performance and direction, working on projects from opera to dance, and completed an M.A. in Contemporary Dance Choreography in 2002.

Tia DeNora teaches Sociology at the University of Exeter, and has special interests in music sociology. Her books are: *Beethoven and the Construction of Genius* (1995); *Music and Everyday Life* (2000); and *After Adorno: Rethinking Music Sociology* (2003).

Philippe Depalle received a Ph.D. degree in Acoustics from the Université du Maine, Le Mans. He was an assistant professor from 1985 to 1988 at the École Supérieure d'Électricité, and a researcher in the Analysis/Synthesis team at the Institut de Recherche et Coordination Acoustique/Musique (IRCAM) from 1984 to 1997. He was visiting professor at the Université de Montréal from 1997 to 1999, and since 1999 he has been Associate Professor in the Faculty of Music at McGill University, Montréal, where he chaired the Music Technology Area from 1999 to 2002. His research interests are related to the modeling, synthesis, analysis, and processing of sound signals for musical applications.

Stephen McAdams received training in music theory and composition, electronic music, computer music, experimental psychology, neurosciences, and hearing and speech sciences. He received his Ph.D. in Hearing and Speech Sciences in 1984 from Stanford University. He has worked since 1981 at the Institut de Recherche et Coordination Acoustique/Musique (IRCAM) where he founded the Music Perception and Cognition team in 1984. He is currently Research Director in the Centre National de Recherche Scientifique (CNRS) and will direct a new laboratory for research in Auditory Perception and Cognition in the Cognitive Studies Department of the Ecole Normale Supérieure in Paris. His research interests include auditory scene analysis, timbre perception, ecological acoustics, and music cognition.

Anthony Pople was a Professor of Music at the universities of Lancaster, Southampton and Nottingham. He was Editor of *Music Analysis* from 1995 to 1999 and co-authored the extensive entry "Analysis" in the 2001 Edition of *The New Grove*. His many publications include books on Berg, Messiaen, Scriabin, and Stravinsky, together with studies of works by Vaughan Williams and Tippett. His *Tonalities* project uses sophisticated but user-friendly computer software to engage with the analysis of music in widely varying styles beyond common-practice tonality. He died in 2003.

Jonathan P. J. Stock is Reader in music at the University of Sheffield. He is author of three books: *Musical Creativity in Twentieth-Century China*, on the key folk musician Abing (1996); *World Sound Matters* (1996)—a three-volume anthology of transcriptions, recordings, and notes for high school teachers and pupils; and *Huju: Traditional Opera in Modern Shanghai* (2002). Recently published articles discuss the interplay of speech tone and melody in Beijing opera, ethnomusicology and "new musicology," and timbral views of formal structure in Mozart's piano concertos. He also edits book reviews for *The World of Music*.

W. Luke Windsor's research has focused on the perception and production of musical rhythm and meter, expressive and cooperative timing in piano performance, and the analysis and perception of electroacoustic music. He is a senior lecturer in the School of Music at the University of Leeds, where he has worked since 1998. Prior to this he worked as a researcher in the UK and Netherlands, was involved in course development at the University of Sheffield. He is the coeditor, with Peter Desain, of *Rhythm Perception and Production* (2000).

EMPIRICAL MUSICOLOGY

CHAPTER 1

Introduction:
What Is Empirical Musicology?

Nicholas Cook and Eric Clarke

I believe there's a real world out there, because not all of my fantasies work.

The words are those of the composer and music theorist Benjamin Boretz (1977: 242), and they articulate a level at which it is hard to envisage work in musicology or theory that is *not* empirical. Any archival musicologist, after all, knows that facts can be very hard indeed—though, as we shall see, it would be more correct to say that facts are a matter of interpretation and that it is the data that are hard. In the same way, different analysts' Schenkerian interpretations of a given passage may well differ (and Schenkerian analysis is supported, or at least surrounded, by a discourse that is largely speculative if not at times metaphysical), but they are closely regulated by the score on which they are based; indeed the trial-and-error process by which music-analytical interpretations develop, with observation leading to interpretation and interpretation in turn guiding observation, is a model of close, empirically regulated reading. Theorists and composers have both on occasion invoked the language of experimentation, too; for example, Marion Guck (1994: 62) has described her analyses as "(thought) experiments," but the best known of such invocations is Milton Babbitt's (1972a: 148) claim that "every musical composition justifiably may be regarded as an experiment, the embodiment of hypotheses as to certain specific conditions of musical coherence."

In short, there is no useful distinction to be drawn between empirical and non-empirical musicology, because there can be no such thing as a truly non-empirical musicology; what is at issue is the extent to which musicological discourse is grounded on empirical observation, and conversely the extent to which observation is regulated by discourse. The idea of regulation is essential in this context. Michel Foucault (1970) has illustrated this point through reference to the comparative illustrations of human and bird skeletons published in 1555 by Pierre Belon: as Foucault says, these illustrations look like the products of nineteenth-century comparative anatomy, but the resemblance is little more than chance, because the interpretational grids of sixteenth-century and of nineteenth-century thought are so different.[1] In other words, what we generally think of as empirically-based knowledge—as science—depends not only on observation but also on the incorporation of observation within patterns of investigation involving generalization and explanation. (That is what turns data into facts.) It also depends on the more fundamental criterion of replication: if an observation is to be regarded as trustworthy, it should be possible to make it on different occasions, and it should be possible for different people to make it. The issue, then, is whether musicology fulfils these conditions—whether, in short, its interface with Boretz's "real world out there" is as well managed and understood as it might be.

Musicologists are certainly aware of the distinction between data and facts (see, e.g., Dahlhaus 1983: 34). Researchers with a background in the hard or social sciences, however, might well question whether most musicologists are sufficiently aware of the methodological consequences of this distinction. Like most humanities scholars, musicologists are prone to build interpretations on very small data sets or even on single instances, and the less the evidence that has survived from the past, the stronger this tendency will be. In the study of medieval music, for instance, so little documentation has survived that what does exist often lacks a secure context, and under such conditions it becomes impossible to avoid circular argument: if your starting point is that there are hidden meanings in fourteenth-century motets, then you are bound to deduce that there were sophisticated contemporary audiences capable of appreciating them, and this then becomes evidence for the hidden meanings (Leech-Wilkinson 2000). Without sufficient evidence to prove or disprove the hypothesis, it is simply not possible to cut through the circle; the problem is endemic. It follows that, as David Huron (1999) has pointed out, the issue is not one of good or bad methodology, but of what is viable in data-poor as against data-rich fields. In most (though not all) of the physical and social sciences, it is possible through systematic programs of observation to acquire large bodies of data, which may then be manipulated statistically and subjected to measures of statistical significance. But in fields like medieval music, this is simply not possible, and so arguments based on statistically insignificant samples or single instances are inevitable; a further result, arguably, is that scholars become wedded to their interpretive hypotheses, since there is rarely the evidence to conclusively overthrow them, resulting in a degree of conservatism that can easily turn into dogmatism.[2] That is the price that has to be paid for working in data-poor fields.

While this is no argument for abandoning such fields, there would be grounds for legitimate criticism if musicologists working in data-rich fields did not take full advantage of the methods available under such conditions, instead restricting themselves to traditional "humanities" approaches developed for data-poor fields—and one of the messages of this book is that musicology is or could be, in many instances, a significantly "data richer" field than we generally give it credit for. (More bluntly, there may be many musicological certainties that would not survive a systematic engagement with the available data.) The same applies to a second characteristic of most work in musicology, which is its retrospective nature. One of the obvious determinants of historical method is that you can't run history again under different conditions and see how it turns out. (What would the history of nineteenth-century music have been like if Mozart had died in 1845, at the age of 89?) Once again, there is no point complaining about this; it is simply how history is. You could reasonably complain, however, if there were areas of musicology in which prospective work—

crudely, making predictions and then testing them—would be possible, but was not carried out, perhaps as a result of the discipline's predominantly historical self-image.

Empirical musicology, to summarize, can be thought of as musicology that embodies a principled awareness of both the potential to engage with large bodies of relevant data, and the appropriate methods for achieving this; adopting this term does not deny the self-evidently empirical dimension of all musicology, but draws attention to the potential of a range of empirical approaches to music that is, as yet, not widely disseminated within the discipline. And just as it is not a matter of empirical versus non-empirical, so we do not wish to draw an either/or distinction between the objective and the subjective. In order to illustrate this point we may return to Guck and her "(thought) experiments." She coins this term with specific reference to Hans David's description of the C♭ in bar 53 of the second movement from Mozart's G minor Symphony K 550 as "unexpected" (a description that Babbitt had in the 1960s characterized as an "incorrigible personal statement"),[3] and goes on to outline a way of thinking about the movement that explains this "unexpected" quality: she likens the C♭ to an "indomitable immigrant" (1994: 72), at its first appearance conspicuously foreign to the tonal environment of the movement, but eventually assimilated within it and even ultimately serving to transform it ("C♭ has succeeded to the leadership of its community" [1994: 70]). In short, she describes a way in which she can hear the music, and invites her reader to share her experience.

In what sense can this be properly called an experiment, "thought" or otherwise? There is no null hypothesis,[4] no control or randomization of potentially extraneous variables, no control group. To say that, however, is not to say—as a perhaps too casual reading of Babbitt might imply—that it is an exercise in uncontrolled, purely subjective speculation. If Guck's frankly fictive account of the immigrant C♭ articulates a way of hearing the music that other people can share, then it can be regarded as a discovery procedure resulting in a replication of experience, and hence in a measure of intersubjective agreement. And indeed resort to measures which are replicable but not necessarily definable in objective terms is quite normal in musicology. An example is the coding of folk songs employed in Alan Lomax's Cantometrics project, which involved a large number of researchers scoring recorded songs for such qualities as nasality: Lomax explained that we don't know how to define nasality in objective or productional terms—but what matters, he said, is that in practice there is "good consensus on the presence of great nasality or its relative absence" (1968: 72).

Guck's and Lomax's arguments, however, would have cut little ice within the culture of objectivity that characterized much postwar musicology and theory (and in which some of the origins of empirical musicology are to be found). Rather like the compositions at the contemporaneous Darmstadt *Ferienkürse für neue Musik*, such work reflected a distrust of conventional approaches and even terminologies; the traditional language of musicology seemed hopelessly compromised by latent subjectivity, and so it seemed necessary to reduce analytical statements to objective propositions or, if this couldn't be done, to abjure them. Arthur Komar (1971: 11) referred to "designing a set of rigorous terms for music" as "the serious but unfulfilled goal of current music theory," but the definitive statement, dating from 10 years earlier, was once again Babbitt's ("there is but one kind of language, one kind of method for the verbal formulation of 'concepts' and the verbal analysis of such formulations: 'scientific' language and 'scientific' method" [Babbitt 1972c: 3, but originally published in 1961]). And when translated into practice, the results included attempts to implement existing analytical approaches as computer programs (Kassler 1967), or to express new ones in the forms of symbolic logic (Boretz 1970) or machine-readable algorithms, as in the case Allen Forte's (1973) pitch class (pc) set theory. They also included some picturesque attempts to extract rigorous content from such "incorrigible" ordinary-language statements as the claim in *Cobbett's Cyclopedic Survey of Chamber Music* that "the spirit of nationalism is felt in all of the best chamber music": Fred Hofstetter, a pioneer of humanities computing, reduced this to the more straightforward claim that "composers differ from one another as a function of their nationalities" (Hofstetter 1979: 105), selected a representative sample of chamber music by French, German, Czechoslovakian, and Russian composers, defined a stylistic measure (the relative frequency of different intervals), and did the sums. His conclusion, perhaps unsurprisingly, was that there are indeed differences between national styles, and that the most distinctive style is the Russian.

The conclusion, of course, was not the important thing. The point of Hofstetter's project was to demonstrate that informal statements about music could be reduced to formal propositions, in which form they could be subjected to rigorous testing. And it is this ideologically motivated idea of reduction that seems so foreign from the vantage point of the twenty-first century, when this kind of unreflective positivism is no longer widespread, even (one might almost say "particularly") in the hard sciences. The "nothing but" kind of objectivity embodied in Hofstetter's project is evident enough, but subtler forms of the same thinking can be more insidious: as Gerald Balzano (1987) has convincingly argued, a chronic problem in music psychology has been the tendency to understand perception as an internalization of objective (e.g., acoustic) categories and structures. Postwar reductionism, then, has left a legacy that has not been entirely shaken off, but it is not the focus of "empirical musicology" as defined in this book: the culture of objectivity in the 1960s and 70s reflected an epistemological world view formed by the ideal of scientific progress, a stance that might be described not so much as "empirical" as "empiricist." The orientation of this book, by contrast, is intended as an essentially pragmatic one, in which reduction is seen—in Huron's (1999) words—as "*a potentially useful strategy for discovery* rather than *a belief about how the world is.*"

In some ways the positivist approaches of the postwar period were more a matter of appearances than of substance; even at the time, Forte's pc set theory was criticized on the grounds that, for all its apparent objectivity, it was based on analytical decisions about how to divide the music up into segments for which there were no properly defined criteria. But there was a quite different problem that early examples of apparently objective analysis tended to present, which is what one was meant to *do* with them, what their value was. An appropriate example, since it achieved considerable exposure at the time, was Matt Hughes's (1977) "quantitative analysis" of Schubert's *Moment Musical* in C major, Op. 94 no. 1. This was certainly objective in the sense that a suitably programmed computer could have carried out the analysis without human intervention: it began with a straightforward note count, not in the serial sense but as a simple computation of how many Cs, C♯s, Ds, and so on there were (that is, it is pitch classes that were counted, and the values were weighted by durations). This provided a measure of the tonal "orientation" of the piece (which turned out to be directed toward G rather than the tonic, C); the values for each pitch class were then mapped onto the cycle of fifths, and analysis of the resulting pattern of peaks yielded a measure of the piece's tonal "complexity." What is of concern here, however, is not the details of the method, but the context in which it was presented, and what came of it. The reason for its exposure is that it formed part of a "symposium" on Op. 94 no. 1 published in a widely disseminated collection edited by Maury Yeston; the other elements of the symposium were a "compositional analysis" by Lawrence Moss and two Schenkerian analyses by Carl Schachter and John Rothgeb. The two Schenkerians engaged with one another, but otherwise—as frequently happens at symposia—the contributors talked (or rather wrote) past one another, without any form of mutual communication being opened up. And since then, Hughes's approach has disappeared more or less without trace.

All this amounts to saying that there was little context within which to understand Hughes's analysis, and that context is essential to value. This can be made clear through a comparison with current work taking place on the border between music theory and cognitive psychology, which embraces the same kind of quantitative approach illustrated by Hughes's analysis but sets it in a more developed context. Fred Lerdahl's *Tonal Pitch Space* (2001) builds on the foundation of his well-known work with Ray Jackendoff (*A Generative Theory of Tonal Music*, 1983), but fills in some of the gaps of the earlier theory by incorporating a model of tonal "pitch space" that goes back in its essentials through Schoenberg and Riemann to Öttingen—a two-dimensional matrix whose axes are minor thirds and perfect fifths. In essence Lerdahl uses this pitch space as a means of evaluating the perceptual distance between different pitch classes, and this enables him to develop a range of quantitative measures for tonal tension and the attraction between pitch classes and chords, including a model of key derivation. What is important here is not the undoubted technical sophistication of Lerdahl's model, but the diversity of its linkages. In the first place, like *A Generative Theory of Tonal Music*, it is based in musical intuition (and Lerdahl is strikingly keen to ground it in his credentials as a composer rather than as a theorist, writing in the very first sentences of the book that, following the publication of *A Generative Theory of Tonal Music*, "fresh theoretical ideas began to intrude on my time for composing. The only way to unburden myself of them was to work them out and write them down" [2001: v]). In the second place, it not only draws on a variety of established theoretical traditions but is also illustrated through a variety of substantial analytical applications. And in the third place, it is expressed in more or less empirically testable terms, that is to say in terms of predictions of what listeners will perceive—and indeed the development of Lerdahl's thinking between 1983 and 2001 in part reflects his collaboration with a number of experimental psychologists, in particular Carol Krumhansl. It is these connections which provide the context that was lacking in Hughes's work.

Krumhansl has been a key figure in the interaction between music theory and cognitive psychology to which we referred; other major theorists with whom she has worked include Eugene Narmour, whose theoretical approach to melodic structure she has tested experimentally, concluding that "the uniformity with which the present results supported the implication-realization model encourages the view that the model has successfully codified psychological principles governing melodic expectations" (Krumhansl 1985: 78). In fact she organized a year-long seminar at Stanford University during 1993–1994 in which both Lerdahl and Narmour took part, along with the music theorist Robert Gjerdingen, as well as the music psychologists Jamshed Bharucha, Caroline Palmer, and of course Krumhansl herself; the outcomes were published in a special issue (1996) of *Music Perception*. All six researchers worked on the first movement of Mozart's Sonata in E♭, K 282, but the result is in some ways reminiscent of the symposium on Schubert's Op. 94 no. 1 in which Hughes's article appeared. Of the music psychologists, both Krumhansl and Palmer engage fully with the music theorists' work, each of them testing predictions derived from Lerdahl's and Narmour's models (with generally rather mixed success); Bharucha at least references the work of all three theorists. Lerdahl's contribution, which anticipates central elements of his 2001 book, includes a final section called "Connections" containing a single sentence on Gjerdingen, and a more extended discussion of Narmour: his aim here is to show how the basic insights of the implication-realization model can be accommodated within his own, more wide-ranging model. Narmour makes single-sentence references to each of Lerdahl and Gjerdingen. As for Gjerdingen, he conspicuously omits any direct citation of either Lerdahl or Narmour (though he does include a pointed reference to "oversimplified assertions based on an imagined calculus of imagined tonal forces," Gjerdingen 1996: 370), instead contributing an exercise in historical musicology that has few if any points of contact with the other articles. A final contribution by Leonard Meyer (who was not present at the seminars) underlines the effect of fragmentation through being structured as a series of separate responses to each of the participants.

The intention of these comments is not to question the significance of such work in its own terms, but to differentiate it from the "empirical musicology" proposed in this book. One obvious point about it is the division of labor: Lerdahl's, Narmour's, and Gjerdingen's work is intrinsically no more empirical than a great deal of music theory, while the work of the psychologists is not, and is not intended to be, musicological (thus Krumhansl specifically writes in the Preface of her *Cognitive Foundations of Musical Pitch* [1990: vii] that "the approach taken is that of cognitive psychology"). The model is rather one in which music theorists develop their ideas on a more or less intuitive basis, following which they are passed along to the psychologists and tested experimentally (a model replicated in the structure of the special issue of *Music Perception*, which presents the work of the three theorists followed by that of the three psychologists); in principle the expectation might be that the theorists would then revise their models in light of the experimental findings, though in practice examples of this are rather hard to find. But the more fundamental lack of communication is *between* the theorists, and the reason for this lies in the nature of the theories. Huron (1999) draws a distinction "between those theories that claim to usurp all others, and those theories that can co-exist with other theories"; in essence Lerdahl's and Narmour's theories fall into the former mould (which is why Lerdahl has to translate Narmour's concepts into his own theoretical language in order to accept them). Another way of saying more or less the same thing is that such totalizing, mutually incommensurable theories place the emphasis less on the analysis as such than on the theory which the analysis serves to illustrate; there is a real sense in which Lerdahl's and Narmour's books are not so much about tonal pitch space and melody, but about their respective theories of tonal pitch space and melody. And this theoretical commitment in turn means that the reductions on which their theories are based give the appearance, at least, of embodying beliefs about how the world is rather than simply representing potentially useful strategies for discoveries (to borrow Huron's words again). Such work, then, has a fundamentally different orientation from the pragmatic, tool-oriented approach to "empirical musicology" presented in this book, whose aim is to document a number of domains in which empirical methods have had an impact on broadly musicological enterprises, to provide some practical guidance in the application of those methods, and to illustrate some examples of the kinds of study that have made use of them, as well as considering some of their theoretical consequences.

The book is organized as follows. Chapter 2 (Stock) provides an overview of empirical methods in ethnomusicology with a particular focus on participant-observational fieldwork—a methodology that, though primarily associated with ethnomusicology, nonetheless has considerable potential for musicology more generally (i.e., it has as much application to Gilbert and Sullivan productions, and perhaps classical concerts at the Lincoln Center, as to ritual music in Taiwan). As Stock points out, the central principle of participant-observational fieldwork is the need for the researcher to become, as far as possible, an "insider" in the culture in question, to observe it and participate in it, and interpret it according to its own standards. Since music is very much more than just the production of certain sorts of sounds, but involves a huge variety of processes (social, financial, technological, organizational), participant observation has the potential to confront a researcher with an enormous mass, and wide variety, of data. The aim of the chapter is to provide practical advice on how to conduct and organize this kind of research—from preparation and planning, through the use of a field log, the organization of field notes and audio or video recordings, and appropriate interviewing techniques, to the manner in which the ideas, attitudes, and "expressive styles" of informants are represented in published accounts of the research. There may be considerable barriers to becoming anything like an insider in some specialized musical subcultures (a participant-observer in the Leeds International Piano Competition, for instance, would need to develop formidable skills as a pianist), but as Stock shows, using examples drawn from a wide range of musical traditions, there is a great deal that can be learned by studying any kind of music from within its own cultural practices.

Chapter 3 (DeNora) is also concerned with ways in which music might be studied and understood as socially embedded, but from the perspective of contemporary sociological theory and practice. Though the work of Theodor Adorno offers arguably the most ambitious and (still) influential theoretical tradition within the sociology of music, it certainly does not offer much encouragement for adopting an empirical approach to the subject. Adorno's approach, perhaps best understood against the backdrop of the appropriation of culture for purposes of propaganda in the Third Reich, was firmly rooted in a conceptually sophisticated analysis of music's ideological dimension; he saw social and ideological structures as replicated within music (as well as acted upon *by* music), and so encouraged "critical" readings that turned away from the actual social circumstances surrounding the production and reception of music, and towards the close reading of musical texts. Like other sociologists of music today (e.g., Martin 2002), DeNora sees serious dangers in the abstraction from social reality that such an approach entails. She identifies the continuing influence of Adorno in the writings of Lawrence Kramer and Susan McClary; such products of the so-called "New" musicology, she argues, maintain the traditional separation between musical works and the contexts of their production, performance, and use, and as a result have no means to describe music as it functions within real social settings, and in specific times and places. By contrast DeNora provides a "toolkit" of different empirical approaches to the analysis of music as a social process, as it participates in people's everyday lives and sense of identity. She gives examples of work that has examined the impact of social factors on composition (including that of commercial competition on innovation in pop music), social factors in the construction of musicians' reputations, the relationship between subcultural identity and musical taste, and music's role in the social construction of subjectivity. These studies use empirical methods ranging from participant observation (as discussed by Stock), through interviews and the analysis of historical documents, to the more impersonal methods of large-scale social statistics and economic surveys.

If DeNora's chapter engages with people's socially constructed experiences of themselves and others through and around music, chapter 4 (Davidson) considers a range of empirical methods to investigate the social character of music, as seen through the lens of a more explicitly psychological approach. Starting from the observation that the overwhelming majority of music-making is social in one way or another, Davidson looks at empirical methods for investigating music as social behavior, ranging from controlled experiments and personality inventories, through video-recorded observation and covert manipulation of people's musical environments, to the use of diaries and interviews as ways of tracking people's involvement in music. The cultural preoccupation with the musical skills of outstanding individuals has led to a significant body of research inquiring into the factors that might explain or predict the appearance of such skills, and Davidson describes the use of large-scale quantitative methods in this field, as well as more focused and intimate enquiries focusing on a single family. This provides an introduction to some of the principles and methods of qualitative data analysis, which are also employed in analyses of the social processes involved in ensemble rehearsal and performance — a domain that has enormous potential but which has only recently been explored within a social psychological context. Finally, a number of authors have proposed that musicians' social interactions and behaviors are a function of their personality types, and Davidson provides an overview of some of the empirical methods by which people have attempted to measure personality attributes.

Performance studies is the area of musicology which has arguably shown the greatest impact of empirical methods, and chapter 5 (Clarke) presents an overview of those methods and influences. As musicology has moved away from its overriding preoccupation with the score, and toward an understanding of music as performance, it has adopted some of the methods—and even some of the explanatory principles—of the kind of research on performance that originated in psychology. Empirical studies of performance go back as far as the end of the nineteenth century, but it is really since the development of cheaper and more powerful desktop computers in the late 1970s and 1980s, with their ability to handle large quantities of data and to record and analyze sound files on hard disk, that detailed empirical performance research has become a practical possibility for a large and growing population of researchers. The chapter gives an outline of this developing pattern of activity, with case studies illustrating the ways in which performance researchers have investigated keyboard performance directly from the instrument, a wider range of performances from sound recordings, and performers' gestures and body movements from video recordings. Practical advice about handling and interpreting MIDI (Musical Instrument Digital Interface) data is provided, as well as a discussion of the advantages and drawbacks of studying performance from the three most commonly used media (MIDI, sound, and video). Finally, the chapter considers the nature and explanatory function of artificial models of performance, arguing that they are best understood not as attempts to supplant or even mimic human expressive performances, but as a way of establishing the general principles or "norms" against which genuinely expressive performance is projected.

Chapters 6 and 7 (Cook and Pople, respectively) move away from music as a cultural, social, or behavioral event, and focus instead on the use of empirical methods in relation to musical scores. Any study of a musical score is empirical in that it pays attention in some fashion to the "data" of the music, but traditional analysis does this only on a very small scale, in relation to single pieces and with very little attention given to the insights that might be gained from a more "data-rich" and comparative approach. Chapter 6 (Cook) is concerned with various ways in which systematic investigations of larger repertories of music can be undertaken, starting with matters of representation (if the aim is to search large databases of music, how do you represent the music in a way that is flexible and appropriate?), and then going on to the kinds of tool that have been developed in order to search for systematic patterns in the data. Following a review of some earlier approaches to score representation and the operations that can be performed on the resulting databases, Cook focuses on David Huron's Humdrum toolkit—an approach to the representation of scores, and associated search techniques, which aims to be as flexible and open-ended as possible, allowing users to create new tools to suit their own purposes. As examples of the ways in which Humdrum can be used, Cook describes studies in which Huron and his coworkers have evaluated, for example, analytical claims regarding motivic structure in Brahms, the relationship between style and geographical location in folk song, and the extent to which trumpet music is idiomatic (i.e., is designed around the particular qualities and shortcomings of the instrument). Like any software, the practical usefulness of Humdrum depends on availability and usability, and the chapter concludes with an assessment of the difficulties of turning cutting-edge research approaches into the everyday tools of musicological enquiry.

Chapter 6 is concerned with the analysis of large bodies of musical data. By contrast, chapter 7 (Pople) takes a closer look at what can be done when systematic methods are applied to individual works—in other words formalized analytical methods. These date back at least as far as the 1960s when, as we have seen, there was a widespread feeling (especially in America) that the analysis of music should be made more scientific, but it is really only since the early 1980s—in particular with the publication in 1983 of Lerdahl and Jackendoff's *A Generative Theory of Tonal Music*—that serious attempts have been made to formalize, and even to automate, aspects of the analytical process. This formalism is not in itself a development in empirical method, but it has important empirical consequences: once a method is formalized, it becomes possible to apply it in a systematic and uniform manner and from this to discover what the empirical consequences of the approach really are. A range of approaches to which this applies is surveyed (from methods based on artificial intelligence to neural nets), but it is particularly applicable to Pople's own "Tonalities" project, with which the chapter ends. Designed specifically with a view to the transition between tonality and atonality in the early twentieth century, but with distinctly wider applications, the "Tonalities" software represents an empirical means by which analysts can become increasingly aware of the consequences of their intuitions concerning a piece's structure. Through testing their intuitions in this way, analysts confront their unconscious preoccupations and blindspots: just as artificial performance models of the kind discussed in chapter 5 confront researchers with the consequences of a given theory, so Pople's approach uses the computer to flush out the sometimes unwelcome consequences that informal methods can all too easily skirt around.

From the relatively clear representational categories of the score, chapter 8 (McAdams, Depalle, and Clarke) turns to the messier empirical reality of musical sounds, and the ways in which those sounds can be represented and empirically investigated. The first half of the chapter deals with a variety of ways in which sound, as a physical signal, can be represented in various kinds of computer-based visualizations, each allowing different kinds of properties to be revealed and different questions to be asked. The chapter provides a detailed and systematic account of the nature of these visualizations and the acoustical principles on which they are based, together with practical advice about how such representations might be generated, and examples from the musicological literature of the use of such methods with a variety of musical styles. The second half of the chapter turns to the ways in which a perceptual (rather than physical) representation of sounds might be used to shed light on musicological questions. Perceptual principles can help to explain how and why sounds group together in both time and vertical texture, which in turn sheds light on a variety of issues involving orchestration, contrapuntal procedure, and rhythmic organization. This discussion of principles, again combined with practical advice about how data might be represented, leads to two final analytical applications—one a perceptually motivated study of orchestration in Schoenberg's music, and the other a perceptual rationalization of traditional voice-leading rules.

Many of the approaches discussed in the book involve the generation of data to which a number of general principles apply, revolving around the conditions under which they are collected and the kind of control that is needed, as well as the identification of optimal forms of data representation and analysis. The purpose of the final chapter (Windsor) is therefore to explain the principles, and some of the specific methods, of experimental design and statistical procedure in a range of musical contexts. Empirical data in broadly musicological research might include any of the following:

- Score data
- Sound recordings
- MIDI data from keyboards (and possibly other instruments)
- Video data
- Diary data from performers, composers or listeners
- Interview data
- Audience questionnaires
- Data from a textual or visual analysis of CD covers or program materials
- Quantitative data relating to the sale of musical "merchandise" (e.g., recordings, fanzines, tee-shirts)

The value or otherwise of such data lies in the larger research context within which they occur, and the musicological uses to which they are put. Reference to data on tee-shirt sales, for example, may look banal and of only bookkeeping significance—but if research into music and identity, for example, found that a powerful index of audience members' sense of identity with classical music was their willingness to buy the merchandise associated with it, then it might be important to know that a rise in tee-shirt sales in one specific year of a particular music festival wasn't just the result of lower prices, fancier designs, or the sudden influx of a new and more style-conscious sector in the audience. Apparently trivial information, in other words, may turn out to be musicologically valuable—but only if appropriately interpreted. The contribution that an empirical approach can make is not to be endorsed (or dismissed) simply *because* of its empiricism, but rather for what it can help to discover or reveal. And in order to discover or reveal anything at all, we need appropriate methods as well as good questions. That is what this book is about.

Notes

1. "The grid through which we permit the figures of resemblance to enter our knowledge happens to coincide at this point (and at almost no other) with that which sixteenth-century learning had laid over things" (Foucault 1970: 22). For a more extended discussion of this quotation and the general issue see Cook 2002: 80.
2. For a characterization of medieval musicology in precisely these terms see Leech-Wilkinson (2002), chapter 4; for the argument that data-poor fields breed interpretational conservatism see Huron 1999, on which we draw at many points in this chapter.
3. Babbitt 1972b (but written in 1965), 11–12; a discussion may be found in Guck 1994.
4. Formally speaking, scientific experiments are designed to refute the "null hypothesis" that no effect is attributable to the factor(s) being tested (you can never *prove* the null hypothesis).

References

Babbitt, M. (1972a). "Twelve-tone rhythmic structure and the electronic medium," in B. Boretz & E. T. Cone (eds.), *Perspectives on Contemporary Music Theory*. New York: Norton, 148–179.

Babbitt, M. (1972b). "The structure and function of musical theory," in B. Boretz and
    E. T. Cone (eds.), *Perspectives on Contemporary Music Theory*. New York: Norton,
    10–21.
Babbitt, M. (1972c). "Past and present concepts of the nature and limits of music," in
    B. Boretz and E. T. Cone (eds.), *Perspectives on Contemporary Music Theory*. New
    York: Norton, 3–9.
Balzano, G. (1987). "Measuring music," in A. Gabrielssen (ed.), *Action and Perception in
    Rhythm and Music*. Stockholm: Royal Swedish Academy of Music, 177–199.
Boretz, B. (1970). Meta-variations: Studies in the Foundation of Musical Thought. Ph.D.
    dissertation, Princeton University [published serially in *Perspectives of New Music*
    8–11].
Boretz, B. (1977). "Two replies." *Perspectives of New Music* 15/2: 239–242.
Cook, N. (2002). "Epistemologies of music theory," in T. Christensen (ed.), *The Cam-
    bridge History of Western Music Theory*. Cambridge: Cambridge University Press,
    78–205.
Dahlhaus, C. (1983). *Foundations of Music History*. Cambridge: Cambridge University
    Press.
Forte, A. (1973). *The Structure of Atonal Music*. New Haven: Yale University Press.
Foucault, Michel (1970). *The Order of Things*. London: Tavistock Institute.
Gjerdingen, R. (1996). "Courtly behaviors." *Music Perception* 13: 365–382.
Guck, M. (1994). "Rehabilitating the incorrigible," in A. Pople (ed.), *Theory, Analysis and
    Meaning in Music*. Cambridge: Cambridge University Press, 57–73.
Hofstetter, F. T. (1979). "The nationalist fingerprint in nineteenth-century chamber
    music." *Computers and the Humanities* 13: 105–119.
Hughes, M. (1977). "[Schubert, Op. 94 No. 1:] A quantitative approach," in M. Yeston
    (ed.), *Readings in Schenker Analysis and Other Approaches*. New Haven: Yale Univer-
    sity Press, 144–164.
Huron, D. (1999). "Methodology: On finding field-appropriate methodologies at the
    intersection of the humanities and the social sciences." 1999 Ernest Bloch lectures,
    University of California at Berkeley, #3 [accessible at http://dactyl.som.ohio-state
    .edu/Music220/Bloch.lectures/3.Methodology.html].
Kassler, M. (1967). "A Trinity of Essays." Ph.D. dissertation, Princeton University.
Komar, A. (1971). *Theory of Suspensions*. Princeton: Princeton University Press.
Krumhansl, C. (1985). "Music psychology and music theory: Problems and prospects."
    Music Theory Spectrum 17 (1985): 53–80.
Krumhansl, C. (1990). *Cognitive Foundations of Musical Pitch*. New York: Oxford Univer-
    sity Press.
Leech-Wilkinson, D. (2000). [Review of] Margaret Bent and Andrew Wathey (eds.),
    *Fauvel Studies: Chronicle, Music, and Image in Paris, Bibliothèque Nationale de France,
    MS français 146. Journal of the American Musicological Society* 53: 152–159.
Leech-Wilkinson, D. (2002). *The Modern Invention of Medieval Music: Scholarship, Ideology,
    Performance*. Cambridge: Cambridge University Press.
Lerdahl, F. (2001). *Tonal Pitch Space*. New York: Oxford University Press.
Lerdahl, F. & R. Jackendoff (1983). *A Generative Theory of Tonal Music*. Cambridge, Mass.:
    MIT Press.
Lomax, A. (1968). *Folk Song Style and Culture*. Washington, D.C.: American Association
    for the Advancement of Science.
Martin, P. (2002). "Over the rainbow? On the quest for 'the social' in musical analysis."
    Journal of the Royal Musical Association 127: 130–146.

CHAPTER 2

Documenting the Musical Event: Observation, Participation, Representation

Jonathan P. J. Stock

Empirical approaches have contributed to research in the field now named ethnomusicology since at least the nineteenth century. Comparative musicologists and folklorists in Europe, the Americas, and elsewhere each drew on the new technologies of sound recording and mass publication in order to develop distinct forms of scholarly empiricism. More recent generations of folk music scholars and ethnomusicologists have measured their work against further empirical norms, and there remains today an intriguing relationship between the discipline's research methods, available technology, and the pattern of its truth claims. Ethnomusicologists have developed empirical approaches to transcription, the analysis of musical sound, the distribution of instruments and repertory, learning processes, and performance interaction, and further chapters could be written on each of these areas as well as on several others. Nonetheless, this chapter focuses on the topic of participant-observational fieldwork, because fieldwork not only is of central importance to enquiry in ethnomusicology but also can be a powerful research methodology for other musicologists. This chapter looks at means of gathering empirical fieldwork data and associated issues of interpretation, authority, and representation. Before looking in detail at fieldwork, however, I shall discuss broader aspects of empirical work in ethnomusicology by means of a brief historical summary.

Introduction: The Empirical Urge in Ethnomusicology and Its Antecedents

The invention of the phonograph in 1877 was almost a precondition for the discipline of comparative musicology as devised by European scholars in the final decades of the nineteenth century. Although some previous studies had used traveling musicians and sets of musical instruments purchased by colonial collectors, the new technology of sound recording made two crucial contributions to the new discipline: first, it allowed researchers to assemble for comparative analysis extensive collections of musical material from all around the world; second, repeated playback permitted the detailed study (and hence the transcription in modified staff notation) of non-Western musical sounds. Pitches were minutely measured and tonal systems postulated from these calculations. Meanwhile, instruments were categorized, not by reference to the contexts of their use within any one cultural system, but strictly in terms of their physical properties and performance technique (see, e.g., Ellis 1885, Stumpf 1886, Abraham and von Hornbostel 1909, von Hornbostel and Sachs 1914). Criticism of the musical styles in question was not undertaken; there was no attempt to explain or rank music in terms of its "greatness." Instead, the close analysis of recorded examples and musical artifacts was ultimately intended to reveal scientific principles underlying all human music making.

Scholars of musical folklore were empirical in a different sense: not for them the careful weighing and measuring of recordings carried out by the comparative musicologists. Rather, many set out to gather and preserve what they saw as the essential music of their own nation. It was not enough to record such music in a haphazard manner, however, whether by means of notation or the phonograph. Instead, researchers conducted their enquiries in a systematic fashion, and they strove to locate those whom they deemed the most authentic representatives of tradition (Sharp 1954: 119). Whole regions were surveyed (Bartók 1931, 1967); folk singers were questioned about their entire repertories; recorded and transcribed materials were deposited in archives—the very real museums of musical works; variant melodies and song texts were tracked down and classified by means of increasingly complex systems (Bronson 1949, 1959, C. Seeger 1966); and national song collections were published and disseminated through educational channels.

Nevertheless, the appeals to empiricism articulated by comparative musicologists and folklorists alike were open to challenge. The comparativists' detailing of cents, 100 to the semitone, and production of "weighted scales" (diagrams that illustrate the relative durations allotted to each musical pitch within a particular extract), look admirably open to replication by any competent scholar armed with the same sound recording and analytical gadgetry. Yet even setting aside the real challenges of deducing a series of fixed, measurable pitches from the continuous sonic fluctuations of live performance (Schneider 1991), it is now clear that the quest for an underlying science of music often overlooked indigenous systems of musical theory and practice, resulting in comparisons between musical apples and oranges.

Likewise, the folklorists' insistence on "authentic" forms, careful tracing of variants (techniques borrowed from manuscript studies in the fields of musicology and literature), and the laying out of melodic and rhythmic types, gives the appearance of contributing substantively to the gradual accumulation of knowledge about the repertory as a whole. However, more recent research recognizes the longstanding changeability of most folk musical traditions. Today's authentic example has all too often proven to be the previous generation's radical innovation. Terms such as authenticity, once so readily affirmed in discussions of sampling and representativeness, now have little credibility except in commentary on specific individuals' or groups' claims of ownership or identity.

If the goalposts of earlier, pre-ethnomusicological empiricism were uprooted by later generations, however, it was only to shift them for replanting elsewhere. First so entitled in the early 1950s, the discipline named "ethno-musicology" (the hyphen was subsequently dropped) represented both a new beginning and a fresh attempt to address existing problems. Comparativist approaches that emphasized the scientific study of physical sound were sustained under the new regime by researchers such as Charles Seeger who attempted to develop electronic transcription devices. These tools, among which the sonograph is perhaps the most widely used, were intended to facilitate the empirical study of non-Western musics through sidestepping the human subjectivity that might compromise aural transcription and analysis.[1] In a separate yet somewhat similarly inspired development, folklorist Alan Lomax (1968) devised a system of song analysis that tabulated some 37 technical traits of selected vocal examples (phrase length, melisma, tempo, nasality, and so on). These musical features were then compared to cultural aspects of the society in question. This system, cantometrics, allowed the detailed comparative study of songs from many societies without the prior translation of recorded sound into the potentially misleading conventions of Western staff notation (see Figure 2.1). Again, Mantle Hood (1971: 123–196), among others, proposed a new system for the classification of musical instruments: his graphic system of "organograms" was designed to accommodate multiple playing techniques, unlike the traditional hierarchical schemes based on performance technique (the high-level subdivision of lutes into bowed and plucked categories, for instance, made it hard to place an instrument like the violin that could be performed both ways). Ultimately, however, these attempts to fine-tune existing modes of empirical enquiry have proven tangential to the main thrust of the new discipline since the 1970s.

It was the adoption of anthropological fieldwork as a primary research model that marked out ethnomusicology as distinct from earlier comparative approaches. In its classic sense, this meant at least one full year's residence within the culture being studied, speaking the local language and learning to perform local musical traditions. Extended *in situ* research was intended to allow sufficient time for the ethnomusicologist to become adept at understanding the contexts within which music making occurs, and to get to know individuals deeply enough for real discussion to take place. Formal interviewing, although sometimes the only way of speaking with particular individuals (and admittedly efficient for checking uncontested details), was seen as the least desirable form of research interaction, and the least likely to generate valuable insights. (Possibly only the mass questionnaire was regarded with greater distrust.)[2] Instead, the ethnomusicologist was to take part in and observe whatever music-related behaviors occurred customarily, becoming part of the existing "community of speech" whose norms and values could be so easily displaced or closed off by the externally imposed constraints of interviewing. Learning to perform was thus seen as a valuable research technique in that it facilitated access to other musical individuals and situations. It also provided personal experience of performance that could generate further research questions and insights. Mantle Hood (1960) coined the term "bi-musicality" to emphasize the researcher's duty to acquire some level of competence as a practical musician within the cultural setting in question.

Nonetheless, and despite the fieldworker's efforts to develop his or her own musical experience, the new ethnomusicologists agreed that interpretative weight was to be given to the musical explanations and evaluations offered by "insiders," that is to say members of the society in question: this constitutes "ethnomusicology" in the

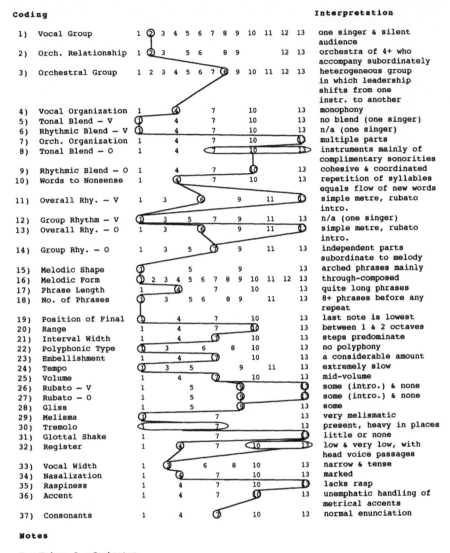

Notes

V = Voice; O = Orchestra
Criteria 15-37 (except 27) are concerned with the voice part only

Figure 2.1. Cantometric profile of an excerpt from *huju* (traditional Shanghai opera) sung by Yang Feifei.

original sense of the term (the musicology of the people), a sense that relates it to ethnopoetics and ethnohistory. Such insider accounts, for which the anthropological term is "folk evaluation," became the authoritative basis of a new empiricism, and the key responsibility of the fieldworker was to ensure that they were not misappropriated in subsequent written analysis. There is, thus, a sense in which self/other distinctions were both collapsed (the ethnomusicologist personally learns the music and the culture that goes with it) and sustained (the ethnomusicologist cedes evaluative and critical authority to local voices). In sum, then, the new methodology could claim to be empirical in that it was based on sustained observation of and participation within the culture in question, interpreted according to indigenous standards.[3]

Investigating Music Through Participant-Observation and Fieldwork

The study of music through fieldwork may be useful to students of Western musical culture in at least two respects. First, it is self-evident that music is more than simply sets of sounds (and the notating of these sounds in symbols). Music is process as well as product, an arena for both social action and personal reflection; it is "emotion and value as well as structure and form" (A. Seeger 1987: xiv). Clearly, many of these essential parts of the whole complex that is music in any concrete setting are not immanent in the sonic material itself. Rather, they inhere, often only temporarily, among particular groups of socially and historically situated individuals. A study of these aspects of musical life will therefore need to integrate close examination of sound structures and symbols with analysis of the patterns of human action and thought that infuse these structures with meaning in specific social situations. Of course, the researcher able to discover what "music" is among a social group at any specific time is then well placed to assess questions of musical value and change within that society. Equally, the musicologist who analyzes what musicians and others actually do on particular musical occasions, and how these individuals explain what they do, is likely to gain enlightening perspectives on the sounds that emerge—there may be differences between theory and practice, for example, that repay close attention.

Second, fieldwork-based approaches offer the socially orientated musicologist access to many kinds of music in Western society that have yet to be extensively written about from a historical perspective, and for which a full range of printed scores, published recordings, and other written documentation may not exist. Church bell ringing, musicals, and amateur popular music offer but three examples. In these cases, personal participation (possibly involving the researcher's performance as part of the musical ensemble) may be not just the best way of gaining access but the only way for the investigator to proceed. Elsewhere, there may be some written materials that can be rounded out through direct personal research. Professional popular music, for instance, is widely written about in journalism and also in several academic disciplines, yet direct interaction with musicians, fans and others provides new perspectives on a range of issues not yet fully addressed in published writings.

These points make it plain that the fieldworker is potentially faced with a huge amount of data: the whole field of musical sound (not only those elements recorded in notation), whole repertories of music-related behavior (from constructing and learning instruments to concert-going practice, modes of shopping for CDs, the use of hi-fi equipment, and habits of in-car listening as well as actual performance), and the social and mental arenas within which equally diverse individuals conceptualize and negotiate aspects of their musical experience. Information within these separate categories may conflict. The members of an ensemble might claim (and believe) that interpretative decisions are made democratically during rehearsal while observation reveals that one individual normally provides most of the direction. Just as theoretical principles may be rarely realized in practice but are still valuable as ideals, so too there may be areas of practice that are not readily talked about. And as in the formal interview, the presence of the investigator may itself become a factor that affects the quality and nature of material collected. Gathering, organizing, and interpreting this heterogeneous body of data with any degree of confidence requires careful consideration of a number of problematic issues.

Prefieldwork Preparation

The first stage in any piece of field research is preparation. Depending on the site of the research, preparation may include language learning, preliminary instrumental or vocal lessons, library or archival research (familiarizing oneself with the musical traditions in question as well as with existing research), theoretical investigation of potential research questions (including looking at similar projects carried out elsewhere), acquisition of technical skills (learning to use, say, a digital audiotape [DAT] recorder or video camera), writing applications for funding, establishing initial contacts within the field, and assembling required materials (DAT cassettes, film, notebooks and medicine, assuming the research is to be conducted in a location where these may not be readily available). A useful technique at this stage is to draw up a plan of research. The plan should sketch the main questions of the research, list known resources, summarize factors that will affect the conduct of the research, and note other conditions that will have to be met for the research to be satisfactorily conducted (see Table 2.1).

Devising a plan makes it possible to cross-relate available resources and conditions in light of the main research questions. Potential problems in the plan might be exposed at once: the plan in Table 2.1 arguably involves so many genres that the researcher is unlikely to be able to acquire real expertise across the whole range. On the other hand, its embracing of instrumental music, vocal music, and dance together with amateur and professional performance contexts may be valuable, and worth sustaining in some form. Perhaps research into two contrasting genres can occur throughout the year with others becoming topics of study for a briefer period at the end, when the researcher has built up more experience. A second criticism might be that although the field looks like being a relatively easy one to gain access to as a participant and observer, its very informality may make it difficult to penetrate deeply. If musicians meet just once weekly and then spend most of that time playing, there may be relatively little opportunity for sustained musical discussion. The researcher may need to try to find another way of meeting some or all of the performers—individual instrumental or vocal lessons, if this is an appropriate model of learning within this community, might be one (though it raises further cost implications). Visiting people in their homes to review recordings or try out instruments might be another; this will require getting to know people well enough to set up such visits and to judge whether one is unreasonably imposing on them.

In contexts where initial access is more difficult, the preparatory stage will include a potentially quite extended phase of writing to or telephoning contacts and intermediaries. Before doing so, it is important to discover potential objections and

Table 2.1.   Sample plan of research: vernacular musics in South Yorkshire.

Main research questions	Resources
1. What role(s) does folk music play in contemporary England? 2. Who is involved in these musics, and why—what's in it for them? 3. What is the role of memorization, composition, and improvisation in these musics?	1. South Riding Chamber Orchestra—every Wednesday at the Red House, Sheffield; uses notation 2. Clog dance group 3. Hathersage carol singers—active only pre-Christmas 4. Listings of folk club sessions in SRFN News and local papers
Significant factors	**Conditions to be met**
1. A well established network of local enthusiasts and scholars; much advice readily available, much material already collected and existing contacts 2. An openness to newcomers both social and technical—no need to be of professional standard in order to take part 3. One year available for main body of field research	1. Easy to meet people collectively at practices and sessions, but will it be possible to talk more deeply in these situations? Will musicians mind being recorded or filmed? (Should I pay for these?) 2. Will it be possible to participate in each of these genres? (Can outsiders join the carol group?) 3. Will it be necessary to memorize large numbers of pieces and songs in order to progress beneath the surface? If so, is there time for this within one year? 4. Transport costs. Other costs? (Beer money!)

think through solutions to them, stressing ways in which the proposed research might advantage those under study (if nothing else, by virtue of an extra pair of hands on site at no cost—some reciprocation for the learning gained is often only fair, even if it is not always demanded). Education staff at a regional professional opera company in the North of England, for instance, were worried that a student who had proposed a period of research into the collective enterprise that constitutes opera production would need constant attention, thereby distracting them from their own work. Nonetheless, they were familiar with work placement schemes, and were supportive of the idea of an initial month-long period of research, a phase during which the student could attempt to gain trust and set up a longer residence. Similarly, school teachers may need to clear an incoming researcher's presence and activities with a head teacher and parents. Certain groups may simply (and perhaps reasonably) object to the idea of being "studied" at all (in such cases it is considered unethical to investigate them covertly), or it may become clear that, to be effective, the research will demand linguistic skills or a commitment of time to on-site residence that the researcher cannot meet. When problems of access or viability cannot be resolved—and courteous persistence often pays off—it may be necessary to abandon the initial research plan and look for another topic altogether.

A final aspect of preparation concerns technical familiarization. The fieldworker may not have operated a video camera before, or may be proposing to record performances or discussions on an unfamiliar DAT, mini-disc, or cassette recorder. He or she may be unsure of microphone placement, selection of recording levels, or typical battery life. In such cases, rehearsal and practice are indispensable.

Field Log and Field Notes

Once a topic has been selected, its viability examined, and funding secured, the field research itself can begin. At this stage, the fieldworker will need to tailor his or her approach to the musical field and context in question, a context that includes the research subjects' assumptions about the researcher. The researcher's gender, age, class, ethnicity, and professional background may encourage the striking of certain attitudes by fieldwork contacts—perhaps they wish to shock, tease, or impress the researcher. While the formal interview or questionnaire is particularly prone to these kinds of distortion, other interactions can easily be affected as well. Two instances will illustrate this observation. A student who started to investigate views on music in gay clubs found that his attempts to initiate informal conversation about the music with individuals outside his group of friends were regularly assumed to be a subtle form of pickup line. Similarly, in educational contexts the incoming researcher may be assumed to be a "teacher," with the result that pupils try to give the "right" answer, or, more mischievously, impose their own agenda. A second student admitted that he had himself some years earlier been a research subject in an investigation into talented young musicians at a specialist music school. Neither he nor his classmates had taken the research project seriously, he claimed, and they had vied with one another in faking data about the amount of practice time they put in.

Fieldwork researchers seek to minimize these kinds of problem through their reliance on participation and observation as well as speaking with "informants" whom they come to know well. (Some writers prefer friendlier terms: consultant or field colleague.) The fieldworker attempts to participate in the life of the community in question for a sufficient length of time that he or she wins the trust and respect of those under study, and to discover through this process of familiarization how to ask questions or encourage conversation leading to genuinely meaningful information. Finally, the fieldworker hopes to become sufficiently aware of the values of the researched community that he or she can produce interpretations or analyses that are well founded. So, in the first example above, it may be that the researcher needs first to expand his circle of contacts among those who attend gay clubs; he needs to gain a clearer idea from experienced regulars about how to approach strangers without being misunderstood, and how best to steer conversation around to musical matters—and this may enable him to reflect more directly on his own musical responses as a listener and dancer, particularly as these develop over time, and to make detailed observations of the responses of others. In the second example, participant-observation might mean becoming a pupil at the music school in question for one academic year (more viable for a younger researcher than an elderly one, perhaps, though the mature student is no more "foreign" than the overseas ethnomusicologist in many another research situation); training (and hiring) one or more pupils as research assistants, thereby involving them personally in the project as researchers and not simply as data-bearers; or taking on a role as teacher in the school in order to gradually win the respect and fuller cooperation of pupils.[4] Whatever the specific solution, personal participation can often break down some of the "us and them" difficulties that otherwise threaten the integrity of a project. Participation as some kind of peer (albeit an unusual one) typically leads to a level of personal experience that can directly inform research questions. Moreover, the researcher is well placed through participation to observe the actions of other individuals, and to set a picture of what people actually do alongside what they say they do.

Whatever pattern of participant-observation is finally selected, a primary technique of planning each day's research is by means of a research log. Helen Myers suggested that the fieldworker maintain a log in which a plan for each day's research is sketched on the left-hand page of each pair; the right-hand page is then used to summarize what actually happened (Myers 1992: 40). This is certainly a means of encouraging good planning and a systematic approach.

Commonly, the researcher keeps two further notebooks. The first is the kind that easily fits into a pocket or small bag; this is used for jotting down thoughts or observations as they occur during the day, for sketching diagrams (layout maps of ensembles, venues, rituals), and for noting information (names, addresses, lists of photos taken). If it is appropriate to take notes during discussions—and one can readily imagine many situations when pulling out notebook and pen would inhibit unselfconscious conversation—then this notebook may be used for that also.

The second notebook is generally a more substantial one. While some researchers carry it around to refer to points, this book is normally used for the writing up of "field notes" (and diagrams) at the end of each day's research. (Relatively few fieldworkers use a portable computer, largely because of the amount of other equipment they already need to take with them.) Field notes are, ideally, an unedited record of all that happened and was said on each day of research, rather like a diary in many respects. Compiling field notes takes discipline and patience, in that there may be a great deal to write down from even a relatively straightforward day's interaction and observation. Furthermore, music events often occur in the evening, meaning that writing up typically occurs late at night; though all ethnomusicologists probably do it sometimes, leaving writing up until the following day seems to place a strain on the frailty of the memory. (Our memories may, nonetheless, be better than we fear, and tape-recorded interviews or lessons can obviously be accurately transcribed days after they occurred.) Each day's entry should be as thorough as possible, and not simply confined to the material pertinent to present research questions, so that future research can make use of these data as well. Some fieldworkers compile an index for each volume of their field notes, and many leave space at the beginning of the book for a detailed table of contents listing date, location, and other key factors or informants by name. A sample extract from one page of my own field notes is illustrated in Table 2.2.

Table 2.2.   Sample excerpt from field notes: ritual ensemble music in Taiwan.

Thursday 12 August 1999, Evening   Baifushequ, Jilong, Taiwan   p. 33

There are twelve to fifteen [Juleshe] members present when I arrive, rehearsing a
qu [kio in Taiwanese: instrumental piece] I have not heard before. They break off
as I come in and immediately ask me to sing Qi cun lian [the simple qu I was set to
learn two days earlier]. I feel somewhat uncomfortable about disrupting the
rehearsal, but it seems that they are happy to break off.

My first attempt goes none too well: I sing the wrong mnemonic (though
right pitch) in line two and mispitch the leap between lines four and five. The
musicians don't criticize me. Wang A'nao (one of the two teachers) simply asks me
to repeat. Now everyone has stopped to listen. Wang tells me to read from the
notation and to beat [da pai] each time there is a "o" symbol in the score. Again,
I perform poorly, hesitating sometimes or singing in time but with incorrect
mnemonics. Wang (and several of the others) emphasize that I need to practice
more, learn how to keep a steady beat, and memorize better than this.

Qiu then fetched a suona [traditional oboe-type instrument] from the wall
rack and played through the qu twice for me, while I sang along. A second
musician joins in the second time. They comment that I seem to know the tune
all right but aren't yet strong enough on the mnemonics to be able to read other
pieces in notation well. Deputy troupe leader Ni fetched a can of beer from the
fridge for me, a gesture that caused some teasing from younger ensemble
members. "Beer! He has beer. How come we don't have any? Let's get some too!"
(In fact, they didn't help themselves to any drinks.) Clearly, I am still a guest. Qiu
and Lin started to chew betel nut, and discussion moved on to the qulu [kiolo]
repertory—music in which an ensemble including stringed instruments
accompanies vocal music. Wang explained that this would involve the bringing in
of outside musicians. None of them are practising kiolo right now. He encouraged
another senior member to sing [the role] Wang Zhaojun but the man declined—
he had no voice (meiyou shengyin). Wang mentioned that the [City?] Cultural
Department [Wenjian hui / Wenhua Jianshe Weiyuanhui] organizes a class for this
in the afternoons but they'll be on holiday at present.

I ask what I might plausibly be able to learn in the remaining six weeks.
There is much declaration of this being too little time—one man states that he
himself has been studying for fifteen years and has learned almost nothing; they
spend four months revising tunes in each guan [kam, mode]. No specific
instruction is forthcoming.

In this extract (approximately one third of the entry for that evening session), the
notes are an unsystematic mixture of present- and past-tense commentary, with occasional reminders thrown in. (A few explanatory comments have been added so that
the passage makes sense to nonspecialist readers.) There is a small amount of direct
quotation, though not very much, largely a result of the mix of languages that characterized the session: some musicians spoke Taiwanese, which I am just beginning to
learn, others then translated this into Mandarin, with which I am more familiar. Direct quotation would be more common in cases where the fieldworker is properly fa-

miliar with the language, in that we are normally concerned with how individuals express themselves, not simply with what they say. Names of individuals are provided, insofar as I knew them at that stage. There are data here on such issues as rehearsal procedures, modes of learning, and informality of interaction within the group, but this particular passage contains few analytical remarks or theoretical reflections. In fact, the writing up of notes is often a process that stimulates analytical thought. When it does, it is a good idea to note these thoughts down immediately (but labeling them clearly as your own ideas and not views that one of the informants offered).

In the literature there are a number of further suggestions concerning the production of field notes.[5] Anthony Seeger, for instance, suggests six questions that the field researcher might seek to document (1992: 90):

1. What is going on when people make music? What are the principles that organize the combinations of sounds and their arrangement in time?
2. Why does a particular individual or social group perform or listen to the sounds in the place and time and context that he/she/it does?
3. What is the relation of music to other processes in societies or groups?
4. What effects do musical performances have on the musicians, the audience, and the other groups involved?
5. Where does musical creativity come from? What is the role of the individual in the tradition, and of the tradition in forming the role of the individual?
6. What is the relation of music to other art forms?

Answers to these questions as recorded in field notes (and subsequently abstracted in analysis) embody empirical information in four respects. First, the information preserved in carefully assembled notes forms a broad palette of personal experience and socially founded perspectives on which specific musical and social interpretations can be based; through participant-observation the researcher not only begins to understand how it feels and what it means to engage in a particular form of music making, but also is well placed to survey the views of other, probably more expert insiders.

Second, this form of in-depth investigation is one in which considerable effort is made to be sensitive to music as made by "real" people in "real" musical contexts. (The quotation marks acknowledge that the specialist denizens and contexts of the university seminar room, philosopher's den, or psychologist's lab are real too.) Context-sensitive field research accordingly exhibits scholarly empiricism in its attention to differences between musical processes and musical products, and between musical practices and musical theories—what John Kaemmer (1993: 14) calls practical consciousness and discursive consciousness, terms intended to emphasize that we may be well able to do things we do not habitually talk about (or vice versa).

Third, the gathering of field notes is empirical in that it pays particular attention to the separation of the researcher's views and interpretations from those of the group or society under examination. Value judgments and assumptions on the part of the scholar are normally avoided, with preference given to the (probably multiple and often contradictory) views of informants. We may personally deem *The Gondoliers* musically superior to *Iolanthe*, say, but the whole point of field research is to discover what members of the Halesowen Light Opera Group and their supporters think, not to impose our views upon them or to use them merely as stooges through whom to put forward our own opinions. When we discover views that are deeply held, we seek to value and respect these, perhaps to analyze or interrogate them, but not to undermine them in our subsequent written studies.

Finally, the detailed recording of data in properly maintained field notes—who said or did what, where, when, and under which circumstances—provides a resource that may be returned to regularly in order to develop new hypotheses about music and culture. (Manuals on fieldwork recommend that the researcher reread the entire collection of field notes at regular intervals as a means of stimulating further reflection, picking up on theoretical musings jotted down earlier on, and catching emerging patterns within the data.) Naturally, it is also possible to return to field notes in later years; the society may itself have already changed in the meantime, and subsequent use of the data will need to acknowledge this possibility (or be accompanied by a restudy).

Interviewing

Some of the problems of interviewing have already been mentioned. Nonetheless, it is a fact of life that the interview is sometimes the only means of speaking with certain individuals. Given that fieldwork is intended primarily to discover how a certain group of people understand their own music making, it is important that the researcher avoids asking leading questions. In certain communities it is impolite to answer in the negative, which means that yes / no questions are of little use. Elsewhere, employment of long or detailed questions may result in short or unrevealing responses, because the interviewee is not allowed space to formulate answers in terms of his or her own categories of thought—categories that may, in the end, prove more important than the specific facts fitted into them. Furthermore, the interviewer's perceived role as a "music expert" may lead interviewees to see the experience as akin to a test, with the result that they feel uncomfortable or struggle to second-guess the "right" answer. David Reck, Mark Slobin, and Jeff Todd Titon (1996: 514–515) illustrate two sample interviews with the same "consultant" in their advice to new fieldworkers: the first fieldworker's questions, it can be seen, imply that particular answers are expected, and thus close off reflection on the part of the interviewee, whereas the second fieldworker keeps the discussion going by asking open questions.

> FIELDWORKER 1: Did you get your first flute when you were a girl?
> CONSULTANT: Yeah.
> FIELDWORKER 1: What was the name of your teacher?
> CONSULTANT: Ah, I studied with Janice Sullivan.
> FIELDWORKER 1: When was that?
> CONSULTANT: In college.
> FIELDWORKER 1: I'll bet you hated the flute when you first started, I can remember hating my first piano lessons.
> CONSULTANT: Yeah.
>
> FIELDWORKER 2: Can you remember when you got your first flute?
> CONSULTANT: Yeah.
> FIELDWORKER 2: Could you tell me about it?

CONSULTANT: Sure. My first flute—well, I don't know if this counts, but I fell in love with the flute when I was in grade school, and I remember going down to a music store and trying one out while my father looked on, but I couldn't make a sound, you know!

FIELDWORKER 2: Sure.

CONSULTANT: So I was really disappointed, but then I remember learning to play the recorder in, I think it was third grade, and I really loved that but I didn't stick with it. Then in college I said to myself, I'm going to take music lessons and I'm going to learn the flute.

FIELDWORKER 2: Tell me about that.

CONSULTANT: Well, I had this great teacher, Janice Sullivan, and first she taught me how to get a sound out of it.

Film and Sound Recording

There is less to say about film and sound recording than field notes, partly because most musicians are already experienced users of cameras and tape recorders, partly because quickly changing technology equally rapidly renders detailed technical advice obsolete (other than the obvious "know your tools"), and finally because the principles that inform the use of film and tape in the field are similar to those that underlie the preparation of field notes. Nonetheless, two aspects of using these media will be briefly discussed here: the special contribution that they may make as research tools in themselves, and issues of preservation and documentation.

Turning our attention first to film, it will be immediately apparent that research into music making in its context is likely to be stronger when the researcher pays attention to the visual dimension of the performance event. Multimedia genres such as opera and ballet offer obvious examples, but almost all musical performance makes meaningful use of location, space, and movement, whether in the form of the spatial deployment of organ and choir in a cathedral, the choreographic hand shifts of Chinese qin zither performance (Yung 1984), audience–performer interaction in Pakistani qawwali devotional singing (Qureshi 1995), the processing of competing brass bands through a Northern English town, or the sending outside in Taiwanese beiguan rehearsals of beginners who practice under the watchful tutelage of an experienced musician (see Figure 2.2). Indeed, it is worth stressing again here the unnecessary restrictedness of the pervasive notion within much of the Western academic community that music is specifically a sonic art. If, apparently like most people outside the academy,[6] we were to assume in our studies that the visual, motional, and emotional aspects of music are just as central as its aural dimension, we would have taken a step toward constructing a musicology well placed to comment on music as social practice.

Video and photographs provide an extra swathe of data, allowing the researcher to look repeatedly and in detail at aspects of the music event that might never be captured in notation. Sometimes these extra data are clearly integral to the cultural practice. Musicians in the Durham-based quintet Juke Box Jive, specialists in the historically informed performance of 1950s–1960s rock, recognized (and demonstrated during performance) the importance of the visual aspect: other than haircuts, clothes, and replica instruments (but replica only visually, as an up-to-date sound

Figure 2.2. A beginner *beiguan* player, assisted by Mr. Qiu, practices outside the main Rehearsal Hall (Baifushequ, Jilong, Taiwan; September 3, 1999; photograph by C. Chou).

system was employed), their dance moves, energy of performance, and—as they stressed in discussion—youth were all part of the 1950s image. (In an irony the quintet understood very well, a genuine 1950s rocker would nowadays appear false, since he'd look too old.)[7] Moreover, study of these nonaural dimensions of performance can reveal the influence they exert on sound structures: for instance, Regula Qureshi (1995: 148–174, 181–186) was able to map (on diagrams she named "videographs" and "videocharts") moments where direct audience encouragement led *qawwali* musicians to offer additional stanzas of certain songs, and where the perceived lack of audience interest led the ensemble to move quickly onto different strains. It is not just that interaction among those present shapes sound structure in certain circumstances, but that musical events can actually create, albeit temporarily, concrete models of social structure through which musically situated individuals move. Examples range from many forms of ritual through to secular dance-centered events: one does not have to be a social psychologist to find social structures in the forming of pairs who move (more-or-less) as one on such occasions.

Unlike field notes, video and photographs can also be conveniently viewed by assembled members of the researched community, thereby encouraging further reflection and conversation on the event by those who were involved, and opening up further informed interpretations to the researcher. (Sound recordings can often be profitably used in this way, too.) This is a particularly useful fieldwork device, in that it leads conversation around to what is significant in performance without the imposed formality of the interview. Video and photography also offer a strong means of sharing ideas with subsequent audiences. In that it is normally the researcher who edits the film, selects the photographs, and composes a script to accompany these images, however, issues of representation pertinent to all social research are particularly marked with regard to the use of film and photography, and I shall return to this in the final section.

Many researchers place the recordings they make (or copies of these) in archives, so that they can be used by others, including members of the researched community. Table 2.3 summarizes the information normally filed with any archived recording (this is in addition to information recorded in the field notes); while each archive may have its own standard formats for noting this material, it is probable that each will require information within the 10 categories laid out here. Much of this information will have been gathered by the fieldworker and entered into field notes, but a special effort will generally have to be made with regard to the question of copyright and permissions. This can be a particularly thorny problem in contexts outside the jurisdiction of the researcher's legal system: for example, religious ritual participants in communist China might well prefer no one to write their names down (as might street musicians in certain locations nearer home). A student attended an ethnic drumming course in Britain where supplies of a mild (yet illegal) inhaled narcotic were shared around to encourage collective relaxation; while names can be changed in any published account that happened to mention this detail, the showing of the group on video (and their identification in the accompanying documentation) might break a tacit confidence.

Coda: Representing Other Voices

This last example has led directly to the issue of representation in social research. The ethnomusicologist and any other music researcher interested in speaking about "other" people faces a potentially complex web of ethical pressures and agendas. Clearly, we have a responsibility to those whom we represent in our writings (and films, lectures, and other offerings). This responsibility is not discharged simply by changing names and places in the published account (although this can help in certain situations) or by specifically asking for permission for all that we do or write (which again can help). Not only are we building our careers on "their" expertise, but also, and particularly in the case of less well-known groups and societies, the scholar's published writings may become the only sources available, and thereby shape other outsiders' expectations about the tradition or people in question. Kay Shelemay's studies of Ethiopian musical traditions suggested to her that the Falasha people (now more commonly known as the Beta Israel), many of whom were seeking evacuation to Israel, might not—as commonly believed—have descended from a formerly unknown Jewish tribe at all: given the potential political impact of this discovery, she had to consider how and where to publish her findings (Shelemay 1991: 136–152). Our role as mediators between our informants and the academic world (and, through textbooks, school pupils) is also one that demands serious consideration. Kofi Agawu (1995) demonstrates how early studies of African music stressed difference to the degree that significant similarities between principles of African and European music making were overlooked. Effects of the construction of African music as "different" in kind included an emphasis on its exoticism (examples

Table 2.3. Sample checklist for data to be preserved for each item recorded in the field.

1. Video or cassette number. These are typically allotted sequentially throughout the research trip as a whole, often with the year (and perhaps general location and medium) as a prefix: TAIWAN VID 99/01, for instance, refers to a video recorded in Taiwan in 1999. Apart from the obvious convenience of a numerical sequence, numbering tapes in this way allows the tapes to be marked up beforehand (on the tape itself as well as on the sleeve) such that errors are avoided when switching tapes over under pressure later on. This code number can be entered into the field notes when the tape is used.
2. Exact date. It may avoid confusion among some potential users if the month is written in letters, for example "12 May 1992," rather than numerically "12/05/92."
3. Exact location. For interview tapes at people's homes, recording their address enables the researcher to send a copy of the tape to those interviewed. (See also 10 below.)
4. One-line title for the event, such as "Beethoven Quartet Cycle at Clothworkers' Hall, Leeds."
5. Technical data: digital or analogue, stereo or mono, PAL or NTSC, noise reduction, duration, etc..
6. Participants. This may involve a list of names (perhaps annotated with instruments, roles or other duties) or be simply a note of ensembles or communities involved: "Choristers of Durham Cathedral directed by James Lancelot" or "c.200 mourners, most apparently from Manchester's Iranian community." When possible, an indication of the size of the group can be valuable. In some cases, a printed concert program can be filed with the recording.
7. Instruments. Unusual or flexible Western ensembles should be summarized and as full details as possible given for all other instrumental groups, including indigenous names as appropriate: "Chou Chien-Er (voice and wood clapper *pie*), Diu Zai-Hing (four-stringed lute *gibei*), Pan Lun-Mui (vertical notched flute *xiao*), Gang Mo-Gen (three-stringed lute *samhen*) and Cua Tiam-Mo (two-stringed fiddle *lihen*)."
8. Items, pieces, or other recording content by track (with real-time durations), including mention of language of speech or singing when other than English (or when use of English is itself significant, for instance in Italian opera performance or German punk rock). Cross-reference to page(s) of field notes where these items are discussed in more detail, or a copy of those pages.
9. Recordist's name and contact details. Other users may need to contact you.
10. Any ethical considerations. Researchers are sometimes permitted to record materials for their own use but not for public broadcast or publication. If this is the case, or if there is doubt about an aspect of the copyright of the performance recorded, reference should be made to special conditions ("for reference use only, no copies to be removed from the library without written authorisation"), to performers (or fieldworker's) contact addresses, or to a detailed copyright release. Where appropriate, it is helpful to discuss all this with the performers prior to archiving their materials; the rise of digitization and automated remote access to archived materials has reinforced this need.
11. Acknowledgments to funding bodies or similar.

that sounded Western were seen as unrepresentative); in seeking to establish African music as a topic worthy of attention, scholars went to great lengths to provide interpretations of African musical activity (polyrhythm, "metronome sense," etc.) that ultimately reveal more about the assumptions of these scholars than they do about African music.

Equally, we have a responsibility to our audiences: we are not simply the mouthpiece of our informants. Our training may give us perspectives on an issue unavailable (and possibly uninteresting) to our informants. We may detect inconsistencies in positions taken by individuals or groups, uncover moments where traditions are constructed by historical revisionism or invention, or wish to compare the views of rival groups; Georgina Born's (1995) analysis of the institutionalization of the Parisian musical avant-garde in the Institut de Recherche et de Coordination Acoustique/ Musique (IRCAM) offers one example of a study in which the author subjects the assumptions of the researched community to (highly revealing) critical examination.

One means of writing that is widely employed is that of letting the researched speak for themselves, and thereby distinguishing clearly between internal views and the researcher's own reading of the situation. But the researcher, as author, still selects which voices get to be heard, how much they are allowed to say, and when they speak—so that the use of quotations does not eliminate the issue of representational ethics. (Indeed, some argue that the potential for scholarly misrepresentation becomes all the stronger.) The onus remains on the researcher to find an honest and sensitive solution to the particular representational challenges exposed during the project. Effective use of informants' voices has been made by Paul Berliner (1994) in his study of jazz; his authorial presence is often limited to introducing each paragraph or summarizing and abstracting key observations from the many musicians he quotes on each new theme. Sara Cohen's (1994) analysis of indigenous views on what constitutes the "Liverpool sound" offers a second, if less extreme, example (see also Herbst 1997).

There is a need, I would argue, for more research on Western musical traditions that seeks to understand how people outside the academy make sense of music. For such study to be effective, traditional academic assumptions about what constitutes music will need to be set aside, the researcher proceeding instead from a sensitive and careful analysis of what those personally involved value, do, and say in real musical situations. Participant-observation offers one well-established means of engaging with these individuals and communities within their own territory and on their own terms. It also offers the student of music a demanding but absorbingly human means of research.

Notes

1. A sonograph (or, in America, melograph) is an electronic device that charts along the vertical axis on graph paper the frequencies, amplitude or, potentially, other features of a stream of sound against duration along the horizontal. The machine is able to detect pitches and details that are inaudible to the human ear, and does not interpret the sound into any preconceived tonal or rhythmic system.

2. Ethnomusicologists do nonetheless interview informants, and a smaller number use questionnaires and other techniques from quantitative sociological research.
3. This empiricism, like that of previous approaches, is not without its own assumptions, and these too have been interrogated in more recent writing. (There is a huge literature on this in anthropology, from which many ethnomusicologists draw; see, e.g., Clifford and Marcus 1986, Geertz 1988, van Maanen 1988, and Jackson 1989.) Most pointedly, perhaps, questions have been asked about the empirical nature of evidence about "other societies" the music researchers themselves help to create (through discussion, recording, and performance, among other means), and then reformulate into a final written account that employs rhetorical devices and theoretical constructs with definite roots in the Western academic tradition.
4. Henry Kingsbury used the first model of research at two American music schools; see Kingsbury 1988, and compare this with Bruno Nettl's more generalist account of these institutions (1995).
5. Several ethnomusicological authors have reflected on the processes, rhetoric, and politics of writing in the field (see, e.g., Barz and Cooley 1997). Fieldwork is, of course, a key research mode in most of the social sciences, including folklore, geography, anthropology, and sociology, and writers in each of these disciplines have written about the preparation of field notes; useful texts from these fields include Briggs 1986, Jackson 1987, Sanjek 1990, and Hammersley and Atkinson 1995.
6. Students of mine over the past six years have as a class exercise each spoken with five so-called "nonmusicians" to attempt to discover these individuals' definitions of music. With a total sample of nearly 1,000 people who have answered these questions, it is perhaps significant that a higher proportion have used words like "identity," "feeling," and "mood" than have referred to "sound" or related sonic terms.
7. In proper ethnomusicological-cum-empirical fashion, this footnote gives the date and location of the specific meetings at which these observations were made: Juke Box Jive in performance (November 14, 1997, Sunderland) and personal communication, November 21, 1997, Durham.
8. A revised or invented tradition is, nonetheless, every bit as valuable, all else being equal, as one with an unchallenged historical record: comments about authenticity above can be reiterated here. The point is that a group may not wish their claims to authenticity or ownership to be critiqued at all.

References

Abraham, O., and E. M. von Hornbostel (1909). "Vorschläge für die Transkription exotischer Melodien." *Sammelbände der Internationalen Musikgesellschaft* 11: 1–25.
Agawu, K. (1995)."The invention of African rhythm." *Journal of the American Musicological Society* 48: 380–395.
Bartók, B. (1931). *Hungarian Folk Music*. London: Oxford University Press.
Bartók, B. (1967). *Romanian Folk Music*, 3 vols., ed. B. Suchoff. The Hague: Martinus Nijhoff.
Barz, G. F., and Cooley, T. J. (eds., 1997). *Shadows in the Field: New Perspectives for Fieldwork in Ethnomusicology*. New York: Oxford University Press.
Berliner, P. F. (1994). *Thinking in Jazz: The Infinite Art of Improvisation*. Chicago: University of Chicago Press.
Born, G. (1995). *Rationalizing Culture: IRCAM, Boulez, and the Institutionalization of the Musical Avant-Garde*. Berkeley: University of California Press.

Briggs, C. L. (1986). *Learning How to Ask: A Sociolinguistic Appraisal of the Role of the Interview in Social Science Research*. Cambridge: Cambridge University Press.

Bronson, B. H. (1949). "Mechanical help in the study of folk song." *Journal of American Folklore* 62: 81–90.

Bronson, B. H. (1959). "Toward the comparative analysis of British-American folk tunes." *Journal of American Folklore* 72: 165–191.

Clifford, J., and Marcus, G. E. (eds., 1986). *Writing Culture: The Poetics and Politics of Ethnography*. Berkeley: University of California Press.

Cohen, S. (1994). "Identity, place and the 'Liverpool sound,'" in M. Stokes (ed.), *Ethnicity, Identity and Music: The Musical Construction of Place*. Oxford: Berg, 117–134.

Ellis, A. J. (1885). "On the musical scales of various nations." *Journal of the Society of Arts* 33/1,688 (March 27, 1885): 485–527. [Repr. in K. K. Shelemay (ed.), *Garland Library of Readings in Ethnomusicology* 7, 1–43. New York, 1990.] See also *Journal of the Society of Arts* 33/1,690 (April 10, 1885): 570 (correspondence from Ellis concerning the article); and "Appendix to Mr. Alexander J. Ellis's paper on 'The Musical Scales of Various Nations,' read 25th March, 1885." *Journal of the Society of Arts* 33/1,719 (October 30, 1885): 1102–1111.

Geertz, C. (1988). *Works and Lives: The Anthropologist as Author*. Cambridge, UK: Polity Press.

Hammersley, M., and Atkinson, P. (1995). *Ethnography: Principles in Practice*, 2nd ed. London: Routledge.

Herbst, E. (1997). *Voices in Bali: Energies and Perceptions in Vocal Music and Dance Theatre*. Hanover, N.H.: Wesleyan University Press and University Press of New England.

Hood, M. (1960). "The challenge of 'bi-musicality'." *Ethnomusicology* 4: 55–59.

Hood, M. (1971). *The Ethnomusicologist*. New York: McGraw-Hill.

von Hornbostel, E. M., and Sachs, C. (1914). "Systematik der Musikinstrumente.'" *Zeitschrift für Ethnologie* 46: 55–90. [Eng. trans. by A. Baines and K. P. Wachsmann in *Galpin Society Journal* 14 (1961): 3–29.].

Jackson, B. (1987). *Fieldwork*. Urbana: University of Illinois Press.

Jackson, M. (1989). *Paths Toward a Clearing: Radical Empiricism and Ethnographic Inquiry*. Bloomington: Indiana University Press.

Kaemmer, J. E. (1993). *Music in Human Life: Anthropological Perspectives on Music*. Austin: University of Texas Press.

Kingsbury, H. (1988). *Music, Talent, and Performance: A Conservatory Cultural System*. Philadelphia: Temple University Press.

Lomax, A. (1968). *Folk Song Style and Culture*. Washington, D.C.: American Association for the Advancement of Science.

van Maanen, J. (1988). *Tales of the Field: On Writing Ethnography*. Chicago: University of Chicago Press.

Myers, H. (1992). "Fieldwork," in Helen Myers (ed.), *Ethnomusicology: An Introduction*. London: Macmillan, 21–49.

Nettl, B. (1995). *Heartland Excursions: Ethnomusicological Reflections on Schools of Music*. Urbana: University of Illinois Press.

Qureshi, R. B. (1995). *Sufi Music of India and Pakistan: Sound, Context and Meaning in Qawwali*. Chicago: University of Chicago Press. [Originally published by Cambridge University Press, 1986.].

Reck, D., Slobin, M., and Titon, J. T. (1996). "Discovering and documenting a world of music," in J. T. Titon (gen. ed.), *Worlds of Music: An Introduction to the Music of the World's People*, 3rd ed. New York: Schirmer, 495–519.

Sanjek, R. (ed., 1990). *Fieldnotes: The Makings of Anthropology*. Ithaca, N.Y.: Cornell University Press.

Schneider, A. (1991). "Psychological theory and comparative musicology," in B. Nettl and P. V. Bohlman (eds.), *Comparative Musicology and Anthropology of Music: Essays on the History of Ethnomusicology*. Chicago: University of Chicago Press, 293–317.

Seeger, A. (1987). *Why Suyá Sing: A Musical Anthropology of an Amazonian People*. Cambridge: Cambridge University Press.

Seeger, A. (1992). "Ethnography of music," in H. Myers (ed.), *Ethnomusicology: An Introduction*. London: Macmillan, 88–109.

Seeger, C. (1966). "Versions and variants of the tunes of 'Barbara Allen' in the Archive of American Folksong in the Library of Congress." *Selected Reports in Ethnomusicology* 1/1: 120–167.

Sharp, C. J. (1954). *English Folk Song: Some Conclusions*. London: Methuen. [First published 1907.]

Shelemay, K. K. (1991). *A Song of Longing: An Ethiopian Journey*. Urbana: University of Illinois Press.

Stumpf, C. (1886). "Lieder der Bellakula-Indianer." *Vierteljahrschrift für Musikwissenschaft* 2: 405–426.

Yung, B. (1984). "Choreographic and kinesthetic elements in performance on the Chinese seven-string zither." *Ethnomusicology* 28: 505–517.

CHAPTER 3

Musical Practice and Social Structure: A Toolkit

Tia DeNora

The sociology of music has a strong empirical tradition, yet retains inspiration from its more philosophically oriented past. For sociologists, especially in recent years as the field has experienced a cultural and interpretative turn, the study of music has been linked to wider questions concerning social structure, stability and change, the interaction between social networks and musical production, the emotions, the body, the study of social movements, identity politics, and organizational ecology. In all these areas, sociologists of music have sought to ground their enquiries through the use of empirical methods designed for the scrutiny of behavioral trends, organizations, and forms of action. In this chapter I take stock of the sociology of music's "toolkit" and present some of the best-known empirical work within the field. My discussion is organized around two broad areas of study: musical production and musical consumption. To contextualize these topics, and to differentiate the empirical sociology of music from musicology's growing interest in social constructionism, I begin with a brief sketch of classic, and more overtly theoretical, work in music sociology.

Sociology of Music: The Classic Legacy

The most sociologically ambitious theoretical perspective to be developed during the last century is to be found in the work of T. W. Adorno (1903–1969). Adorno's perspective is distinguished by its comprehensive vision, and for the central place it accords to music within modern (and, as Adorno perceived, often repressive) culture and social formation.

In contrast to Max Weber's more formal concern with the origins of musical-technical practices specific to the West (Weber 1958), Adorno focused on the question of music's ideological dimension. In line with classical philosophers such as Plato and Aristotle, he pursued the question of music's ability not only to reflect but also to instigate or reinforce forms of consciousness and social structures. For Adorno, different forms of music were homologous with (structurally parallel to, and thus able to inculcate) cognitive habits, modes of consciousness, and historical developments. As he saw it, music's compositional processes—its degree of conventionality, the interrelation of musical parts or voices, the arrangement of consonance and dissonance—could serve as means of socialization. This ultimately structuralist notion is perhaps best exemplified by considering Adorno's views on the contradictory possibilities for consciousness posed by twentieth-century musical forms. On the one hand, he believed that Schoenberg's music could enable critical consciousness because, through its processes of composition—for example, its use of dissonance and formal fragmentation—it modeled a mode of critical attention to the world that refused to offer "false" musical comfort. On the other hand, jazz, Tin Pan Alley, and other popular genres inculcated psychological regression and infantile dependency (Adorno 1990; Witkin 1998), providing, in the age of "Total Administration," a medium that "trains the unconscious for conditioned reflexes"(Adorno 1976:53). "Wrong" music thus had to be denounced, and for this reason, Adorno considered socio-musical study to possess a special urgency: given music's capacity to "aid enlightenment" (Adorno 1973:15), socio-musical analysis was nothing less than a tool for liberation.

These are certainly profound questions and ones to which musicologists are increasingly drawn. During the 1970s, interest in Adorno's work was located peripherally within musicology (e.g., Subotnik 1976, 1978, 1983; see also Subotnik 1990 and McClary 1991:175n). During the 1980s and 1990s, by contrast, musicologists increasingly turned to Adorno. While they generally rejected his dismissal of popular culture and his notion that truly great, liberatory music was that which had "escaped from its social tutelage and is aesthetically fully autonomous" (Adorno 1976: 209), they took up Adorno's concern for music's social and ethical character. In particular, they sought to "ground" musical works, and the values embodied in them, either through showing how musical representations inscribed social relations (Subotnik 1983; Leppert and McClary 1987), or through relating them to a cultural history or psychology of music consumption (Cook 1990, Frith 1996, Johnson 1995). Consideration of how musicologists responded to Adorno, and more broadly of the way in which they adopted a social-critical perspective, helps to illuminate some of the differences between musicology's and sociology's "toolkits." It also provides a springboard into contemporary sociology's more "action-oriented" focus on music as social practice, its shift away from a homology-centered, structuralist paradigm, and its quite different take on the "social construction" of music.

Ten years on from Goehr (1992) and Randel (1992), a form of social constructionism thrives in musicology, one that opposes itself to traditional understandings of what is "natural" in music. Even basic, previously taken-for-granted concepts such as the musical "work" have been deconstructed, shown to be purely social constructions of restricted historical and geographical application. Today, most musicologists would probably agree with Randel's apt observation that musicology's traditional "toolbox" was designed for the construction and maintenance of a canon of acceptable topics, namely, works and composers. But, as I shall suggest in this chapter, the forms of constructionism now prevalent within musicology are, from a current sociological perspective, not so different from the structuralism characteristic of Adorno's work. Although there are some notable exceptions, particularly studies of musical listening, reception and use, constructionist approaches in musicology still center on works, and on critical readings of them that aim to reveal the music's social content.

In the writings of Lawrence Kramer and Susan McClary, for example, we are di-

rected to see music as structurally similar (homologically linked) to social phenomena, or as a "representation" of some extramusical phenomenon. The methodological toolkit here—uncovering intertextual allusion, identifying conventional tropes
and the ideological connotations and functions of these tropes, comparing (some aspect of) music's structure with (some aspect of) the structure of something else—
maintains a separation between works and the actual contexts of their production
and reception. While social contexts and contents are the ultimate quarry of this
type of "New" musicology (as the work of such writers as Kramer and McClary was
termed in the 1990s), they are typically pursued through the analysis of texts, rather
than through more ecological, empirically oriented investigations of the production,
distribution, and consumption of music. Such a move also sidesteps the contested
meanings that arise within particular contexts, for example, through resistance to
particular musicological interpretations. In short, it is impossible to specify music's
mechanism of operation: there is no methodology for describing music as it acts
within actual social settings, specific spaces, and in real time.

I do not here wish to imply that sociology cannot benefit from or be compatible
with this type of text-based musicological constructionism; on the contrary, a weak-
ness of sociology has been its failure to deal with music's specifically musical materials, and here textual interpretation and analysis can help to draw sociological studies on to more firmly musical terrain. Nor do I wish to imply any clear division of
labor between musicology and sociology; some of the best "sociological" work on
musical topics is currently being done by musicologically trained scholars (e.g.,
Pasler forthcoming). Rather, I wish to contrast the textual focus of "New" musicology
with the emphasis of the sociology of music, particularly since the late 1970s, on an
action-based paradigm—one that is concerned with the matrices and milieus in
which action is framed and effected. Howard Becker (1989: 282) put his finger on the
difference when he wrote, with disarming clarity, that sociologists of his persuasion
(generally termed "social interactionists") "aren't much interested in 'decoding' art-
works [but rather] prefer to see these works as the result of what a lot of people have
done jointly." This version of constructionism treats music as a social *process*, focusing on how musical structures, interpretations, and evaluations are created, revised,
and undercut with reference to the social relations and contexts of this activity. It is
also concerned with how music provides constraining and enabling resources for social agents—for the people who perform, listen, compose, or otherwise engage with
it. As the sociologist Pete Martin (1995: 42) has observed, "in general this 'turn to
the social' in musicological studies has not led to a sustained engagement with the
themes and traditions represented within the established discourse of sociology"—
themes and traditions that are at some remove from Adorno and his structuralist
perspective. Martin calls instead for a focus on music as it is lived and experienced,
quoting the Swedish musicologist/ethnomusicologist, Olle Edström, on how the
members of his group at Gothenburg responded to Adorno: "we gradually gained a
deeper insight into the pointlessness of instituting theoretical discourses on music
without a solid ethnomusicological knowledge of the everyday usage, function and
meaning of music" (Edström 1997: 19, quoted in Martin 2000: 42).

Edström and Martin both allude here to a shift in focus from abstract theory and
"macro" issues (such as systems, societal structures, and norms) to grounded theory

and "micro" concerns (such as a focus on individual and collective practice). Part of this shift centers upon the concept of social agency, on how both social and musical forms (including meanings) are put together or accomplished jointly, in Becker's sense. This focus on activity is, as I shall argue intermittently throughout this chapter, a very useful perspective. It is dedicated to elucidating the links between social and musical structures in ways that are more than hypothetical. It conceives of the music-society nexus in terms of the pragmatic contexts within which musical works take shape and come to have "effects" in real situations. This focus on action provides an alternative to homological models and their text-centered methodological toolkit—to the emphasis, *pace* Adorno, Attali (1985), and Shepherd (1991), on how music "reflects," "anticipates," or is structurally analogous to social developments or social structures. From a social-interactionist perspective, then, neither Adorno-inspired sociology of music nor musicology's version of constructionism is sufficient for illuminating ("grounding") music's sociality. The problem with both these inherently structuralist, text-centered modes of study is simply this: they are oriented to the recognition of patterns and structural affinities between two or more realms (music and some aspect of society—ideology, gender or class relations, identities, cognitive styles), but they are not able to document the mechanisms that create these patterns, that is, to describe how music informs or enters social life, and vice versa. They assert links between music and society, but their methodological toolkits do not equip them to show these links in terms of how they are established and how they function within actual musical and social contexts.

By contrast, newer sociological perspectives concerned with social agency investigate the social processes through which these links are forged. As the French sociologist Antoine Hennion says, "it must be strictly forbidden to create links when this is not done by an identifiable intermediary" (1995:248). By this, Hennion means that while music may be, or may seem to be, interlinked to "social" matters, for example. patterns of cognition, styles of action, ideologies, institutional arrangements, such links should not be assumed. Rather, they need to be specified (observed and described) at their levels of operation, for instance in terms of how they are established and come to act. We need, in short, to follow actors in and across situations as they draw music into (and draw on music as) social practice. And this is where empirical methods come into their own within the sociology of music. There are good parallels and precedents to be found in the social study of another "technical" realm: science and technology, in particular in the study of science-in-the-making (Knorr-Cetina 1981; Latour and Woolgar 1986; Bijker, Hughes, and Pinch 1987; Latour 1987). It should be underlined here that these studies of scientific practice and knowledge formation, most of which have been conducted by sociologists with advanced training in the sciences, have concentrated on action—on the situated production of scientific matters of fact, step by (sometimes contested) step. In this respect, such action-based studies move well beyond more general concerns with the parallels between science and society. And some recent studies of this sort have begun to focus explicitly on music technology and musical culture (e.g., Pinch and Trocco 2002).

It is, then, in the focus on culture-producing worlds that the sociology of music has found its empirical feet, and thus a way to ground its claims about the links between music and society. More specifically, as I will describe below, such work centers on action: on musical practices in and across musical and extramusical realms. For example, it is concerned with musically engaged actors as they constitute (and negotiate the constitution of) music through performance, through coordination, and through reception. It is also concerned with how these constitutive processes in turn draw upon music to constitute other social realities, realities that may exceed the musical but that may, simultaneously, be articulated with reference to music. And with this focus it is possible to dispense with the music-society dichotomy, and to think instead of musical practice as, inevitably, social practice.

Sociology of Music: Musical Production and Its Milieux

During the 1970s and 80s, and particularly in the U.S. and U.K., new paradigms were developed that sought to explore music's links to social processes and contexts rather than structures. Here, music was conceptualized, simply, as social activity. Known as the "production of culture" approach, and developed by scholars such as Peterson (1976), Wolff (1981), Becker (1982) and Zolberg (1990), this perspective provided an effective antidote to the overly theoretical character of Adorno-influenced models. It reinvigorated the sociology of music in its emphasis on action and action's matrices. It reconceptualized the composer, or music producer, as a member of a musical world or community, and as working with and abiding by (or reacting against) conventions and work practices in order to make music. This view was deliberately prosaic; the production of culture approach sought to demystify the romantic notion of "the composer" and its attendant ideology of the genius in the garret.

Karen Cerulo's (1984) study of change in musical composition across six countries during the Second World War serves to illustrate these points. Cerulo focused on the social disturbance brought about by war and its relation to music-compositional practice. She examined the prewar and wartime activities of composers whom she divided into two groups, those located in combat zones and those who operated in more stable environments. She began with the hypothesis that the work of composers located in areas most characterized by social upheaval due to war would exhibit most evidence of stylistic change, with composers based in non-combat zones showing less evidence of change in their compositional styles and practice. She established a sample of wartime works, focusing on pieces that were intended by their composers explicitly as reactions to the war, and compared these with prewar works by the same composers so as to identify any changes in style during the war years. Government-sponsored works were excluded, on the grounds that they may have needed to portray official sentiments (through uplifting march rhythms and so on).

Thus delimited, Cerulo's sample consisted of 16 works by 14 composers over six countries—combat zone (wartime England, France, Hungary, Germany, and Russia) and noncombat zone (prewar England and the U.S.). These works were examined in terms of the following features, conceived of as dependent variables (see this volume, p. 219, for a definition of dependent variables): melodic structure, tonality, dynamics, rhythm, medium of expression and form. ("For purposes of pedagogical vividness and ease of exposition," however, Cerulo's discussion of her findings focused primarily on melody.) In particular, Cerulo sought to measure the degree to which melodies were conjunct ("smooth gradations") or disjunct ("leaping motion") before and after the onset of war in each zone. She plotted melodic pitches using crotchets—one for each new pitch—so as to achieve a graph of melodic spacing for each work. She concluded that while before the onset of war the works of all composers in the sample—combat zone and non–combat zone composers, exhibited jagged melodies, after the beginning of the war those in combat zones became conjunct and lengthy, while those in noncombat zones remained unchanged (1984: 892). From this, Cerulo concluded that she had found evidence for the impact of disruption on compositional practice. She then turned to the critical question: how was one to explain this apparent shift in compositional practice?

While older sociological paradigms might have pointed to a homology (or reverse homology) between disruption in society and conjunction in music, with perhaps an associated psychological explanation of trauma and its impact on composers' needs for consonance and congruence of musical material, Cerulo took a different and more pragmatic tack. She emphasized instead how war-zone composers were cut off from normal music-world interactions, from information and communication with fellow composers, and from access to music publications: "The loss of contact with peers experienced by Combat Zone composers destroyed their professional community." This, in turn, Cerulo suggested, "led to the unraveling of the normative prescriptions that govern techniques of composition. Consequently, in the absence of both a supportive system and its enforcement by contemporaries of normative adherence, composers deviate from their current paradigm of musical construction" (184: 900).

To be sure, these conclusions may provide a source for fruitful debate by music historians: why, for example, if changes in stylistic practice were a function of loss of normal networks and communication patterns, should the deviation of isolated war-zone composers all exhibit the same basic tendency—the shift from disjunct to conjunct melodic lines? How might the study benefit from more detailed consideration of the individual work-lives of composers? Does the graphical method of plotting melodic movement provide a valid means for comparing different melodic structures? Could identification and measurement of the parameters of compositional material be combined with an ethnographic understanding of the meanings (local, regional, biographical) associated with musical materials and practices? I suggest that the value of Cerulo's work (and the justification for reading it today) lies in her general interrogative strategy, her bold attempt to specify measurement techniques for the study of compositional practice and, in particular, her focus on production networks and communication as a determinant of this practice.

Cerulo's study is important in the present context not only because it was one of the first sociological works to deal with musical forms and stylistic change, but also because it can be regarded as a pivot between the older homological model and the newer approach, with its emphasis on music-producing worlds and on the social contexts of artistic production. As Cerulo (1984: 885) put it: "the limited body of literature dealing with the transection of artistic creation and social structure consists almost entirely of large-scale, speculative theories which are heavily influenced by sociohistorical arguments, and whose illustrative support often rests on the stylistic and structural changes in the music of a single composer, or a particular musical tradition." While seeking to distance herself from "speculative theory," Cerulo also set her sights on matters that connected back to the grand tradition within music sociology—concerns that were addressed by the earlier homological perspectives she sought to transcend. On the one hand, her work can be read as in contrast to structuralist approaches, such as Lomax's (1968) "cantometric" investigation of correspondences between song styles and societal structures. (For Lomax, song styles reflect societal forms and, thus, thus habits of mind congruent with these forms—see this volume, p. 17, for further details.) On the other hand, Cerulo wished to retain Lomax's concern with musical style and its variation across social space—too often, she argued, ignored by the new perspectives and their focus on production, markets and patronage—while linking that concern with a focus on the production circumstances of composers. In this sense Cerulo's study represented a pioneering attempt to illuminate the "transection," as she put it, of structure and creation: that is, to devise means of measuring the impact of a changed social context on creative activity in music.

By 1989, the "production" perspective was firmly established in not only the anglophone but also the francophone world, after Pierre Bourdieu's (1984) work on taste publics and social classification systems, and Bruno Latour's studies of science worlds and science in the making (1987). These perspectives and the various publications that issued from them drew upon detailed empirical study—ethnographies, cultural and social histories, quantitative surveys, and studies of institutions. It was precisely what Becker referred to as "what a lot of people have done jointly" that formed the focus of sociological investigation between, roughly, 1978 and the middle 1990s. In retrospect, the contributions of these years may be set in one of three broad categories: (1) conditions of production (2) the construction of musical value and reputation, and (3) musical tastes, consumption, and social identity.

Conditions of Musical Production

Cerulo's work is representative of a large number of studies aiming to show how the content of musical works is shaped in relation to musicians' working conditions. Elias's (1993) pioneering consideration of Mozart, for example, suggests that Mozart's compositional scope was hampered by his location between two patronage modes and his inability to escape the shackles of aristocratic control. Similarly, Becker's (1963) study of dance musicians documents how career patterns and occupational opportunities are shaped by patrons and by the need to find a fit between musicians' aspirations and tastes and what their publics will tolerate. Not only are individual compositional practices affected by productional organization, but so too is the selection of compositions that are ultimately produced and marketed. Peterson and Berger (1990 [1975]) illustrated this point in a highly influential study that revealed how musical innovation was enabled and constrained by infrastructural features of the pop music industry; their work suggested that innovation in pop arises from competition between large record companies and their smaller rivals, showing that diversity in musical forms (as they are produced and reach their publics) is inversely related to market concentration. At the time their article was published, Peterson and Berger were trailblazers for the "production of culture" perspective, and their study still serves as a model of how to conduct work in this tradition.

Peterson and Berger examined number one hit songs over 26 years of record production, from 1948 to 1973, dividing this period into five eras of greater and lesser degrees of market concentration. Eras of high market concentration were those in which a high proportion of the annual production of hits was produced by one of the four leading companies: during such eras, these companies controlled over 75 percent of the total record market (in fact just eight companies produced nearly all the hit singles). Peterson and Berger considered whether such concentration bred homogeneity of product, pursuing this question by examining the sheer number of records and performers who recorded the hits during their five eras; the thinking was that there might be little incentive to introduce "new" products under conditions of market concentration. They also examined the lyrical content of hits, tracing these variables through the five eras as competition between record companies grew and then diminished over the 26-year period. Simultaneously, they considered indicators of what they termed "unsated demand," such as changes in record sales and the proliferation of music disseminated through live performance and backed up by independent record producers—genres such as jazz, rhythm and blues, country and western, gospel, trade union songs, and the urban folk revival. They then considered the conditions under which the independent producers were able to establish more secure market positions as the top four producers lost control of merchandising their products over the radio. Finally they traced how the record industry and its degree of market concentration expanded and contracted cyclically over time.

By studying conditions of record production and marketing, relating these conditions to new developments in the communications industry, and examining trends in record output and product diversity, Peterson and Berger concluded that changes in concentration lead rather than follow changes in diversity, and that this finding "contradicts the conventional idea that in a market consumers necessarily get what they want" (p. 156). Their study not only highlighted the impact of production-organization on musical trends and styles; it also outlined how popular music production is characterized by cycles, and detailed some of the mechanisms that affect cyclic development.

Peterson and Berger's study set the scene from the 1970s onward for the concern, in popular music studies, with the production system. Negus (1992), for example, has suggested that working practices within the popular music industry are linked to an artistic ideology associated with college-educated white males who came of age in the "rock generation" of the 1960s and 70s. This occupational stratification has consequences for the types of pop that are produced: women and unfamiliar styles and artists, for example, are marginalized (Steward and Garratt 1984). Such forms of gender segregation may also be seen in pedagogical settings (Green 1997), particularly with regard to instrument choice—a topic that overlaps with work by social psychologists (O'Neill 1997).

In the "production" studies discussed so far, the primary methodological strategy consists of a focus on organizational contexts of musical production, and an attempt to conceptualize musical work as not so different from other types of work, insofar as it requires collaboration, resources in the form of materials, conventions, and communication. Through this strategy, music's link to social structure is specified: musical structures are examined in terms of their links to the local contexts or musical worlds in which they are produced, distributed, and consumed. The production perspective thus illuminated the impact of social structure on music in highly concrete ways; it highlighted the mundane circumstances under which musical work gets done, the circumstances under which careers are forged and styles developed and changed. On the heels of the production focus and its attention to creative milieux, came sociological studies of the construction of both musical value and reputation.

The Construction of Musical Value and Reputation

The stratification of composers, styles, and genres is a rich seam of socio-musical research. Historical studies have helped to unveil the strategies by which the musical canon and its hierarchy of "Master [sic] Works" was constructed and institutionalized during the nineteenth century in Europe (Weber 1978; 1991; Citron 1993) and America (DiMaggio 1982). Both an aesthetic movement and an ideology for the furtherance of music as a profession, the fascination with "high" music culture during the nineteenth century was simultaneously a vehicle for the construction of class and status group distinction. It was also a device of music marketing and occupational advancement.

More recent work in this area has gone beyond the distinction between "high" and "low" musical forms. It now includes the issue of how "authenticity" is constructed and contested (Peterson 1997), dismissing the idea of the "work itself" in favor of particular configurations of the work in and through particular performances (Hennion 1997; see also chapter 5, this volume). And it examines the practices and strategies through which particular versions of aesthetic hierarchies are stabilized. For example, Hennion (1989) has drawn comparisons between the recording studio and the scientific laboratory, showing how musical value and scientific fact are both produced through producers' liaisons with various groups such as the public and the media. Similarly, Maisonneuve (2001) has focused on the way in which the twentieth-century technology of the gramophone afforded music's users new and more intensely personal modes of experiencing the love for music. Drawing upon record reviews, catalogues, liner notes, and other documents, Maisonneuve suggests that this technology facilitated a music user actively engaged in constructing her or his tastes and monitoring self-responses. By comparing the two major technological revolutions in music distribution during the century, she shows how both musical listening and the listening subject were technologically transfigured. Her study thus builds upon and gives a new type of spin to William Weber's pioneering work on the emergence of modern musical consumption and notions of "music appreciation." Similarly, it highlights the extent to which the consumption of music involves more than listeners and works, consisting also of networks or, as Maisonneuve puts it, "set-ups" of objects, postures, habits, and evaluative discourses.

Sociological studies of musical value can be regarded as critical or even deconstructive in that they suggest that apparently self-evident judgments of inherent quality are socially constructed. In my own work on Beethoven's reputation, for example (DeNora 1995), I was interested in the interaction between Beethoven's reputation and the organizational culture and practices that allowed Beethoven to be increasingly perceived (and behave) as Vienna's "greatest" composer. This project was by no means posed in contradiction to the idea of musical value (as some musicological critics believed, e.g., Rosen 1996, DeNora and Rosen 1997), but was rather concerned with two main sociological issues. The first was how, to be a social fact, value of any kind needs to be recognized socially. Unlike gravity or the sound barrier, artistic value is an institutional fact, not a natural one; hence, if it is to be valued, music must be socially recognized and institutionalized as valuable, particularly when it is perceived as violating the norms and conventions that characterize a musical field—when in other words, as with Beethoven, its acceptance constitutes a significant reorientation of taste. (The point is not to presume there is anything automatic about these recognition processes, but to explore them to see how they took shape.) The second issue concerned how the musical field was in flux during Beethoven's first decade of operation in Vienna, being increasingly transformed in ways that were conducive to the perception of Beethoven's "greatness": somewhat like a financier, Beethoven gathered increasing means with which to launch increasingly ambitious aesthetic ventures, while simultaneously augmenting his power within the evaluative terrain of that field. In short, I tried to document the fundamentally practical aspects of how one can emerge as a socially recognized "genius," so highlighting the way in which genius, as a social fact, emerges from a particular configuration of evaluative criteria, aesthetic orientation and convention, social acts, discourses, and material culture. The study thus focused on the complex interaction between what Beethoven did, what he could do, and how he was perceived.

Methodologically, the work began with an investigation of three interrelated factors: the organizational context of music patronage as Beethoven entered it in 1792, his social network as it expanded over time, and his social situation as compared to that of some of his competitors. From there, I adapted methods of ethnographic observation for use on historical data, focusing on agents and actions within this musical field—and specifically on the entrepreneurial activities of Beethoven and his patrons as they presented him in contexts that would flatter his talent. Here the data were letters, other accounts, and contemporary descriptions of the ways in which Beethoven was presented to the public and quasi-public worlds of Viennese musical culture. These were, as I have said, highly pragmatic activities accomplished by Beethoven and his supporters, and they included such things as Beethoven's own negotiations with the editor of the *Allgemeine musikalische Zeitung* (a leading music periodical of the day) and his interventions in the world of piano technology. While the study's aims were ultimately sociological rather than musicological—to theorize, via a case study, key issues concerned with the politics of identity—the book also sought to highlight the contingent nature of the writing of history: in relation to music scholarship, this can be understood as a move away from hagiography and toward an ethnomusicological perspective as applied to the canon.

This line of enquiry has been pursued by sociologists in relation to other art forms—for example, Heinich's (1996) study of van Gogh's posthumous reputation. It has also been pursued as a collaborative project between a musicologist (J.-M. Fauquet) and a sociologist (Antoine Hennion), in a recent study which argues that the present-day understanding of J. S. Bach is a particular "use" of the composer within a social context (Fauquet and Hennion 2000). By this they mean that the way in which Bach is configured—his value and the ethos for which he is said to stand—represents a form of cultural "work": it is a tool with which social realities are established and elaborated. The nineteenth-century discovery of Bach and his installation as the "father of music," Fauquet and Hennion argue, were also a means of configuring the present; Bach's presence was a resource for articulating the meaning of what it was to be "modern" (Hennion and Fauquet 2001). In this case the empirical strategy was anthropological: Fauquet and Hennion followed various musical (and musicological) actors as they appropriated Bach and so simultaneously produced "Bach" and themselves, defining their own identities in relation to music and, through music, to the social world.

Musical Taste, Consumption and Identity

By definition, sociological studies of musical value and its articulation address the matter of how music is appropriated and how music consumption is linked to status definition. This program is implicit in the work discussed in the previous section, and is in turn buttressed by quantitative studies of arts consumption that document links between musical taste and socioeconomic position.

In a review of the 1982 national Survey of Public Participation in the Arts, collected for the National Endowment of the Arts by the U.S. Census Bureau, Peterson and Simkus (1992) examined arts participation in relation to occupational group (as a measure of social status). Their aim was to test the notion, as elaborated in Bourdieu (1984), that there is a direct correlation between high social status and the consumption of "high" cultural goods. To do this they considered the case of musical taste, examining items from the survey that addressed musical genre preferences, and attendance at types of music performances. They concluded that, in recent years, perhaps particularly in the U.S., the traditional highbrow/lowbrow division of musical taste has been transformed in favor of an omnivore-univore model. The latter model suggests that individuals with high occupational standing are omnivore-type music consumers: they attend and consume a variety of musical genres. Members of lower status occupational groups, by contrast, exhibit more restricted taste preferences (univores) and are also more likely to defend those preferences vehemently.

Quantitative modes of analysis have an important place within the sociology of music. Representative sampling techniques permit reliable and generalizable portraits of populations, which in turn permit the testing of hypotheses—in this case, concerning cultural consumption and social exclusion. But, as with all methods, quantitative techniques pose limits, even when practiced at their best. Peterson's and Simkus's work (1992), for example, points directly to questions concerning music and the construction of self- and group-identity; most of these concern the social-psychological and cultural aspects of musical consumption and practice—music's link, for example, with the social identities of its consumers, its role within sub- and small-group cultures, and its social uses within music-consuming worlds. And nowhere is this tradition better illustrated than in the pioneering work of Paul Willis (1978; see also Frith 1981), with its ethnographically oriented work on the sociology of popular music consumption.

Willis was concerned with how, in and through musical practice, through situated consumption of (and talk about) music, musical structures could be seen to have social-organizational properties and capacities. Methodologically, his study drew upon participant-observation techniques (see chapter 2, this volume). The great advantage of this kind of ethnographic observation is its ability to illuminate the nondiscursive dimensions of action (such as emotions and embodiment)—the very dimensions overlooked by survey questionnaires and quasi-formal interview techniques (and also the dimensions of human existence most closely associated with music and musical response). Because of its aims, ethnography is conducted in real time and on the social territories germane to the research subjects themselves. If the aim of one's research is to understand how music functions, for example, how it inscribes social relations, or how it may serve to inculcate modes of agency within social settings (questions that hark back to Adorno's concerns), then the advantages of this approach more than outweigh its practical disadvantages (i.e., that it is labor and time intensive, focused on a particular milieu, and not conducive to generalization). In particular, ethnography's advantage lies in its holistic focus and the emphasis on the emergent and negotiated character of meaning within social settings (Hammersley and Atkinson 1995). Ethnography, in short, can illuminate music as it functions as a resource for meaning construction and for the structuring and organization of social settings.

Describing ethnographic work with two groups of music consumers, the "hippies" and the "bike boys," Willis made his theoretical and methodological perspective clear in the book's appendix, where he emphasized the virtues of participant observation and its ability to follow actors in natural environments and situations. When allied with other methods, he argued, it provided a means of understanding members' practices and meanings while suspending theoretical notions that might otherwise be externally imposed. His study involved "hanging around" with members of a motorbike club in an English city, engaging the men in group discussions (tape recorded) where records were played and discussed, and where conversation took off without prompting by the researcher; in the same way, Willis investigated the hippy scene by visiting three groups at their "pads" and holding similar discussion sessions with them. Through this unobtrusive mode of inquiry, held on the respondents' normal territory and following their ordinary conversation and action, Willis was able to observe how deeply music was implicated in the life worlds of his informants: compared to those of the hippies, the preferred songs of the bike boys were fast-paced and characterized by strong beats and pulsating rhythms. It is here that we can see the great advance of Willis's study, particularly in its handling of the "homology" concept. While Willis suggested that the preferred music of each group resonated with or was homologous to his groups' values and habits of being, his concern was to show how the boys themselves established these connections, how they themselves constructed the links between their preferred forms of music and social life. This point bears underlining: the structural similarities between music and social organization documented in Willis's book were forged through the cultural practices and lay classifications of the group members. And it follows from this that, as Willis (1978: 193) put it, "objects, artifacts and institutions do not, as it were, have a single valency [one could read here also 'single social significance']. It is the act of social engagement with a cultural item which activates and brings out particular meanings."

In Willis's work, then, we can observe a theory of musical meaning as located in the interaction between musical objects and music's recipients; in this respect, Willis's work connects with other, more theoretically oriented, perspectives within music sociology that conceptualize musical meaning as the result of an interaction between music's properties (its mobilization of familiar or "stock" materials, conventions, styles, gestures) and the ways these properties are received and responded to (DeNora 1986; Martin 1995). While emphasizing the social construction of meaning, then, Willis is by no means dismissive of the ways in which music's specific properties may lend themselves with greater or lesser degrees of fit to particular interpretations and appropriations. In the theoretical appendix to his work (1978: 200–201), he describes how cultural items possess "objective possibilities," but suggests that

> The same set of possibilities can encourage or hold different meanings in different ways. They can reflect certain preferred meanings and structures of attitude and feeling. On the other hand, because they relate to something material in the cultural item, something specific, unique and not given from the outside, the "objective possibilities" can also suggest new meanings, or certainly influence and develop given meanings in unexpected directions. This uncertain process is at the heart of the flux from which the generation of culture flows. The scope for the interpretation or influence of the "objective possibilities" of an item is not, however, infinite. They constitute a limiting as well as an enabling structure. It is also true that what has been made of these possibilities historically is a powerful and limiting influence on what is taken from them currently.

Willis's work demonstrates that if our aim is to understand music's social significance and dynamic relationship to social structure, we need to move beyond an exclusive concern with "the music itself" and investigate the processes of its reception and use. This line of thinking has been developed by sociologists of other cultural media: literature (Griswold 1986), television (Moores 1990), and theatre (Tota 1997). Across these studies, attention has been devoted to the more general fabrication of meaning and aesthetic response (including nonverbal response) through interaction with cultural texts, in ways that are directly linked to identity and world construction. The observation that agents attach connotations to things, and orient to things on the basis of perceived meanings, is a basic tenet of interpretivist sociology. But its implications for theorizing the nexus between aesthetic materials and society are profound. It signals a shift in focus from aesthetic objects and their content to the cultural practices in and through which aesthetic materials are appropriated and used to produce social life. And with this shift, we have moved from the cultural constructionism characteristic of recent trends in musicology (as described at the outset of this chapter) to the interactionist constructionism of sociology proper.

In Willis's study, "the boys" are seen as interpretatively active; their group values are "almost literally seen in the qualities of their preferred music" (p. 63). The focus is directed at the question of how particular actors make connections or, as Stuart Hall later put it, "articulations" (1980, 1986) between music and social formations. This approach grounds the concept of homology by focusing on the way in which homologies are created (articulated) and experienced, rather than seeing them as inherent in the relationship between pre-given musical texts and pre-given social contextual factors. The further development of this perspective is, arguably, one of sociology's greatest contributions to the understanding of culture, insofar as it has provided concepts and descriptions of how aesthetic materials come to have, as Willis puts it, social "valency" in and through their circumstances of use. And to see how this valency is produced, ethnographic methods of observation are required—methods that, through their very time-intensity, allow the researcher to observe articulations in the making, in real time and within naturally occurring situations.

In the two decades that have followed the publication of Willis's book, the field of audience and reception studies has advanced considerably. But the early interactionist promise of the classic works of Willis, Frith, and Hall is too often neglected in favor of a preoccupation with the specifics of one or another interpretation of a particular cultural work. The great contribution of these writers was their focus on what the appropriation of cultural materials achieves *in action*, what culture "does" for its consumers within the contexts of their lives and how these processes can be observed ethnographically. Thus one of the most striking (and usually underplayed) aspects of Willis's study is its conception of music as an active ingredient of social formation. The bike boys' preferred music didn't leave its recipients "just sit[ting] there moping all night" (1978: 69): it invited, perhaps incited, movement. As one of the boys put it, "if you hear a fast record you've got to get up and do something, I think. If you can't dance any more, or if the dance is over, you've just got to go for a burn-up" (1978: 73).

Willis's work was pioneering in its demonstration of how music does much more than "depict" or embody values. It portrayed music as active and dynamic, as constitutive not merely of "values" but of trajectories and styles of conduct in real time. It reminded us of how we do things to music and we do things with music, dance and ride in the case of the bike boys, but beyond this, work, eat, fall asleep, dance, romance, daydream, exercise, celebrate, protest, worship, meditate, and procreate with music playing. As one of Willis's informants put it, "you can hear the beat in your head, don't you . . . you go with the beat, don't you?" (1978: 72). As it is used, both as it plays in real time and as it is replayed in memory, music also serves to organize its users' actions and experiences.

Musically Inscribed Music Consumers

Studies such as those conducted by Willis and Frith during the 1970s have proposed that, for the sociology of music, one of the most fruitful analytic strategies is the focus on musical practice. In recent years, the ethnographic focus on musical consumption and musical practice has embraced sociological questions concerned with collective behavior and social institutions, as well as questions concerned with the emotions and embodiment.

A common thread running through nearly all of the new sociology of music is the concern with music as a resource for social action and for agency broadly conceived. Within social movement theory, for example, music has been conceptualized as providing "exemplars" or models within which social action and movement activity is constructed and deployed (Eyerman and Jamieson 1997). In this respect, music provides, as earlier ethnographers of musical subcultures suggested, a resource for articulating meanings that apply beyond the sphere of music itself. Following actors ethnographically, as they explain themselves in terms that make reference to music, and as they compare themselves or their action styles to musical works, shows how music may actually "get into" action in specific ways, how it functions as an analogue or paradigm for action and cognition. This perspective develops the assumption outlined by Willis' work on the bike boys, that music provides homologous resources for imagination and conduct. This is saying much more than that there are parallels between music and social forms; it is saying how such parallels are drawn and acted upon—how, as Middleton puts it in his description of Levi-Strauss, music *comes to offer* "a means of thinking relationships . . . as this note is to that . . . so X is to Y" (Middleton 1990:223). Examining music as it provides media for building social and conceptual relations both extends and operationalizes Attali's (1985) vision of music's "annunciatory vocation," its ability to presage social structural developments. It does this by shifting sociomusical interrogation away from a focus on "reciprocal interactions," homologies or structural similarities between "music" and "society" (as if these were two distinct realms): instead, it directs focus to the interactive relationship between music and social activity, music and interpretation. This is a pragmatic approach to the topic of musical meaning, one that sidesteps the text/context dichotomy (and the idea of the musical object) in favor of a notion of music as it is drawn into and becomes a resource for action, feeling, and thought.

This focus on music as resource has recently been applied to the question of subjectivity and its cultural or social construction (Hennion 1993, Gomart and Hennion 1999, Bull 2000, DeNora 2000, DeNora 2001). Here music is portrayed as a resource for the production and self-production of emotional stances, styles, and states in daily life, and for the remembering of emotional states. The predominant methodological strategy within this work has been the ethnographic interview, designed to uncover, in the first instance, musical practices of the kind that often pass unnoted by respondents—for example, whether they listen to certain types of music in particular circumstances but not in others, or whether they ever choose to listen to works to realign their emotional or energy state. Although this work clearly connects with research in social psychology (Sloboda 1992, Sloboda 2000) and ethnomusicology (Crafts, Cavicci, and Keil 1993), it also indicates an explicitly sociological focus on self-regulatory strategies in particular social contexts. It reveals some of the ways that individuals and groups engage in emotional management and in self-production across a range of circumstances.

Concurrent with sociological studies of music and emotion management, there has been a renewed interest in music's effect on and relation to the body. This focus moves beyond the interest, within musicology, in body imagery (Leppert 1993, Walser

1993) to a concern with bodily praxis and bodily phenomena. In this respect, it connects with recent work by music scholars on the topic of performance "ergonomics" and the socially communicative body in performance (viewing music performance as just one type of social performance [Clarke and Davidson 1998]), and with work on the body as implied and afforded by musical form (McNeill 1995). In keeping with sociology's emphasis on the situated construction of musical response, new research by sociologists on how music may be understood to mediate corporeal states (such as energy, coordination, entrainment, and bodily self-awareness) downplays a conception of music as stimulus and highlights instead music's capacity to "afford"—to provide resources for and to enable forms of corporeal organization and states of being. In its focus on music's connection with modes of being and modes of attending to the social environment, this work connects with Schutz's classic emphasis on the phenomenological dimension of music making (Schutz 1964).

These issues can be illustrated through a study of my own on the role played by music within fitness classes (DeNora 2000: 88–102). The research site—the aerobics class—was chosen because, given the music-led, choreographed character of aerobic exercise, it provided a venue in which music's role in relation to bodily phenomena (energy, stamina, pain perception, coordination, and motivation) was critical, and where it could, potentially, be observed. The central aim of the research was to illuminate the way in which music structures physical activity and the subjective dimension of that activity. To that end, the study was designed to observe what was conceptualized as "human-music interaction"—the points where music came to serve as an organizing device for bodily activity. It drew together a range of methodological strategies, employed in the following order with overlap between the different types of data collection: participant observation of fitness sessions (primarily "hi/lo" aerobics; the research was undertaken by Sophie Belcher, the extremely fit research assistant); in-depth interviews with music producers; in-depth interviews with class instructors and class members; and quick questionnaires, administered to class members.

Given the aims and subject matter of the study, participant observation was a critical investigative technique. As with most embodied practices, there are many things about aerobics that one can only know about by doing. Being physically stretched, for example, experiencing "the burn," sweating and tuning into the rhythm of a session, feeling at the point of fatigue and then re-energized when the music changes, wanting to move with gusto to the musical pulse—these are all experiential matters. The first form of data in this study thus consisted of the (junior) researcher's own experience of exercising to music, her "knowing-by-doing." The second form of data was the record provided by the videotapes of each session. These enabled the researcher not only to recall the embodied experience of class sessions, but also to see and freeze otherwise fleeting and subconscious moments of class experience, to play them back and so enable reflection upon what it was about the music that enabled or constrained forms of physical activity. This reflection was facilitated through conversations (in-depth interviews) with the senior researcher (myself), such that the research assistant was, simultaneously, researcher and key informant in the study. These conversations (analytically oriented debriefing sessions) in turn generated hypotheses and ideas for further observation. Key among these was the strategy of examining "breakdowns" in sessions and of comparing "good" sessions with "bad" ones, that is, sessions characterized by a high degree of aerobic order with sessions where such things as fatigue, lack of coordination, and boredom occurred.

The third form of data came from interviews with professional aerobics music providers. Here the focus was on what these providers said about music's features and their usefulness for exercise. The data from these interviews were compared with what class participants themselves thought about particular musical numbers and passages, types of movement, and their associated motivational states.

The research highlighted ways in which specific musical devices were enabling or constraining at certain points in the aerobic session. The key point was that some of these devices were effective for some aspects of the exercise session but not for others, and this finding helped to highlight music's structuring properties in relation to the body and embodied activity. From there, the key research question became why certain features were effective at certain stages of the aerobic process. Analysis of all the data, and particularly the videotapes, suggested that music could be seen to work with and for the body (and against the body) by profiling bodily movement, by entraining movement, and by modeling and enabling the adoption of motivational stances (and energies) appropriate to different segments of the session. So, for example, slower-paced, more "lyrical" formats were useful for the stretching movements of the warmup, while music with a highly prominent beat and powerful orchestration (e.g., lower brass tutti) was useful during the core of the session characterized by a vigorous movement style. The study concluded that music could serve as a "prosthetic technology" (Ehn 1988: 399) of the body, a device that has the capacity to extend and restructure bodily phenomena, including embodied states such as emotion and motivation. This capacity is by no means confined to the totalizing environment of the exercise session, but can be perceived across a range of settings in daily life—in the workplace, within organizations (Lanza 1995), and in commercial environments such as restaurants and shops.

Indeed, this study was followed by an ethnography of music in retail outlets, with an explicit focus on these outlets' attempts to configure modes of agency (here understood as predispositions for and styles of action or subjectivity) by configuring the sonic environment (DeNora 2000, chapter 5). Overall, we were interested in how shops used music to target preferred types of consumers, and to structure the temporal and other aspects of the environment; and we were also interested in how shoppers interacted with music in-store—for instance whether they noticed it and, if so, what they thought about it. As with the aerobics work, our own autobiographical experiences in relation to in-store music were used as a basis for generating interview questions and as a ground against which to analyze the in-store conduct of other shoppers.

To these ends, and with the permission of the stores in question, the research assistant and I posed as shoppers to observe the scene in-store, and in particular to take note of (and compare) in-store ambience and the conduct of other shoppers. With tape recorders unobtrusively held in our hands (they pass as personal stereos) and clip-on microphones on our coat collars, we simultaneously recorded the in-store soundtrack and our various observations about the conduct of other shoppers (such as whether shoppers showed signs of engaging with the music by singing along, snapping their fingers, or making dance movements). We combined this with semi-structured interviews with shop managers and staff about their music policies and how the music seemed to work in-store, as well as exit interviews with consumers as they left the shops (we did not have permission to speak to shoppers in-store). In addition, as a pilot study, we followed volunteer shoppers whom we "wired for sound": we asked them simply to "think out loud" as they moved through the shop, commenting on anything that came to mind and anything they might notice about the music in particular. Simultaneously, we shadowed these shoppers, one-on-one, recording our own observations about their behavior (e.g., "she is looking at an orange jumper now"). The two tapes could be synchronized precisely because they shared the same musical soundtrack, and this enabled us to overlap the two transcripts.

Conclusion

I have sought, in this chapter, to unpack the sociology of music's toolkit, and to feature, in particular, the tools designed for the exploration of musical practice; some of these tools are new, and their utility over the long term is yet to be determined. I have also sought to highlight how the sociology of music currently elaborates a particular version of constructionism, one that takes as its object of analysis music as it is made, used, and responded to within specific contexts and settings. Sociologists of music have drawn upon a range of empirical strategies for the collection and analysis of music's social role, from analyses of networks and the impact of associations and information exchange on music-stylistic choices, to comparative analyses of institutional and organizational structures of music making and their influence on musical works and producers. Survey methods have been used for mapping musical participation and taste, and in-depth interviews for exploring reception issues; ethnographic methods have been adopted for the examination of music as it is involved and mobilized in culture creation, group culture, and the noncognitive dimensions of social being and social life.

Over the past three decades, the sociology of music has shifted from its status as a somewhat abstract endeavor located on the margins of sociology, to a grounded and empirically oriented mode of enquiry directed to many of sociology's core concerns—social structure, consciousness, and social difference and division. In undergoing this change, the sociology of music has not only been empowered within sociology as a whole, but has simultaneously retooled in ways that are significant for musicology, as that field develops toward an understanding of music as a fundamentally social enterprise.

References

Adorno, T. W. (1973). *Philosophy of Modern Music*. New York: Seabury.

Adorno, T. W. (1976). *Introduction to the Sociology of Music*. New York: Seabury.

Adorno, T. W. (1990). "On popular music," in S. Frith and A. Goodwin (eds.), *On Record: Rock, Pop and the Written Word*. London: Routledge, 301–314.

Attali, J. (1985). *Noise: Toward a Political Economy of Sound*. Manchester: Manchester University Press.

Becker, H. S. (1963). *Outsiders*. New York: Free Press.

Becker, H. S. (1982). *Art Worlds*. Berkeley: University of California Press.

Becker, H. S. (1989). "Ethnomusicology and sociology: A letter to Charles Seeger." *Ethnomusicology* 33: 275–285.

Berger, B. (1996). *An Essay on Culture*. Berkeley: University of California Press.

Bijker, W. E., T. P. Hughes, and T. Pinch (eds., 1987). *The Social Construction of Technological Systems*. Cambridge, Mass.: MIT Press.

Bourdieu, P. (1984). *Distinction: A Social Critique of the Judgement of Taste*, Cambridge, UK: Polity Press.

Bull, M. (2000). *Sounding out the City*. Oxford: Berg.

Cerulo, K. A. (1984). "Social disruption and its effects on music—an empirical analysis." *Social Forces* 62: 885–904.

Citron, M. (1993). *Gender and the Musical Canon*. Cambridge: Cambridge University Press.

Clarke, E., and Davidson, J. (1998). "The body in performance," in W. Thomas (ed.), *Composition—Performance—Reception. Studies in the Creative Process in Music*. Aldershot: Ashgate Press, 74–92.

Cook, N. (1990). *Music, Imagination and Culture*. Oxford: Clarendon Press.

Crafts, S., Calvacci, D., and. Keil, C. (1993). *My Music*. Hanover, N.H.: Wesleyan University Press.

DeNora, T. (1986). "How is extra-musical meaning possible? Music as a place and space for work." *Sociological Theory* 4: 84–94.

DeNora, T. (1995). *Beethoven and the Construction of Genius*. Berkeley: University of California Press.

DeNora, T. (2000). *Music in Everyday Life*. Cambridge: Cambridge University Press.

DeNora, T. (2001). "Aesthetic agency and musical practice: New directions in the sociology of music and emotion," in P. Juslin and J. Sloboda (eds.), *Music and the Emotions*. Oxford: Oxford University Press, 161–180.

DeNora, T., and Rosen C. (1997). "'Beethoven's genius': An exchange." *New York Review of Books* XIV/6 (April 10, 1997): 66–68.

DiMaggio, P. (1982). "Cultural entrepreneurship in nineteenth-century Boston: The creation of an organizational base for high culture in America." *Media, Culture and Society* 4: 35–50, 303–322.

Edström, O. (1997). "Fr-a-g-me-n-ts: A discussion of the position of critical ethnomusicology in contemporary musicology." *Svensk Tidskrift för Musikforskning*, 79: 9–68.

Ehn, P. (1988). *Work-oriented Design of Computer Artifacts*. Stockholm: Arbetslivscentrum.

Elias, N. (1993). *Mozart: Portrait of a Genius*. Cambridge, UK: Polity Press.

Eyerman, R., and Jamieson, A. (1997). *Music and Social Movements*. Cambridge: Cambridge University Press.

Fauquet, J-M., and Hennion, A. (2000). *La grandeur de Bach: L'amour de la musique en France au XIX siecle*. Paris: Fayard.

Frith, S. (1981). *Sound Effects: Youth, Leisure, and the Politics of Rock 'n' Roll*. New York: Pantheon.

Frith, S. (1996). *Performing Rites: Evaluating Popular Music*. New York: Oxford University Press.

Goehr, L. (1992). *The Imaginary Museum of Musical Works: An Essay in the Philosophy of Music*. Oxford: Clarendon Press.

Gomart, E., and Hennion, A. (1999). "A sociology of attachment: Music amateurs, drug users," in J. Law and J. Hazzart (eds.), *Actor Network Theory and After*. Oxford: Blackwell, 220–247.

Green, L. (1997). *Music, Gender and Education*. Cambridge: Cambridge University Press.

Griswold, W. (1986). "The fabrication of meaning." *American Journal of Sociology* 92: 1077–1117.

Hall, S. (1986). "On postmodernism and articulation: An interview with Stuart Hall." *Journal of Communication Inquiry* 10: 45–60.

Hall, S. (1980). "Recent developments in theories of language and ideology: A critical note," in S. Hall, D. Hobson, A. Lowe, and P. Willis (eds.), *Culture, Media, Language: Working Papers in Cultural Studies 1972–79*. London: Hutchinson, 157–162.

Hammersley, M., and Atkinson, P. (1995). *Ethnography: Principles in Practice* (rev. ed.). London: Routledge.

Heinich, N. (1996). *The Glory of van Gogh: An Anthropology of Admiration*. Princeton, N.J.: Princeton University Press.

Hennion, A. (1989). "An intermediary between production and consumption: The production of popular music." *Science, Technology and Human Values* 14: 400–424.

Hennion, A. (1993). *La Passion musicale*. Paris: Metaille (forthcoming as *Music as Mediation*, Manchester: Manchester University Press).

Hennion, A. (1995). "The history of art—lessons in mediation." *French Journal of Communication* 3: 233–262.

Hennion, A. (1997). "Baroque and rock: Music, mediations and musical taste." *Poetics* 24: 415–435.

Hennion, A., and Fauquet, J.-M. (2001). "Authority as performance: The love for Bach in nineteenth-century France." *Poetics* 29: 75–88.

Johnson, J. (1995). *Listening in Paris: A Cultural History*. Berkeley: University of California Press.

Juslin, P., and Sloboda, J. (eds., 2001). *Music and the Emotions*. Oxford: Oxford University Press.

Kingsbury, H. (1991). "Sociological factors in musical poetics." *Ethnomusicology* 35: 195–219.

Knorr-Cetina, K. (1981). *The Manufacture of Knowledge: An Essay on the Constructivist and Contextual Nature of Science*. Oxford: Pergamon Press.

Lanza, J. (1995). *Elevator Music: A Surreal History of Muzak, Easy Listening and Other Moodsong*. London: Quartet Books.

Latour, B. (1987). *Science in Action*. Cambridge, Mass.: Harvard University Press.

Latour, B., and Woolgar, S. (1986). *Laboratory Life: The Construction of Scientific Facts*. Princeton, N.J.: Princeton University Press.

Leppert, R. (1993). *The Sight of Sound: Music, Representation, and the History of the Body*. Berkeley: University of California Press.

Leppert, R., and McClary, S. (eds., 1987). *Music and Society*. Cambridge: Cambridge University Press.

Lomax, A. (1968). *Folk Song Style and Culture*. Washington, D.C.: American Association for the Advancement of Science.

Maisonneuve, S. (2001). "Between history and commodity: The production of a musical patrimony through the record in the 1920–1930s." *Poetics* 29: 89–108.

Martin, P. (1995). *Sounds and Society: Themes in the Sociology of Music*. Manchester: Manchester University Press.

Martin, P. (2000). "Music and the sociological gaze." *Svensk Tidskrift för Musikforskning* 82: 41–56.

McClary, S. (1991). *Feminine Endings*. Minneapolis: University of Minnesota Press.

McNeill, W. H. (1995). *Keeping Together in Time: Dance and Drill in Human History*. Cambridge, Mass.: Harvard University Press.

Middleton, R. (1990). *Studying Popular Music*. Milton Keynes, UK: Open University Press.

Moores, S. (1990). *Interpreting Audiences*. London: Sage.

Negus, K. (1992). *Producing Pop: Culture and Conflict in the Popular Music Industry*. London and New York: Edward Arnold.

North, A. and Hargreaves, D. (1997). "Music and consumer behaviour," in D. Hargreaves and A. North (eds.), *The Social Psychology of Music*. Oxford: Oxford University Press, 268–289.

O'Neill, S. (1997). "Gender and music," in D. Hargreaves and A. North (eds.), *The Social Psychology of Music*. Oxford: Oxford University Press, 46–66.

Pasler, J. (forthcoming). *Useful Music, or Why Music Mattered in Third Republic France*. Berkeley: University of California Press.

Peterson, R. (ed., 1976). *The Production of Culture*. Los Angeles: Sage.

Peterson, R., and Berger, D. (1990). "Cycles in symbol production: The case of popular music," in S. Frith and A. Goodwin (eds.), *On Record: Rock, Pop and the Written Word*. London: Routledge, 140–159.

Peterson, R., and Simkus, A. (1992). "How musical tastes mark occupational status groups," in M. Lamont and M. Fournier (eds.), *Cultivating Differences: Symbolic Boundaries and the Making of Inequality*. Chicago: University of Chicago Press, 152–186.

Pinch, T., and Trocca, F. (forthcoming). *Analog Days. The Invention and Impact of the Moog Synthesizer* Cambridge, Mass.: Harvard University Press.

Randel, D. (1992). "The canon in the musicological toolbox." In K. Bergeron and P. Bohlman (eds.), *Disciplining Music: Musicology and its Canons*. Chicago: University of Chicago Press, 10–23.

Rosen, C. (1996). "Did Beethoven have all the luck? Beethoven and the construction of Genius." *New York Review of Books* XLIII/18 (November 14, 1996): 57–63.

Schutz, A. (1964). "Making music together: A study in social relationship," in A. Brodersen (ed.), *Alfred Schutz: Collected Papers* (vol. 2). The Hague: Martinus Nijhoff, 159–78.

Shepherd, J. (1991). *Music as Social Text*. Cambridge, UK: Polity Press.

Shepherd, J., and Wicke, P. (1997). *Music and Cultural Theory*. Cambridge, UK: Polity Press.

Sloboda, J. (1992). "Empirical studies of emotional response to music," in M. R. Jones and S. Holleran (eds.), *Cognitive Bases of Musical Communication*. Washington, D.C.: American Psychological Association, 33–46.

Sloboda, J. (2000). "Everyday uses of music listening," in S. W. Yi (ed.), *Music, Mind and Science*. Seoul: Western Music Research Institute, 354–369.

Sterne, J. (1997). "Sounds like the mall of America." *Ethnomusicology* 41: 14–50.

Steward, S., and Garratt, S. (1984). *Signed, Sealed and Delivered. True Life Stories of Women in Pop*. London: Pluto Press.

Subotnik, R. (1976). "Adorno's diagnosis of Beethoven's late style: Early symptoms of a fatal condition." *Journal of the American Musicological Society* 29: 242–275.

Subotnik, R. (1978). "The historical structure: Adorno's 'French' model for the criticism of nineteenth-century music." *19th-Century Music* 2: 36–60.

Subotnik, R. (1983). "The role of ideology in the study of Western music." *Journal of Musicology* 2: 1–12.

Subotnik, R. (1990). *Developing Variations: Style and Ideology in Western Music*. Minneapolis: University of Minnesota Press.

Tota, A. (1997). *Ethnografia dell' arte*. Rome: Logica University Press.

Walser, R. (1993). *Running with the Devil: Power, Gender and Madness in Heavy Metal Music*. Hanover, N.H.: Wesleyan University Press.

Weber, M. (1958). *The Rational and Social Foundations of Music*. Carbondale: Southern Illinois University Press.

Weber, W. (1978). *Music and the Middle Class*. London: Schocken.

Weber, W. (1991). *The Rise of Musical Classics in Eighteenth-Century England: A Study in Ritual, Canon, and Ideology*. Oxford: Clarendon Press.

Willis, P. (1978). *Profane Culture*. London: Routledge.

Witkin, R. (1998). *Adorno on Music*. London: Routledge.

Wolff, J. (1981). *The Production of Culture*. Oxford: Blackwells.

Zolberg, V. (1990). *Constructing a Sociology of the Arts*. Cambridge: Cambridge University Press.

CHAPTER 4

Music as Social Behavior

Jane W. Davidson

Introduction

In the vast majority of music-making contexts, the real or implied presence of others means that at some level social communication or interaction takes place: singing a lullaby, a work song, a hunting song, or a school song; chanting as the member of a football crowd; participating as either a musical performer or a spectator in a symphony orchestra concert or at a Hindu wedding. In fact, individual practice is one of the rare musical occasions when there is no involvement with a co-performer or spectator, but even here there is generally a social goal: the preparation of a performance. Recordings might seem to be another exception, but the social element is still implied: there is a need to communicate the musical content to someone else, even if for the duration of the recording the audience is imaginary. Music is a social act, but investigating how social behaviors function in different musical contexts, and what significance they have, is a very recent research interest in psychological approaches to Western music (for an overview see Hargreaves and North 1999). The delayed development of social psychological research seems to be the result of a largely reductionist approach to music which has tried to understand it in terms of its structural elements: melody, harmony, rhythm, and so forth. But, as general interest in issues related to attitudes and beliefs, and individual and group behavior, has grown, so too has the interest in music as a social-behavioral phenomenon.

Within the psychology of music, Farnsworth (1954) was one of the first to exhibit an explicit interest in such issues, arguing that it was not sufficient to look at how a song functioned musically; rather it was important to know how the performing context operated, and how it affected both performer and audience. Anecdotal accounts can go some way toward describing social behaviors, but the motivation behind the work of researchers such as Farnsworth was to undertake more systematic investigations. They wanted to generalize from their observations, measuring the frequencies of musical behaviors and the interrelationships of these behaviors within and across individuals. Thus they adopted quantitative research designs employing statistical techniques in the analysis of data. By the 1970s and 1980s, however, experimental studies were increasingly complemented by work influenced by the writings of theorists like Harré (1979, 1992a, 1992b), who demonstrated that controlled manipulation under experimental conditions was not always an appropriate methodology when looking at beliefs and behaviors. Out of these kinds of theoretical discussion emerged New Paradigm Research, which adopted qualitative research techniques such as in-depth semistructured interviews and participant observation in an attempt to capture the subjectivity of individual experience (Smith, Harré, and van Langenhove 1995.)

As a consequence, there is now a much more diverse palette of research techniques available for investigating music as a form of social behavior than there was at the time of Farnsworth's work. At one extreme, there is the tradition based on the reductionist approach which manipulates conditions so that specific variables can be examined. An example of this is Burland and Davidson's (2001) study of the effects of different social groupings (single sex, mixed sex, friends, strangers, and classmates) on the quality of musical compositions, exploring the effects of different social combinations on problem-solving in a musical composition task; without the controlled manipulation of the independent variable (the social group in which the children were working), the study would not have been able to demonstrate the impact of social processes on the dependent variable (the musical composition).[1] Formal questionnaires, surveys, and tests have also been used. For instance, Finnäs (1987) wanted to explore the musical preferences of young people; in order to do this, he designed an experiment in which participants listened to and then rated excerpts on a preference scale—a typical quantitative design that is then subjected to statistical analysis. Since Finnäs believed that most participants of this age group would prefer rock over other forms of music, he designed the experiment in such a way that participants always had to compare a test excerpt (a piece of classical music, for instance) with a rock item, so that the relative preference for an item in relation to the best liked piece could be determined.

Other investigations have combined qualitative and quantitative methods. Davidson and Scutt (1999) used a quantitative measure of musical achievement (a musical examination grade) as an objective point around which to assess the role of students', parents', and teachers' beliefs and practices in preparing for these examinations, collected by means of qualitative interviews. By contrast, work of an entirely qualitative nature, like that of Kanellopoulos (1999), demonstrates the New Paradigm approach in which the researcher plays an active role in the generation and interpretation of the data.[2] Kanellopoulos wanted to know how a class of children worked on free improvisation. The analysis emerged from examining the content of conversations Kanellopoulos had with the class of children, semistructured interviews, and tape recordings of the musical and social interactions during the improvisation process. Kanellopoulos also became a co-improviser, attempting to enter the children's world by participating in the creative process alongside them. The data revealed the critical role of social context, with classmates and the teacher assisting in the development of musical improvisation skills.

In summary, a broad spectrum of research approaches has developed, each approach serving a slightly different purpose. In Burland and Davidson's study, only a short period of time was available in which to explore the impact of social group on the ability to compose, and so the most effective approach was an experiment that deliberately formed groups and so manipulated the social context in the study. For Finnäs, rating scales produced easily quantifiable data in response to a straightforward question: what are young people's musical preferences? Davidson and Scutt used data of a more objective nature and compared them with reports of thoughts, feelings, and practices in the preparation, execution, and follow–up periods to a public examination; these longitudinal qualitative data permitted emergent social relationships and key themes to be described and explored over a six-month period. Finally, Kanellopoulos undertook qualitative interviews similar to those of Davidson and Scutt, but involved himself fully in the process, reflecting on his own input as teacher and guide to the children.

The aim of this chapter is not only to illustrate the breadth of social-behavioral research, but also to look in detail at how music has been analyzed as a form of social behavior, and to pinpoint why particular methods of analysis might be appropriate to specific research questions. It will not be possible to provide an overview of all the forms of social musical behavior, nor to explore the vast range of strategies that might be employed to examine research questions. Instead, the focus will be on a number of specific areas from within the Western art tradition: the music learning environment; social influences on musical behaviors; individual differences in musical behavior; and the social context of musical performance.

Social Factors in Musical Skill Acquisition

Research techniques applied to questions of skill acquisition have drawn on a whole spectrum of approaches, from large-scale quantitative questionnaire studies to detailed qualitative case studies. Two contrasting research approaches are considered here: the first involves the collection of biographical data to provide quantitative and generalizable results, while the second considers material focused on the individual and derived from a longitudinal case study.

The Biographical Survey

If you want to find out how musical skills are acquired within a social context, musicians' biographies can be an effective source of information. Biographies are useful because they can trace the factors, social and otherwise, that have led to musical achievement. In terms of existing social-psychological research in music, retrospective biographical accounts have provided the major source of information about key influences on the development of musicians, particularly those of prodigious achievement. Such research has been undertaken in a variety of ways, but principally through interviews in which parents and children talk about their lives and what happened at particular stages of their musical development (e.g., Sloboda and Howe 1991). This is not an optimal research technique, since human memory is notoriously unreliable, but it is often possible to verify retrospective accounts at least in part by asking how, for instance, a child was practicing at a certain time, or looking for data of a more objective nature such as the dates of examinations and grades achieved.

Biographical research has clear and established precedents in historical musicology, which can provide a useful resource for subsequent analysis. Lehmann (1997), for instance, carried out an analysis of historical documents relating to famous individuals, cross-referencing a variety of texts to provide both confirmatory evidence and extra detail. While this is a useful method of collecting data, it is also problematic. Historical documents can be unreliable, with accounts from similar periods often being summaries of one another and no opportunity available to fill the gaps in what may be an incomplete record. Furthermore, the accuracy of the data can be questionable when it relies on second-hand reports written many years after the actual events. Despite such drawbacks, however, primary source material such as the considerable correspondence between Clara and Robert Schumann (Weissweiler 1984)—or the diaries of Berlioz (Searle 1966), which tell of concert life and the role of various individuals in the development of his musical skills—are important documentary resources, rich in self-reflection and insight. And similar kinds of diary data have been widely used in socio-behavioral enquiries. For instance, in research on pregnancy, Smith (1994) gained all manner of insights into a woman's sense of changing self from the diary she kept during the course of her pregnancy. But the key to understanding the free accounts in the diaries was the follow-up interview: by asking similar questions of all the women participating in his study, Smith was able to undertake a comparative analysis of both sets of data. The interviews provided information that then permitted all the material to be systematically structured and thematically arranged. This, obviously, is not possible in the case of historical data.

In looking at the events underlying musical development, an alternative to the historical biography is a real-time survey over the life-span of many individuals. Researching music over the life span is a tricky business, since in Western culture not everyone learns an instrument, and a very large population survey would be needed to ensure the inclusion of a sufficient number of participants who developed musical skills and then progressed to high levels of accomplishment. Sloboda went some way toward collecting this kind of data by adding a section of questions on music to the Mass-Observation Project based at the University of Sussex, which involves around 500 people in an ongoing recording of their daily lives (Sheridan, Bloome, and Street 1998). In autumn 1997, data on individual involvement with music was sought, with family and other influences being explored in order to find out what proportion of the population engage in music and how this process occurs. Although some elements of these data have been reported by Sloboda in conference proceedings (1998), the main analyses have yet to be undertaken as they are dependent on further data collection.

It is generally very difficult to find ways of separating out the many potential factors that may have an effect on an individual or a social group. The next section shows how this difficulty can be addressed through biographical research projects involving empirical methods and comprehensive data collection. There are many possible research techniques, but I discuss the two principal techniques used in behavioral research: the quantitative and the qualitative questionnaire.

Developing a Quantitative Biographical Questionnaire Study

In most quantitative, survey-style research, considerable effort is put into making sure that the right sorts of question are asked so that the data collected are appropriate to the particular aims of the investigation. While reviewing the relevant literature can help to give a preliminary indication of potentially valuable lines of enquiry, it is common for a small number of in-depth interviews to be undertaken prior to the main questionnaire, so that the focus of questions can be clarified and developed. At this stage, new issues that emerge can be easily integrated into the design. Similarly, there is often a phase of "piloting" the questions and response categories in order to make sure that the data are collected in an appropriate format for analysis, as well as to identify the relevant statistical analysis techniques. Once the questionnaire and analysis technique have been developed, individuals from the sample to be surveyed are often given "trial" interviews to make sure that they can deal with both the types of questions proposed and the interview environment itself.

The fine details of preparing questionnaires can be found in Oppenheim's (1992) text on the topic. However a useful set of examples is provided by a series of studies in which a small-scale biographical study was used as a pilot to develop a major investigation of young musicians with a variety of backgrounds and interests in music (Howe and Sloboda 1991a, Howe and Sloboda 1991b, Sloboda and Howe 1991, Davidson, Howe, and Sloboda 1995/1996, Davidson, Howe, Moore, and Sloboda 1996, Davidson, Howe, Moore, and Sloboda 1998). Initially, Sloboda and Howe wanted to find out what social and other factors such as motivation, practice habits and so on were shared by musicians of prodigious talent; the intention was to unravel the issue of how far musical ability is the product of nature or nurture. The researchers chose to survey 42 young musicians of between 8 and 18 years of age, who were all in specialist musical education and had musical accomplishments well beyond those expected of a normal child. This number of children was chosen so that shared factors could be more easily identified and grouped: it would be difficult, for instance, to say that a particular social factor was influential in the development of musical ability if only two out of three interviewees shared it. The 42 children were statistically representative of their group, and were sufficiently numerous to generate statistically analyzable results relating to the behavioral influences on young, talented musicians in Britain.

Sloboda and Howe initially worked from the existing research literature on high achievement in order to identify a number of key areas for the interviews: the impact of parents, teachers, siblings, and role models. They also wanted to find out information that was specific to the musical tasks, such as how often the children practiced and what examinations they had taken. Having identified these broad areas of interest, they then constructed an open-ended interview schedule—that is, a schedule that would be delivered in an informal conversational style. In open-ended questioning of this kind, the interviewer needs to know the interview topic areas very well, and be prepared to go along with the flow of a conversation from one topic to the next at the participant's pace; he or she needs to pursue areas that may emerge spontaneously in the interview, and that may end up providing important insights into the participant's thoughts about an issue. Despite the open nature of these interviews, however, Sloboda and Howe made sure that they began with general, noninvasive areas of questioning, and then as the interview went on, proceeded to more specific questions, with the ultimate aim of finding out more personal or potentially sensitive information. As Smith, Flowers, and Osborn (1997) have pointed out, this kind of funneling of questions allows for a rapport to be established between interviewer and interviewee prior to tackling questions of a personal nature.

After carrying out their interviews with the young musicians in this semi-structured manner (one-to-one and tape recorded), Sloboda and Howe developed a second schedule for the musicians' parents, who were all interviewed independently. Each interview lasted approximately 40 minutes and full transcripts of all interviews were made. At this stage, the researchers examined all the data for common themes, and for any corroboration between the parent and child interviews that might validate what had been said; this approach produced more themes and topics than the researchers had initially anticipated, resulting in a rich data set that was highly specific to the individuals interviewed.

Once they had grouped the data according to theme, the researchers undertook statistical analyses of the frequency of different behaviors and the correlations between practice and achievement, exploring those factors that contributed most to these children's musical progress. These statistical analyses (reported in Sloboda and Howe 1991) were used to show that the children they interviewed were significantly supported by social networks of family, friends, and teachers. Although the data were dependent on retrospective memory, and for that reason potentially unreliable, the independent interviews with children and parents allowed for differences in recollections to be accounted for. Moreover, by interviewing children still in education, the interviewers made a deliberate attempt to collect data as near as possible to the time that the relevant events occurred.

In the three publications that resulted from their biographical investigation of the 42 children (Howe and Sloboda 1991a, Howe and Sloboda 1991b, Sloboda and Howe 1991), Sloboda and Howe highlighted different elements of the data. The first paper looked for quantifiable results to show trends for the particular group of individuals investigated, while the subsequent two papers dealt much more directly with the data as they were collected, for instance providing extensive quotes to illustrate how children from professional musician families saw music as an integral part of their lives. In a text on research techniques in the social sciences, Robson (1993) notes that some of the best research is that which combines the generalizability of statistical findings—for example, that 73% of those interviewed had supportive parents—with the particularities of individual cases. The study reported above, however, was not only an end in itself, but also provided pilot data for a much larger-scale and more formally structured questionnaire study which combined past and current accounts of musical engagement.

Developing and refining the research questions and expanding the population to be surveyed to include children who had given up music as well as those who had music as a second or third hobby, Sloboda and his colleagues developed a formal multiple-choice questionnaire suitable for 45-minute interviews with over 250 children and their parents. Like the initial study, this larger-scale survey involved interviewing all children and parents individually so that comparisons between the data could be made. Besides the more formal retrospective interviews concerning family, sibling, and teacher influences, the children were asked to maintain diaries of their lessons, practicing, and other forms of engagement with music. These diaries produced a more accurate survey of what children were actually doing by reducing the problems of reconstruction and retrospection.

One group of children investigated by the researchers (those who had aspirations to become professional musicians but were not receiving a specialist musical education) came from a wide geographical spread, so postal survey techniques were adopted in order to collect data from them. Oppenheim (1992) observes that it is not untypical for return rates on postal surveys to be as low as 15%. Such low returns may be a depressing prospect, but an astute researcher can increase potential return rates in a number of ways. First and most obviously, material rewards such as a free CD can be offered to participants, putting them under a certain obligation to respond. Second, the questionnaire should be designed and expressed in such a way that the participants feel that what is being requested of them will be of value to the research. Third, the questionnaire should not be too long or complex. Careful piloting of how questions are constructed and set out on the page is just as important as the content and relevance to the potential respondent: for instance, a questionnaire might begin with easy, general questions and work toward more specific and "difficult" ones (such as those that are of a personal nature or require a lengthy written description as opposed to a one-word response). Sloboda and his colleagues meticulously piloted their postal questionnaire, modifying wordings of questions and response sheets in the light of their face-to-face interviews, and their careful planning resulted in a return rate of around 50 percent.

This large-scale study demonstrated that children who regarded musical participation as a second or third hobby alongside sports or other activities, or gave up musical participation completely, had entirely different family, school, and peer circumstances compared with those children who attained high levels of achievement. From this, the researchers were able to gain some insight into the role of environmental influences in the development of musical ability, which in turn enabled them to engage in a much broader theoretical debate concerning the relative roles of nature and nurture in musical development. (These specific debates can be found in Sloboda, Davidson, and Howe 1994a, Sloboda, Davidson, and Howe 1994b, Howe, Davidson, and Sloboda 1998a, Howe, Davidson, and Sloboda 1998b.)

In summary, Sloboda and his colleagues aimed their research at discovering general characteristics and overall trends, and they used the semistructured interview primarily as a starting point from which to develop a fully structured questionnaire. By contrast, the next case study uses the semistructured interview as a means of producing a very detailed case study of a single family's views and behaviors with regard to music.

The Case Study and Interpretative Qualitative Analysis

A series of publications by Borthwick and Davidson tackles the issue of how the family, as a social unit, supports children's musical learning (Borthwick 2000; Borthwick and Davidson 2002; Davidson and Borthwick 2002). Borthwick noted that although researchers like Sloboda and Howe had considered the influence of others in the child's acquisition of musical skills, they had not looked at interactions within the immediate family and how these might influence musical development. She therefore focused her work on the complexity of the interactions within a specific family: parent–child, parent–parent, and sibling–sibling. Overall, her work demonstrated not only that the elder sibling provided a role model for the younger one, but also that the parents established a strong "script" in relation to their children's music. The concept of a script was adapted by Borthwick from the work of Byng-Hall (1995), a family therapist, who defines a "script" as a set of beliefs and behaviors that regulate the social roles played by each individual within the family. By keeping detailed records of observed and reported behaviors and beliefs over a period of 18 months, Borthwick was able to argue that music scripts exert a powerful influence on children's musical development and their perception of themselves in relation to other family members. For instance, exploring parent–child coalitions, she discovered that the father seemed to project his own musical identity as a professional pianist onto his eldest daughter, and that the daughter took on the script as part of her self-identity, believing that she was the inheritor of her father's abilities.

This approach is interesting for two reasons: first, the "script" theory provides a framework within which to interpret the highly subjective material that Borthwick collected from the family; and second, Borthwick took on the role not only of interviewer, but also of observer of, and participant in, the family's life. Visiting the family every two weeks for interviews, she was able to observe the children's music making in the home and how it was discussed and supervised by the parents. She was also invited to participate in family events like Easter egg making, so that from early in the research period she faced few of the "outsider" difficulties that an interviewer coming to a family for the first time might encounter.

Borthwick's approach generated a depth of data far in excess of that produced by Sloboda and his colleagues. However it was extremely time consuming, and the data analysis (based on transcripts of interviews, conversations, and a series of diaries that she maintained) was very detailed and labor intensive. Although the use of such material is well established in ethnomusicology (see chapter 2, this volume), it is only recently that interview, discourse, and diary text has been used for the psychological analysis of musical behavior (e.g., Davidson and Smith 1997). Within psychological, sociological, and educational frameworks more generally, however, the 1990s saw an increase in qualitative research of this kind. Techniques such as verbal protocol analysis, discourse analysis, grounded theory, and interpretative phenomenological analysis have emerged (for an overview, see Robson 1993), all of which use small numbers of participants or even single case studies. In all these techniques, the intersubjectivity between the participant and the researcher is acknowledged as part of the research process, requiring that the researcher's own thoughts and feelings about the participant are discussed and included as a critical part of the analysis. Measures of reliability are not attainable in the same way as in quantitative research (that is to say, by conventional statistical methods), but this problem can be tackled in two different ways. One approach is for the researcher to ask another person with similar analytical skills to examine both the raw data and the analysis in order to evaluate the internal consistency of the researcher's analysis. An alternative is for the researcher to collect multiple forms of data (e.g., interview and diary data) and to use these different sources to "triangulate" the data—that is, to access the participants' thought processes from a variety of convergent perspectives. In either case, the analyses are often taken back to the participant, who may be asked whether or not the interpretations are plausible.

The research methodology adopted by Borthwick is highly interpretative and has its roots in the belief that individuals construct a sense of reality on the basis of understanding and interacting with a social world (see Gergen and Davis 1985). The data are discussed as constructions rather than realities, and as a researcher Borthwick considered reflexivity to be central to her work. This involved making explicit the processes by which her data and analyses are produced, acknowledging her personal interests and values as a researcher and the way in which these influenced the research process. Unlike Sloboda and Howe's approach, which does not mention the role of the interviewer in eliciting particular responses from the interviewees, Borthwick acknowledged that the interview data she collected are negotiated between her and the interviewee at a particular point in time. As part of this, she discussed her own family background and how this may have influenced her in the development of her questionnaires and the way in which she approached her interviewees.

Basing her work on individuals' accounts rather than attempting to produce an objective statement, Borthwick compared the interpretation of her interviewees' experiences with looking for meaning in a text. She assumed that what was said by the participants was significant, and that there was some relationship between this and their more enduring beliefs or constructs. She drew on a particular analytical technique which has emerged out of theoretical work on social constructionism and reflexivity—in this case, interpretative phenomenological analysis (IPA). Used extensively by Smith (1996, 1999), this technique is based on the assumption that interviewees do not express all their thoughts and feelings, so that what they say must be interpreted in the light of other observations of their behavior. The procedure involves examining transcripts and other forms of data for themes. The researcher does this pragmatically, making summaries of interviews, lists of associations and potential connections between them. Main themes and subthemes are created and then discussed, the aim being to produce a "grounded analysis"—that is, an analysis based in and emerging from the data. Smith's work has been in the area of health psychology, and the objective entity of the patient's body provides a solid backdrop onto which subjective psychological accounts of the physical processes can be projected. In the same way, Borthwick used the musical instrument and progress on it (assessed through examination results and reports from teachers) as the evidence in terms of which she could interpret the interviewees' accounts of themselves, their relationship with the instrument, and the role of others in shaping their musical development.

The advantages of IPA are that it produces very detailed data specific to a particular group or individual, and that it facilitates an intimacy with the data (and arguably the participants), in a way that formally structured quantitative analyses do not; at the same time, the technique of triangulation serves to counteract what might otherwise be seen as the excessive informality or subjectivity of the approach. While the analysis of verbal or written material may appear to be less technical than quantitative analysis, and in that sense easier, qualitative techniques require sensitivity and critical insight that depend on a rigorous training: qualitative research is by no means an easy option, as it is heavily dependent on the researcher's skills with text and interpretation, and the ability to write about his or her experiences. This is not to say that quantitative research does not also require skills of interpretation, but the results obtained from quantitative research are usually contained within a more generally agreed interpretative framework, and make reference to more formally defined notions of significance.

These considerations demonstrate the importance of finding an appropriate theoretical and practical approach to the issues and materials of a research topic. Nowhere is this more evident than in the subject of the next section: research into the influence of social factors on the shaping of musical tastes.

Social Factors in Musical Taste

People nowadays have access to a huge range of musics from across the world, through both live performance and broadcast or recorded media. Yet, despite this global potential, research demonstrates what most of us probably suspect already— that different types of music appeal to people of differing social groups. As Russell (1997) points out, the audience at a Country and Western concert will probably have little in common with the members of an opera house audience. People's tastes are heavily influenced by a huge variety of social factors, and a primary aim of research in this area has been to pinpoint the principal sources of influence. The results have typically shown consistent social class, age, and gender biases (DiMaggio and Useem 1978, Pegg 1984, Abeles and Chung 1996, Russell 1997).

Research into musical tastes has generally made use of surveys or questionnaires, in the same way as the large-scale study by Sloboda and his colleagues. The techniques Sloboda et al. employed were straightforward: structured questionnaires consisting of closed questions designed for the specific groups targeted, with the completed questionnaires analyzed simply by counting the frequency of different responses. The researchers did not attempt to survey large numbers of the population, but they drew upon representative samples from different age groups and both sexes, in order to give focus to their research while at the same time avoiding undue narrowness. But social psychological research in the domain of musical taste has not always involved simply asking people to rate or report how much they like or dislike a particular kind of music. Surreptitious methods of data collection have also been used, and these raise a further set of issues. A concrete example is provided by North and Hargreaves's (1996) study of responses to music in a university canteen.

Surreptitious Methods of Data Collection

The aim of North and Hargreaves's study was to test a theory of aesthetic response to music proposed by Berlyne (1971). The theory proposes a relationship between structural complexity and liking (listeners prefer music that is neither too simple nor too complex), so North and Hargreaves used music with low, moderate, and high levels of complexity. Since the study drew on university students as participants, they decided to play a kind of music that they believed that the students might recognize: New Age. They undertook a series of pilot investigations in order to ensure that the specific musical materials were unfamiliar (so that previous knowledge of a particular track could not influence judgment), but nonetheless readily recognizable as belonging to the same genre. This meant that comparisons between the different musical examples would be valid, ideally reflecting only differences in complexity. In order to ensure appropriate differences in musical complexity, the pilot investigations were also designed to confirm that the materials conformed with Berlyne's general definition of aesthetic complexity: high-complexity excerpts were "unpredictable, erratic, and varied," while low-complexity excerpts were "predictable, simple, and uniform." All excerpts for the pilot study were 30 seconds long, and were selected to be representative of the piece from which they were taken. In the experiment proper, they played the tracks over loudspeakers in the canteen, and in a random order.

The authors were concerned that the study should be as "ecologically valid" (i.e., naturalistic) as possible. For this reason the questions about musical preference were concealed within a general questionnaire survey that asked the students about the canteen environment. So as to give credibility to this apparent aim, the experimenters went around the canteen, asking the students what aspects of the environment they might like to change. The surreptitious assessment of the students' musical preferences was accomplished by noting how readily they cited the music as an aspect of the environment which they might like to change, or how much they liked it; the researchers also recorded the times at which each questionnaire was filled in, so that they could cross-refer it to the music being played at that time. The results were in line with Berlyne's theory, with moderately complex music being preferred. The surreptitious nature of the research technique enabled the researchers to show that as dislike of the music increased, the music became more salient. Had the experimenters asked the students about the music in a more direct fashion, they would have drawn attention to the music, eliciting a more self-conscious assessment of these students' musical preferences.

After this brief consideration of work on audience behavior, the next section considers research into social interaction between performers, with a specific focus on how people work together to create a musical performance.

Ensembles as Musical and Social Groups

There have been only a few studies exploring group processes in music, most of them either small-scale qualitative investigations or single case studies. The principal reason for this is that in order to assess how a group operates, it is necessary to have a detailed account of their daily practices and operating procedures, and qualitative approaches permit this depth of enquiry. Murnighan and Conlon's (1991) work is the closest to a more generalizable investigation, combining quantitative analysis with qualitative techniques. They initially contacted 21 string quartets by letter and phone, of which all but one agreed to take part. The study took the form of semistructured interviews with individual quartet members, which lasted between 45 minutes and four hours. The data were then quantified where possible, and quotations were used as a basis for discussions between the experimenter and the players, in which thematic issues were developed. From the broad range of data collected, it seems that the success of a quartet depends on social factors within the group (such as the way in which the second violinist interacts with the other players), as well as on issues of skill and repertoire.

Murnighan and Conlon's work emerges out of the same tradition exemplified by Sloboda and his colleagues' work on musicians' biographies. An alternative to the questionnaire approach is to study ensemble behavior in a more direct manner, an example of which is a study by Davidson and Good (2002); this used various kinds of directly recorded data to focus on the rehearsing and performing of a student string quartet.

A Direct Approach to Ensemble Research

Davidson and Good (2002) studied the musical and social processes of this quartet both in their general interactions with one another, and when rehearsing and performing. They did this by adopting a number of research techniques. First, in individual semistructured interviews, they asked the members of the quartet to give background details about how the ensemble had formed. Then questions were asked about who led both the musical and the social interactions between the quartet members (how the music should be played, how repertoire was chosen, which individuals were dominant, and so on); this revealed the players' own views about the dynamics of the group. Then, in a second stage, the researchers simply placed a video camera in the rehearsal room. They analyzed the recordings using the following categories, for which detailed criteria were drawn up:

- Social conversation (general topics related to friendship, jokes, etc.).
- Nonverbal social interaction (related to nonmusical issues, and including physical contact, gestures, degree of proximity, looking behaviors, etc.).
- Musical conversations (discussions about technical or expressive points in the music).
- Nonverbal musical interactions (gestures demonstrating a musical purpose: coordinating entrances and exits, expressive gestures for particular passages, etc.).
- Musical interactions (dynamics, timing profiles, and when the music starts and stops).

The two authors carried out the analysis together, checking with one another to confirm or disconfirm their ideas. Examples of each of the categories were also checked by an independent evaluator as a measure of the reliability of the researchers' assessments. Performance data—a video recording of the concert for which the quartet had been rehearsing—were analyzed in the same manner as the rehearsal data. All members of the quartet were then asked to view the rehearsal and performance videos, giving feedback on the nature of their musical and social behavior. These discussions were also videotaped, so that they could be aligned with the original video footage, and they were themselves subjected to a similar form of analysis. Finally, when all this material had been analyzed, the researchers took their analysis back to the four players for further commentary. This was in part to ensure that the analysis was a fair representation of the players' experiences, but more importantly, it served as an opportunity for further issues to emerge. One of these issues (the dominance of the male second violinist and a sexual dynamic between him and the female first violinist) caused a little embarrassment, but all players spoke about the role this individual had in the group, and how it had shaped both the general conversation and the first violinist's style of leadership. Had the researchers not fed their analysis back to the players, this issue might never have been clarified.

The high level of participation in this project by the players made it a dynamic enterprise. The data have a degree of richness and detail that is often missing in social studies. The advantages of this kind of research are that the data are collected under real-world conditions; that the participants are able to give their interpretations and provide points of clarification for the analysis; and that it provides results that are very specific to the individuals concerned, through accessing their individual and collective experiences. The disadvantages are the cumbersome and time-consuming data collection and feedback procedures.

The research described above has hinted at the role of the individual in the formation of group dynamics and so in the creation of a musical performance. It is appropriate, therefore, to conclude this chapter by considering how the differences between individual musicians have been researched, and what kinds of traits have been found.

Individual Differences

In general psychological research, there was a surge of interest during the 1930s and 40s in the extent to which individuals differed from one another, and how the differences between them could be categorized (see Atkinson, Atkinson, Smith, Bem, and Hilgard 1990 for details). This research was fueled by the need to find measures of skill and ability for recruitment to the armed services. Broadly speaking three kinds of personality test were developed: questionnaires or inventories, projective tests, and objective tests. These can be classified under two headings (Kline 1994): nomothetic, that is looking for aspects of personality that are common to different individuals; and idiographic, attempting to assess those that are peculiar to the individual. Personality inventories tend to be nomothetic, while projective tests are idiographic; objective tests may be of either type. The examples below will give a flavor of these tests.

Personality Questionnaires or Inventories

Personality questionnaires consist of sets of items (statements or questions) relevant to the personality variables that the test measures, and to which subjects have to respond. When designing a test, the choice of variables to be examined is a complex matter, and researchers have shown that there is a vast number of personality traits which might be measured. Some have argued that there could be as many personality traits as there are descriptive terms for behavior. However Digman (1990) has shown that there is a considerable degree of overlap between the variables, as a result of which five broad traits, together with about 50 independent traits, account for a large proportion of the variation between individuals.

The five broad traits have been studied for many decades and inventories have been designed to access them; these usually comprise items which have to be rated as true or false about preferred forms of behavior—for instance, "I always lock my door at night." The traits are labeled as extraversion, agreeableness, conscientious-ness, neuroticism, and openness (see Goldberg 1993 for more details). As for the in-dependent traits, a number of tests have again been developed, but the most rele-vant here is Cattell's Sixteen Personality Factor questionnaire (Cattell, Eber and Tatsuoka 1970): this is now widely used and standardized, and it is Cattell's inven-tory that has been used in the most well-known research on musicians' personali-ties. This research is summarized in Kemp (1996), and shows that musicians have different types of personalities from nonmusicians. Within musicians, composers are found to be more imaginative and sensitive than others, while brass players are more outgoing and boisterous than string players. As a group, however, there is a general tendency for musicians to be introverted, and they display much higher levels of an-drogyny in their personalities than nonmusicians. Kemp uses these findings as the focus for a discussion of whether it is an individual's personality *per se*, or the social factors surrounding him or her, that leads to these rather uniform behaviors. This is, of course, the central issue: what can these results usefully demonstrate? Clearly they can show that there are group characteristics (the brashness of brass players, for in-stance), and these can be compared with those of other groups (visual artists, say, or white middle class males). The data do not, however, enable researchers to say *why* such behaviors occur: the question which Kemp addresses has the look of chicken-and-egg about it.

The details of such personality measures need to be carefully studied before empirical work is undertaken, but many investigators find these standardized tools very useful and they have a long track record. They are also publicly available and easy to score, and have been extensively tested for reliability. Moreover, because they are standardized, an individual's personality can easily be tested by administering the same inventory on a number of occasions, and the resulting profile can be com-pared to norms derived from the typical profiles of various sample groups.

Kemp's book is a good starting point for exploring such inventories; the detailed discussion of his own research shows how the standard questionnaires can be mod-ified for use with musicians, and how specific data can be tested against the norms. There are, however, two main disadvantages of the inventory technique. First, items have to be short in order to cover all the dimensions of the personality, and such brevity can lead to simplistic statements which fail to capture the complexities of an individual and his or her behaviors. Second, responses can be faked. For instance, if you complete an inventory in a job interview which bluntly asks whether or not you are shy, unreliable or erratic, you may not be inclined to give an honest answer.

Open-Ended or Projective Tests

Projective tests emerged from Freudian psychodynamic theory, with its emphasis on imaginative production and its attempt to gain insights into subconscious or hidden aspects of the personality. A typical test of this kind is Rorschach's inkblot (Ror-schach 1921; see Kline 1994, for details). In the test a series of 10 cards, each with a different size and color of inkblot, is shown to the participant and she or he is asked to report everything that each inkblot resembles. The responses are examined according to three main categories:

- Location (whether all or part of the inkblot is referenced)
- Determinants (whether it is shape, texture, or shading that is reported as being important)
- Content (what the blot represents)

Although some systematic criteria have been applied to the response categories in order to allow for comparisons between individuals, the responses typically provide a qualitative impression of the participant's general disposition, for instance in terms of competition or cooperation, or a focus on positive or negative images.

The advantages of projective tests are that they are a rich source of data. They seem particularly useful in the exploration of subtle aspects of personality that cannot easily be categorized and described, such as an individual's contrariness. However, these are highly subjective interpretations, and although the rationale is that the participant's inner world is tapped, guiding a person through a test, and the subsequent interpretation of the data, can be problematic unless the questioner has psychoanalytical skills.

Objective Tests

The essential feature of objective tests is that their purpose cannot be guessed by subjects. Typically questionnaires are used in these tests, but the data are not the answers to the questions: rather it is the behavior accompanying the completion of the questionnaire that counts. For example, the degree of acquiescence demonstrated in answering oral questions might be used as a measure of the participant's anxiety level. Another measure of anxiety level is the "Fidgetometer," which uses a special chair with electrical contacts which are sensitive to the subject's movements; a score is derived by calculating the number of movements over a fixed amount of time. Objective tests seem appealing because they are hard to "fake," but as Kline (1994) points out, despite his own efforts and those of other psychologists interested in individual testing, the validity of these objective tests has yet to be ascertained.

In summary, individual differences can be tested in a number of ways. The essential problem facing the researcher is finding a tool which will access an individual's traits in a manner that is both sensitive and reliable. From the discussion above, it is clear that there are problems as well as advantages with all the different research techniques available.

Personality and Preferences

In addition to looking at personality per se, tests can be used to examine the way in which individuals' preferences and tastes are affected by their personality. An example of this in music is Rawlings and Ciancarelli's (1997) use of the Neuroticism, Extraversion, Openness (NEO) Personality Inventory (developed by Costa and Mc-Crae 1985), to explore which types of personality correlate with a preference for specific types of music. Given the accessible nature of this study, it is a useful model of how individual difference research can be carried out in musical contexts.

Rawlings and Ciancarelli employed 10 categories of question, each made up of several items that identify specific types of music. In framing their questions they made use of a standardized measure of musical preference (Litle and Zuckerman's Music Preference Scale, 1986), to which the researchers added more recent types of music such as "acid jazz" to update the measure, basing their modifications on discussions with representatives of a large music store. Working from a typed questionnaire sheet, participants rated how much they liked each item. The resultant data were analyzed using the NEO Personality Inventory; typical findings were that females liked popular music styles more than males did, and that individuals who scored strongly on the personality dimension "openness" enjoyed a wide range of musical styles.

Conclusion

This chapter has sampled just some of the wide variety of techniques available to address research into music as social behavior. But a few key issues emerge which apply to all such work, and these might be summarized as follows. In the first place, the quantity of research in music behavior is quite limited, which means that researchers need to be creative and open-minded in their approach. In other words, do not be put off by a lack of precedent: some of the most engaging and penetrating research emerges out of lateral thinking and an eclectic approach to empirical design. At the same time, you need to be systematic, persistent, and reflexive: it is essential to apply the appropriate research technique correctly, in the sense of fully understanding what data are being collected, and how these data may be analyzed. The research technique you adopt will determine how explicitly you set out your hypotheses, or how far you follow up emergent themes; however it is always important to look for ways of examining the data as fully as possible, and to be aware of possible problems. Constant reflection on working processes is necessary if the result is to be coherent. Finally, analyzing music as social behavior means analyzing how people engage with music and with one another at individual, group, and societal levels, and that in turn means that ethical considerations cannot be ignored. Most academic institutions, health authorities, and other public sector institutions in which research takes place run ethics committees; these monitor proposed research projects so as to ensure that no one is exploited, mistreated, or deliberately subjected to physical or psychological discomfort. If you are going to undertake social research, make sure your proposal is seen and approved by an ethics committee, or failing that by at least three experienced researchers. Getting the design right in the planning stages can save a lot of anxiety later.

Exploring music and social behavior is both stimulating and challenging. Face that challenge with energy, an open mind, and sensitivity to others, and your research could make an important contribution to an ever-expanding field.

Notes

1. For a discussion of independent and dependent variables, see chapter 9, this volume.
2. A comparison may be drawn with the participant-observation approach common in ethnomusicology; see chapter 2, this volume.

References

Abeles, H. F., and Chung J. W. (1996). "Responses to music," in D. A. Hodges (ed.), *Handbook of Music Psychology*, 2nd ed. San Antonio: IMR Press, 285–342.

Atkinson, R. L., Atkinson, R. C., Smith, E. E., Bem, D. J., and Hilgard, E. R. (1990). *Introduction to Psychology*. Fort Worth: Harcourt Brace Jovanovich College Publishers.

Berlyne, D. E. (1971). *Aesthetics and Psychobiology*. New York: Appleton Century Crofts.

Borthwick, S. J. (2000). "Parenting Scripts: The Pattern for a Child's Musical Development." Ph.D. dissertation, University of Sheffield.

Borthwick, S. J., and Davidson, J. W. (2002). "Developing a child's identity as a musician: A family 'script' perspective," in R. MacDonald, D. J. Hargreaves and D. Miell (eds.), *Musical Identities*. Oxford: Oxford University Press, 60–78.

Byng-Hall, J. (1995). *Rewriting Family Scripts*. London: Guilford Press.

Burland, K., and Davidson, J. W. (2001). "Investigating approaches to musical composition with eleven year olds." *Research Studies in Music Education* 16: 46–56.

Cattell, R. B., Eber, H. W., and Tatsuoka, M. M. (1970). *Handbook of the Sixteen Personality Factor Questionnaire*. Champaign, Ill.: Institute for Personality and Ability Testing.

Costa, P. T., and McCrae, R. R. (1985). *The NEO Personality Inventory Manual*. Odessa, Fla.: Psychological Assessment Resources.

Davidson, J. W., and Borthwick, S. J. (2002). "Family dynamics and family scripts: A case study of musical development." *Psychology of Music* 30: 121–136.

Davidson, J. W., and Good, J. M. M. (2002). "Social and musical co-ordination between members of a string quartet: An exploratory study". *Psychology of Music* 30: 186–201.

Davidson, J. W., Howe, M. J. A. and Sloboda, J. A. (1995/6). "The role of parents and teachers in the success and failure of instrumental learners", *Bulletin for the Council of Research in Music Education* 127: 40–45.

Davidson, J. W., Howe, M. J. A., Moore, D. M., and Sloboda, J. A. (1996). "The role of parental influences in the development of musical ability," *British Journal of Developmental Psychology* 14: 399–412.

Davidson, J. W., Howe, M. J. A., Moore, D. M., and Sloboda, J. A. (1998). "The role of teachers in the development of musical ability." *Journal of Research in Music Education* 46: 141–160.

Davidson, J. W., and Scutt, S. (1999). "Instrumental learning with exams in mind: A case study investigating teacher, student and parent interactions before, during and after music examination." *British Journal of Music Education* 16: 79–95.

Davidson, J. W., and Smith, J. A. (1997). "A case study of newer practices in music education at conservatoire level." *British Journal of Music Education* 14: 251–269.

Digman, J. N. (1990). "Personality structure: Emergence of the five factor model." *Annual Review of Psychology* 41: 417–440.

DiMaggio, P. and Useem, M. (1978). "Social class and arts consumption: The origins and consequences of class differences in exposure to the arts in America." *Theory and Society* 5: 141–161.

Farnsworth, P. R. (1954). *The Social Psychology of Music*. Iowa: Iowa State University Press.

Finnäs, L. (1987). "Do young people misjudge each other's musical tastes?" *Psychology of Music* 15: 152–166.

Gergen, K.J. and Davis, K. E. (eds. 1985). *The Social Construction of the Person*. New York: Springer-Verlag.

Goldberg, L. R. (1993). "The structure of phenotypic personality traits." *American Psychologist* 48: 24–34.

Hargreaves, D. J., and North, A. C. (1999) "The functions of music in everyday life: Redefining the social in music psychology." *Psychology of Music* 27: 71–83.

Harré, R. (1979). *Social Being*. Oxford: Basil Blackwell.

Harré, R. (1992a). "The discursive creation of human psychology". *Symbolic Interaction* 15: 515–527.

Harré, R. (1992b), "Introduction: The second cognitive revolution." *American Behavioral Scientist* 35: 5–7.

Howe, M. J. A., and Sloboda, J. A. (1991a). "Young musicians' accounts of significant influences in their early lives: 1. The family and the musical background." *British Journal of Music Education* 8: 39–52.

Howe, M. J. A.., and Sloboda, J. A. (1991b) "Young musicians' accounts of significant influences in their early lives: 2. Teachers, practising and performing." *British Journal of Music Education* 8: 53–63.

Howe, M. J. A., Davidson, J. W. and Sloboda, J. A. (1998a). "Innate gifts and talents: Reality or myth?" *Behavioral and Brain Sciences* 21, 399–407.

Howe, M. J. A., Davidson, J. W., and Sloboda, J. A. (1998b). "Natural born talents undiscovered." *Behavioral and Brain Sciences* 21: 432–442.

Kanellopoulos, P.A. (1999). "Children's conception and practice of musical improvisation." *Psychology of Music* 27: 175–191.

Kemp, A. E. (1996). *The Musical Temperament*. Oxford: Oxford University Press.

Kline, P. (1994). "Personality tests," in S. E. Hampton and A. M. Coleman (eds.), *Individual Differences and Personality*. London: Longman, 77–96.

Lehmann, A. (1997). "The acquisition of expertise in music: Efficiency of deliberate practice as a moderating variable in accounting for sub-expert performance," in I. Deliège and J. A. Sloboda (eds.), *Perception and Cognition of Music*. Hove: Psychology Press, 161–187.

Litle, P., and Zuckerman, M. (1986). "Sensation seeking and music preferences." *Personality and Individual Differences* 20: 33–45.

Murnighan, J. K., and Conlon, D. E. (1991). "The dynamics of intense work groups: A study of British string quartets," *Administrative Science Quarterly* 36, June 1991: 165–186.

North A. C., and Hargreaves D. J. (1996). "Responses to music in a dining area." *Journal of Applied Social Psychology* 24: 491–501.

Oppenheim, A. N. (1992). *Questionnaire Design, Interviewing and Attitude Measurement*. New York: Pinter.

Pegg, C. (1984). "Factors affecting the musical choices of audiences in East Suffolk," *Popular Music* 4: 51–74..

Rawlings, D., and Ciancarelli, V. (1997). "Music preference and the Five-Factor Model of the NEO Personality Inventory." *Psychology of Music* 25: 120–132.

Robson, C. (1993). *Real World Research*. Oxford: Blackwell's.

Rorschach, H. (1921). *Psychodiagnostics*. Berne: Hans Huber.

Russell, P. A. (1997). "Musical tastes and society," in D. J. Hargreaves and A. C. North (eds.), *Social Psychology of Music*. Oxford: Oxford University Press, 141–158.

Searle, H., ed. (1966). *Hector Berlioz: A Selection from his Letters*. London: Gollancz.

Sheridan, D., Bloome, D., and Street, B., eds. (1998). *Writing Ourselves: Literacy Practices and the Mass-Observation Project*. London: Hampton Press.

Sloboda, J. A. (1998). "Everyday uses of music listening." *Proceedings of the Fifth International Conference on Music Perception and Cognition, Seoul, Korea, August, 1998*, 55–60.

Sloboda, J. A., and Howe, M. J. A. (1991). "Biographical precursors of musical excellence: An interview study". *Psychology of Music* 19: 3–21.

Sloboda, J. A.., Davidson, J. W., and Howe, M. J. A.. (1994a). "Is everyone musical?" *The Psychologist* 7: 349–354.

Sloboda, J. A., Davidson, J. W., and Howe, M. J. A. (1994b). "Musicians: Experts not geniuses." *The Psychologist* 7: 363–365.

Smith, J. A. (1994). "Reconstructing selves: An analysis of discrepancies between women's contemporaneous and retrospective accounts of the transition to motherhood". *British Journal of Psychology* 85: 371–392.

Smith, J. A. (1996). "Beyond the divide between cognition and discourse: Using interpretative phenomenological analysis in health psychology." *Psychology and Health* 11: 261–271.

Smith, J. A. (1999). "Identity development during the transition to motherhood: An interpretative phenomenological analysis." *Journal of Reproductive and Infant Psychology* 17: 281–299.

Smith, J. A., Flowers, P., and Osborn, M. (1997). "Interpretative phenomenological analysis and health psychology," in L. Yardley (ed.), *Material Discourses of Health and Illness*. London: Routledge, 68–91.

Smith, J. A., Harré, R., and van Langenhove, L., eds. (1995). *Rethinking Methods in Psychology*. London: Sage.

Weissweiler, E., ed. (1984). *The Complete Correspondence of Clara and Robert Schumann*. New York: Peter Lang.

CHAPTER 5

Empirical Methods in the Study of Performance

Eric Clarke

Introduction

From the perspective of musicology, the empirical study of performance has coincided with a move away from the primacy of the score and toward increasing interest in music *as* performance. The rise of performance studies as a research area has brought a focus on different performance traditions, the nature of performance interpretation and its relationship to analysis, and the legacy of historical recordings (now dating back 100 years) and what it can tell us about changes in performance styles. Musicologists have been interested in empirical studies of performance as ways of documenting what goes on in performance, and for their ability to make performance a concrete object of study with the same tangibility that was previously confined to scores and sketches.

Although performance occupies a central position in just about every musical culture, systematic studies of performance go back only to the turn of the twentieth century. The reason for this is the problem of transience: only once methods had been developed to record either the sounds of performance, or the actions of instruments, was any kind of detailed study possible—and so the piano roll, record, magnetic tape, and computer have all played their part at different stages in the short history of empirical studies of performance. Gabrielsson (1999) provides a survey of empirical studies starting with Binet and Courtier's (1895) study of piano playing, and demonstrates the rapid growth in the field—particularly since about 1980, while the 37 separate chapters in Rink (2002) and Parncutt and McPherson (2002) indicate how active the field continues to be. A significant factor in this development has been the involvement of psychologists, to whom music performance has appealed as an area of study on various grounds. It represents an example of a very sophisticated and complex motor skill, on which there is a wider research literature in psychology; it has affinities with language (about which there has been a great deal of psychological research), but represents a distinct form of nonverbal communication; it provides an opportunity to study rhythmic and other temporal skills at various levels of expertise; and it provides a "window" onto hidden cognitive processes in music. For these and other reasons, and because of the converging interests of psychologists and musicologists, performance research is perhaps the most developed area of empirical musicology—though the differing motivations for studying performance have given rise to certain problems, as I discuss at the end of this chapter.

Because of the specific issues investigated, and for technical reasons, the great majority of empirical work on performance has looked at keyboard performance. The keyboard offers a number of specific advantages for empirical research:

- It provides a ready-made context in which to study the coordination and control of concurrent tasks, because the two hands essentially "do the same thing" (albeit in mirror image).
- There is a large and varied repertoire of solo music for the instrument, providing the opportunity to study individual performance in an entirely realistic way, as well as a large ensemble repertoire (including piano duets and four-hand material).
- The percussive character of the instrument makes it an effective way to study rhythmic skills, and makes accurate timing analysis from sound files possible (due to the sharp onsets of events).
- It is easier and less intrusive to take direct mechanical measurements from the keyboard than from almost any other instrument, due to the physical separation of the instrument from the performer.
- Since the early 1980s a range of commercially available keyboard instruments has existed that can be directly monitored by computer, allowing performance data to be captured and analyzed easily and with considerable precision. Since the mid-1980s this range of instruments has included real pianos.

The principal focus of this chapter is therefore on the study of keyboard performance.

Landmarks

To give a quick overview of how the empirical study of performance has developed, the following is a list of some of the publications that have played an important part in defining the field:

- In the early 1930s, Seashore and his research associates developed an extensive research program in music performance at the University of Iowa, much of which is brought together and reported in Seashore's summative book [1967 (1938)]. This represents the earliest extensive and systematic empirical work on performance, and identified many of the issues that have remained the preoccupations of subsequent research.
- Povel (1977) describes expressive timing in a number of Bach harpsichord performances, and Bengtsson and Gabrielsson (1977) in performances of Swedish folk tunes. Together, these represent the first significant publications of the "modern" period of performance research.
- Shaffer (1981) is the first substantial paper to report results obtained from direct computer monitoring of the piano. The paper concentrates on timing, coordination, expression, and the cognitive representation of complex movements.

- Sundberg, Fryden, and Askenfelt (1983) is the first published attempt to produce an artificial model of performance expression, using a collection of separate rules that relate to local features of the music. Todd (1985) is a subsequent attempt to achieve the same goal using only a single rule applied recursively.
- Repp (1990a) is the first paper to look at a larger body of performance data, using commercial recordings and extracting performance data from the recorded sound. Since that first paper, Repp has gone on to investigate larger collections of performances, in some cases analyzing over 100 recorded performances of the same work.
- Davidson (1993) is the first published work analyzing the visual component of expressive performance.
- Rink (1995) represents the first large-scale publication bringing together musicologists and psychologists in the study of performance.

With this overall pattern of development in mind, the following sections discuss the different methods that have been used and some of the issues that have been tackled.

Using MIDI to Study Performance

As already observed, a survey of the existing empirical work on performance demonstrates that by far the largest body of research has examined data derived from the direct measurement of keyboard performances. Until the mid-1980s, this was only possible by building a specialized technical setup (examples of which are Seashore's piano camera in the 1930s, and Shaffer's piano/computer interface designed by him in the 1970s), or by using synthesizer keyboards. From the early 1980s, synthesizer keyboards could be connected to tone generators and computers using a specific digital communications protocol called the Musical Instrument Digital Interface (MIDI), making it possible to record and store on a computer all the keyboard events of a performance. But because MIDI was initially implemented on keyboards with poor touch characteristics and that produced unconvincing approximations to piano sound, little in the way of serious research was possible. In the mid 1980s, however, Yamaha produced first a synthesizer keyboard with more realistically weighted keys, and then a MIDI grand piano—a standard acoustic grand piano fitted with a photo-electric cell system which picked up the movements of the piano's keys, hammers, and pedals, and translated them into MIDI signals. This was essentially a commercial implementation of the type of system devised by Shaffer (see above), but with the advantage that it used a standardized method of data transfer, and could therefore be connected to any MIDI compatible computer. Soon after this, Yamaha came up with their Disklavier system (which is essentially the same as the MIDI piano, but with the added facility that the piano can be used to play back files, as well as to record them), while Bösendorfer developed their own sophisticated (and expensive) equivalent.

Although the following discussion is based on MIDI data from keyboards, it is worth noting that other kinds of MIDI controllers exist and can be used for performance research. There are MIDI drum pads, wind controllers, guitar, and other string controllers, as well as pitch-to-MIDI conversion systems designed to take input from a microphone and to convert the signal into MIDI information. This last category of device has the potential to extend the direct measurement method to the study of any instrument, including the human voice, and to make it possible to take ordinary sound recordings and convert them to MIDI. However there are serious limitations with existing pitch-to-MIDI conversion systems: they are not yet reliable or robust in performing the conversion and thus provide rather inaccurate and unreliable data, they cannot deal with anything other than a single melodic line, and they are sensitive to any sounds that might mask, or interact with, the instrumental signal. Nonetheless, advances in signal processing technology and software are likely to make this kind of conversion a practical reality in the future.

General introductions to MIDI can be found in a number of readily-available sources (e.g., Penfold 1990, Manning 1993). What follows is a simple and non-technical description of only those features of MIDI that are relevant to performance research. MIDI is essentially a digital coding of the features of a controller (i.e., a performance instrument of some kind) into a form that can either be used to manipulate a sound source to which the controller is connected, or simply stored in a file on a computer. Since the keyboard is the only controller represented in the existing research literature, the discussion here is confined to the way in which MIDI encodes keyboard events. Six features of keyboard performance are captured by MIDI:[1]

1. The identity of any key that is struck
2. The time at which a note starts
3. The time at which a note stops
4. The velocity of the key press or of the piano hammer as it hits the string (which is directly correlated with the loudness of the sound produced)
5. The time at which either the sostenuto or soft pedal is depressed
6. The time at which either the sostenuto or soft pedal is released

These data can be captured and stored by most desktop or laptop computers running any one of a large number of commercially available software packages—usually a sequencer of some kind (common ones include Vision, Cubase, and Logic, as well as the more sophisticated graphical programming environment called Max). Most of the data described above provide information that is completely self-explanatory: the resulting file records which notes are played, at what time, with what velocity, at what time they are released, and what pedaling might affect them. Two further pieces of data are also available, but not quite so directly: interonset interval (IOI), and articulation. The interonset interval of a note, usually taken to be a note's primary rhythmic property, is defined as *the time from the start of any note to the start of the next note in the same part*. The identification of a "part" in the definition given here can be tricky, but is equivalent to the rhythmic stream to which a note belongs (the relationship between the onset of a note in one part and the onset of an adjacent note in the other part is usually meaningless as a *rhythmic* property—though it can indicate something interesting about synchronization). In the case of a note-against-note texture (such as a two-part invention), the definition of each part is clear enough. Other textures may be rather more difficult to partition into streams, and may necessitate making pragmatic (rather than strongly theoretically founded) decisions.

The second piece of "hidden" data is articulation. The articulation of a note on a keyboard instrument is determined by the relationship between the sounding and silent parts of a note's time span: a staccato note is one in which the sounding portion of a note's IOI is shorter than the total IOI (i.e., part of the IOI is silent), and a legato note is one in which the sounding portion is either the same, or greater, than the total IOI—in this last case overlapping with the following note in the same part. The information to determine a note's articulation, therefore, is found in the relationship between the value of the IOI, and the period during which the key is actually depressed (given by the time difference between features 3 and 2 in the list of six above). This value can be further influenced by pedaling: if the sostenuto pedal is depressed prior to, or during, the sounding part of the note, then the critical value which determines the offset (end) of the note is either the release of either the note or the pedal—whichever is the later.

Most sequencer programs store MIDI information in a format that is appropriate for studio use but awkward for analytical purposes. In order to overcome this difficulty, and to provide various analytical and transforming possibilities, a software environment called POCO has been developed that can convert standard sequencer files into a variety of more readable text formats, provides the means to strip out selectively all kinds of information from the original performance file, and allows the transfer of data directly into a variety of statistics and graphics packages. The software can be used via the Web, and its rationale and structure (at an earlier stage of development) are described in Honing (1990).[2] At the most basic level it converts the timing of events from the "bars, beats, and ticks" format that most sequencers use into seconds and milliseconds (ms), and the velocity (dynamic) data from the 0 to 127 values that MIDI employs into a scale from 0 to 1.

Other than this simple conversion, MIDI velocity data need no transformation: they give a direct and immediately interpretable picture of the variations in loudness over time.[3] The IOI values are rather less transparent, since the duration of any note in a performance is a product of the duration specified by the notation combined with any stretching or contraction of that value introduced by the performer. It is these relatively small departures from what can be termed the "canonical value" of a note (as specified by the notation) that tend to be of interest in empirical studies of performance, since they are taken to indicate expressive effects (see below). For this reason, it is not usually the absolute value of the difference between a note's actual duration and its canonical value that is of interest, so much as its proportional increase or decrease. Take the case of crotchets alternating with pairs of quavers at an indicated tempo of 60 crotchets per minute. If played exactly as notated, each crotchet should last for exactly 1,000 ms and each quaver for 500 ms. Imagine some data from two keyboard performances of these notes with the IOIs shown in Figure 5.1. Two things are evident from these data: neither performance is metronomically precise (the IOIs vary from their canonical values of 1,000 and 500 ms); and as a whole the first sequence is played slower than the indicated tempo (most of the IOIs exceed their canonical value), while the second sequence is played close to the in-

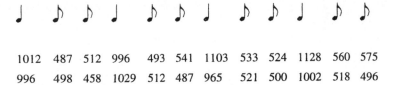

1012   487   512   996   493   541   1103   533   524   1128   560   575

996   498   458   1029   512   487   965   521   500   1002   518   496

Figure 5.1. Sample performance data (in milliseconds) for two performances of a simple rhythmic pattern.

dicated tempo (there is something like a balance of IOIs that exceed and fall short of their canonical values). It is not easy, however, to compare these two sets of data directly: Figure 5.2 shows the raw data in a graphical form, and although it is possible to see that the data of performance 1 tend to lie above those of performance 2 (i.e., the tempo of performance 1 is somewhat slower), the zigzag profile makes it hard to see what is going on. There are various ways to transform the data to bring out specific features and make comparisons between data easier: a common approach is to divide the duration of each note by a number representing the note's written value, usually expressed as a multiple of some underlying metrical value. For the sequence of crotchets and quavers being considered here, crotchets are represented by the value 2 and quavers by the value 1, and the result of dividing the two sets of data by the appropriate sequence of ones and twos is shown in Figure 5.3.

It is now a great deal more obvious that performance 1 is slower than performance 2, and furthermore it is also clear that performance 1 gets slower as it proceeds (it rises in the graph) while performance 2 stays more or less stable in terms of overall tempo. Figure 5.3 is essentially a tempo map, showing the momentary tempo of each note for the two performances—except that what is shown is actually the in-

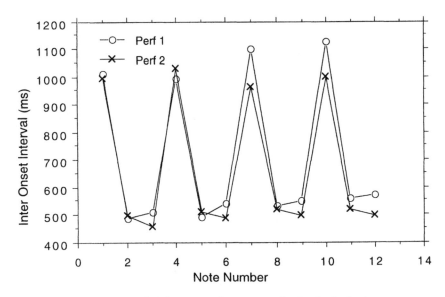

Figure 5.2. Raw timing data for two performances of a simple rhythmic pattern.

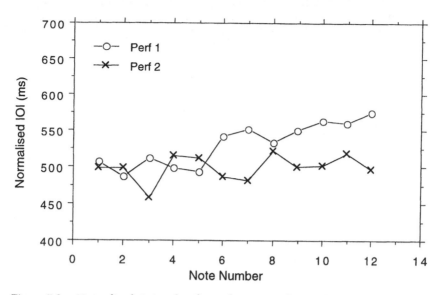

Figure 5.3.   Normalized timing data for performances of a simple rhythmic pattern.

verse of tempo (sometimes called "normalized IOI"). Because tempo is a more familiar concept, it is common for a further transformation (inversion of the data)[4] to be applied, with the result shown in Figure 5.4.

At least one more feature can be extracted from even such simple and small-scale data—a difference in the treatment of the tempo of quavers in the two performances. In performance 1 the second of each pair of quavers (the quavers are data

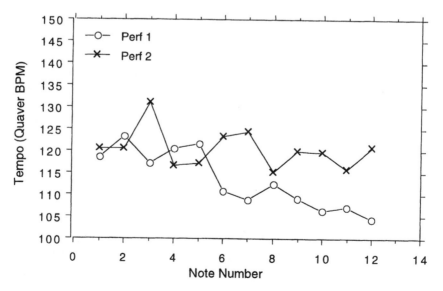

Figure 5.4.   Timing data represented in terms of momentary tempo (in quaver beats per minute).

points 2 and 3, 5 and 6, 8 and 9 and 11 and 12) is played consistently slower than the first, while in performance 2 it is the other way around, a result that could be used as evidence either for a difference in performance style between the two sets of data, or for a distinction between cognitive strategies in the two performers who were the source of the data.

Expression in Performance: Its Definition and Analysis

A central preoccupation in research on performance has been the nature and function of expression. A crucial question is how expression should be defined and characterized, and whether (and how) it might be measured. From some of the earliest work on performance [Seashore 1967 (1938)] has come the idea that expression should be defined as departures from some neutral norm, this norm itself being inexpressive as far as performance is concerned. For Seashore, and many others who have followed a Western, score-based tradition, this has translated into defining expression as departures from the values (principally rhythmic and dynamic) specified in the score. The rationale for this approach is that what makes a *performance* expressive is what the *performer* brings to the piece beyond what the composer has specified in the score. Thus expression consists of systematic departures from the explicit notation of the score—whether these departures are deliberate and conscious on the part of the performer or not (for further discussion, see Clarke 1995).

A problem with this approach is that it regards the score as "the piece" in a kind of disembodied, ahistorical fashion, apparently divorced from any of the cultural assumptions about how the notation might be understood and interpreted. For example, it was an assumed convention of the French Baroque to play passages of equally notated quavers in an alternating long-short pattern (*notes inégales*), and to play dotted notes with variable amounts of over- and underdotting. An analysis which concluded that the performer consistently applied an expressive emphasis to the first of a pair of quavers, or to the dotted note in dotted rhythms, might be thought to have missed the point since these "departures" from the notation are implicit within the notation itself, and thus do not constitute the performer's contribution. However, exactly the same might be said of the overwhelming tendency for performers to slow up toward the end of phrases or sections, an equally pervasive cultural expectation within the Classical and Romantic repertoire—but this phenomenon has become probably the most intensively studied *expressive* property of performance. The problem comes down to whether expression should be regarded as the specific contribution of an individual performer, or in more social terms—as the combination of widely shared cultural norms with the particular input of the individual performer. If it is the former, then where one places the boundary between cultural norms and individual expression becomes a critical consideration; if the latter, then a more relaxed attitude to the source of the phenomenon (cultural convention or individual intention) is possible. In practice, few researchers have devoted much attention to these issues.

A more concrete methodological issue is how to distinguish between random or accidental variations in timing, dynamics, or articulation, and properties that might legitimately be considered expressive. The problem of distinguishing deliberate (hence expressive) features from mistakes is problematic: the most widespread solution adopted in the literature is to make use of the principle of reproducibility, and to pay attention only to those features that emerge from the average of a number of repeated performances, rather than individual data points. While this approach is consistent with the standard approach to empirical data used in the behavioral sciences, it runs counter to a fundamental principle in musical performance—the idea that performance is a recreative, rather than reproductive, act: each performance is a specific realization of a piece of music, and there is no reason why any two such realizations should converge toward identity. Variation between notionally "identical" renderings of the same piece cannot therefore be regarded as random, and the average of a set of performances, by collapsing together distinct approaches to the piece, may have little value.

An alternative is to use internal consistency within a single performance, and to analyze the data guided by principles of musical coherence to distinguish expressive features from errors. There are still problems here: first, internal consistency within a single performance is subject to the same "uniqueness" argument as applies to separate performances (there may be good reasons to play the same, or a similar, passage occurring in two places with deliberately different expressive features); and second, musical analysis is not an exact science and cannot be relied upon to provide an unequivocal basis for distinguishing between errors and intentions. The approach actually adopted in the published literature has often depended on the nature of the task and the quality of the data. When the performance data come from relatively simple musical materials, collected under controlled conditions with performers who are not of concert standard, repeated performances and groups of subjects have been used, with standard statistical methods (e.g., Clarke 1993). By contrast, when the data are from concert pianists performing concert repertoire, there is often no opportunity to collect repeat performances, and in these cases the authors may depend on the expertise of the performers and the consequent standard of the data to justify the abandonment of standard statistical methods (e.g., Palmer 1996). A further possibility, demonstrated in work by Widmer (2002), is to apply data mining methods to large bodies of data taken from skilled performers in order to extract general principles from unique performances that all belong to a narrowly focused performance style and repertoire.

Example: Chopin's Prelude, Op. 28 No. 4, in E Minor

The data shown in Figure 5.5 come from an analysis of two performances of Chopin's E Minor Prelude by a concert pianist playing on a MIDI grand piano (Clarke 1995). The performer was a professional pianist who played on a Yamaha MIDI grand piano in one of the teaching rooms of the Music Department at City University, London. The only people present were the pianist himself and three researchers involved in the study. The performer was originally asked to provide three performances of the prelude in succession, but for a variety of reasons (not least his own interest in the study) he ended up playing the piece six times in the space of about an hour. There were no instructions as to how he should play it on any occasion, and between performances he spontaneously provided an idiosyncratic commentary on his playing. The performances therefore took place in a rather unusual—even artificial—situation, but one with which the performer seemed entirely comfortable. The data were recorded on a desktop Macintosh computer using a commercial sequencer (Vision), and were processed using POCO and a statistics program (Statview) in the ways that have already been described.

The piece consists of a rhythmically differentiated right hand melodic line accompanied for the most part by a constant stream of three-note left hand quaver chords,[5] and this immediately raises questions about how the data should be examined and represented. The data from the right hand are an obvious target for analysis, since the right hand (particularly in this kind of texture) is conventionally regarded as the primary carrier of expression, and in this piece consists of a stream of single notes. The disadvantage is that it provides rather sparse and intermittent data (many bars contain only two notes—a dotted minim and a crotchet) compared with the regular quavers of the left hand. The problem with the left hand is that it consists of three- and four-note chords, each note of which has its own dynamic and timing value. One solution is to simplify the left hand data by regarding each chord as a unit, resulting in a single timing and dynamic measure for each chord. There are various ways in which this might be done, but for the purposes of this example the dynamic value for each chord is represented by the average dynamic value of the notes played in the chord, and the IOI for the chord is calculated as the time from the first note of the chord to be struck (whichever note that is) to the first note of the subsequent chord (whether that note is in the same voice or not). The rationale for this is that the most fundamental rhythmic property of any event sequence is its attack-point pattern, and that the primary dynamic attribute is a property of the whole chord regarded as a fused entity. Figure 5.5 thus shows sequences of single data points for the tempo and dynamic level of each chord in the left hand, for each of two performances.

The large-scale, two-part shape of the performances can be seen in the tempo and particularly the dynamic data; the bar-by-bar pattern of expressive timing can be plainly seen at the start; and various differences between the expressive shaping of the two performances can also be seen. In the original publication (Clarke 1995), these differences were used to argue for two different interpretations of the piece (articulated in these two performances) relating to an ambivalence in its underlying formal structure. The purpose of the example here has been simply to illustrate the kinds of data that can be gathered and some of the questions that they can be used to address.

The Limitations of MIDI

A number of sources of information available from MIDI were not considered in the study described above (pedaling, articulation, synchronization within chords and between parts), while other features of piano performance are impossible to study using MIDI: because MIDI data are derived from the mechanism of the keyboard action and not the sound, anything that relates to acoustical properties of the instrument is excluded from the kind of analysis shown above. This includes a whole variety of

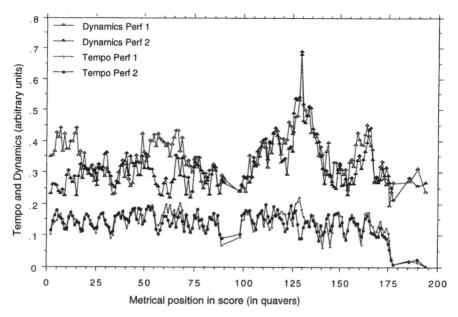

Figure 5.5. Tempo and dynamic data from two expert performances of the Chopin Prelude in E minor, Op. 28 no. 4.

timbral properties, which are the consequence of complex interactions between simultaneously and consecutively sounding strings and the whole body of the instrument, as well as of pedaling and the specific actions of the hammers and dampers. These are, of course, properties over which a skilled performer exercises considerable control, and may even be regarded as the primary expressive parameters in certain kinds of repertoire: MIDI data from a performance of Steve Reich's *Piano Phase*, for example, would entirely miss the resonance and "streaming" effects that take place between the two pianos in a performance of the piece, and are arguably its most important features.

Then there are the physical and social dimensions of the performance: neither the interactions with any listeners who may be present, nor a whole variety of visual data (most obviously the movements, demeanor, and facial expressions of the performer) can be considered. Some of these have been studied separately (see below), but there is little work that tries to bring these different sources of information together to provide a more multidimensional view of performance (though see Clarke and Davidson 1998, for a preliminary and partial attempt, and Juslin, Friberg, and Bresin 2001–2002 for a rather different approach).

Finally, there is one simple but rather practical limitation to the use of MIDI: the performances have to be *new* performances given by living performers who are willing to give up their time to give a performance on a MIDI instrument of some sort. This immediately excludes the huge resource and historical perspective that commercial recordings can provide, and also limits research to the study of those performers who are willing to take part in these "research" performances—often recorded in unnatural circumstances (usually without an audience or any sense of occasion) and on instruments that may not be of concert standard. For this reason, methods have been developed for obtaining performance data from existing recordings, as the next section describes.

Performance Data from Recordings

The attractions of working with recordings are self-evident: not only is there is no other way to study Cortot or Michelangeli, but you can also deal with instruments other than the piano, and you are working directly on the real artifacts of musical culture. Moreover an enormous heritage of recordings, now going back over a century, is becoming easily accessible to scholars, partly through CD reissues of historical recordings, but also through the efforts of major collections such as the British Library Sound Archive (London).

There are, however, significant drawbacks. One is that the data are much more difficult to extract than MIDI data: retrieving useful information is at best laborious, and at worst impossible. The other is that historical recordings present problems of interpretation comparable to those that apply to other forms of documentary evidence, but less well recognized owing to the comparative novelty of this area of research. One such problem is the fact that recording speeds were not standardized in early recordings (and were in any case subject to mechanical variation). Early recording techniques were also highly intrusive: in the mechanical era (up to 1925) players had to crowd around a large horn, and this not only drastically affected the balance between instruments but also disrupted the social environment of normal performance. (Such recordings may be no more true to life than the carefully posed studio portraits of Victorian families, with their suspiciously well-scrubbed and immaculately dressed children.) Ironically, when the technology to make high-fidelity recordings became available, with Decca's full-frequency-range recordings (ffrr) from 1945 and the adoption of magnetic tape from 1950, it was rapidly used to create recordings of performances that had never been, by means of editing techniques: "it was not uncommon," writes Day (2000: 26), "for the master-tape for an LP, lasting perhaps fifty or fifty-five minutes, to be the result of 150 splices." This in no way invalidates the recording as an object for musicological study: it may not be a direct representation of an actual performance, but at the same time such recordings represent one of the principal forms in which music was made available in the twentieth century, and was consumed by an ever-increasing public. The point to be made is simply that there is nothing straightforward or transparent about recordings as historical sources.

There have been two approaches to obtaining performance data from existing sound recordings: one has been to try to derive something like the same level of detail that MIDI recordings provide, while the other has been to focus on a slightly coarser-grained approach, usually limited to timing. The first of these two approaches has been used most extensively by Repp in a stream of publications investigating in some cases very large repertoires of recorded performances (e.g., Repp 1998, 1999).

His method has been to digitize the music and then use a digital waveform editor (SoundEdit16) to display the waveform at a suitable level of temporal resolution. A cursor is positioned at clearly recognizable note onsets and used to label those points, using auditory feedback from playing the waveform to decide on the onsets of any difficult notes. These labels identify the times of note onsets, and are saved to a file for subsequent analysis. The method is primarily designed to retrieve IOIs, but has also been used to measure asynchronies among nominally simultaneous note onsets. A meaningful analysis of dynamic levels is even more difficult to derive from sound recordings than is timing, because of the problem of estimating the *effective* dynamic level of simultaneously occurring events (multinote chords). Repp has, however, undertaken such a study (Repp 1999) using software (Signalyze) that provides the amplitude envelope of the signal. His approach is to take the peak amplitude of the envelope after the onset of a note (or chord) as the index of its dynamic level, and to make no attempt to separate out different streams (voices) within the texture;[6] clearly the appropriateness of this approach depends on the texture of the music, and it would be of dubious value in a polyphonic context. Repp's method can in principle be used with any instrument or combination of instruments, although it becomes increasingly difficult to use as the texture becomes more complex, or with instruments that have indistinct note onsets (e.g., the voice). It should also be noted that it is laborious and time-consuming, involving a number of operations to extract the data for each single event.

A second approach has been to focus on timing at a variety of levels, and to extract the timing information by tapping on some device (usually a computer keyboard, or a MIDI instrument connected to a computer) in synchrony with the music (e.g., Cook 1995, Bowen 1996, and for a study that also considers dynamic shaping see Martin 2002). This "tap along" method has the merits of simplicity and economy, but clearly depends on the precision with which the researcher can synchronize with the music. For relatively large musical units (sections, phrases, sub-phrases, and even bars) this is not a problem, since the synchronization error will be a small proportion of the measured unit. However, for smaller units (beats or single notes) it can become a serious problem, and the method has generally not been attempted below the level of the beat. One reassuring point is that the synchronization error is not cumulative, since it is monitored and adjusted at every unit onset, and a check on the reliability of the method can be made either by making multiple passes at the material, or by enlisting independent judges.[7]

Example: Beethoven's Ninth Symphony

In a chapter broadly concerned with the relationship between analysis and performance, Cook (1995) explores Furtwängler's conducted performances of Beethoven's Ninth Symphony in the context of Schenker's analysis of the music. The study focuses on tempo in performance, and uses the "tap along" method to extract bar-by-bar tempo information for the first movement of two live performances available on CD (the use of live recordings helped to minimize the problems resulting from editing, which are particularly acute in studies of performance timing). The technique involves playing the CD in the CD-ROM drive of a computer, and tapping the space bar of the computer keyboard in synchrony with the onset of each bar. The computer then stores the times for the inter-tap intervals in a file, which can be shown as a bar-by-bar tempo chart. Cook (1995: 114) observes:

> Because it is sometimes difficult to decide exactly where the downbeat falls, and because of factors of motor control, this process is not entirely reliable. In repeated tests based on the same passage of music, my responses varied by an average of 60 milliseconds, which is around 3 percent of the total duration of each bar; deviations of 100 milliseconds (5 percent) were quite frequent. For this reason it would be foolish to make too much of small transitions which appear on the bar-to-bar level; the data are not sufficiently accurate. But the discrepancies are not cumulative, and this means that inferences regarding the broad shaping of tempo (which is what [the] chapter is about) are robust.

The study goes on to use the data to refute the assertion that Furtwängler's tempo fluctuations were arbitrary and uncontrolled, and to show that his performances correspond to Schenker's analytical view of the piece. Cook (1995: 109) points out that, simply from listening to the performances, it appears that

> Furtwängler shapes his phrases, balances his instrumentation, or articulates formal junctures in ways which do match what Schenker says, or that at least seem to belong within the same language of performance that Schenker is talking. But judgments of this sort are inevitably vague and impressionistic, especially in view of the limited sound quality and control over balance that was possible in live recordings around 1950. And close listening, by itself, is even more inadequate when it comes to large-scale tempo modifications; waves of accelerando and decelerando are clearly audible, but it can be difficult to disentangle them from dynamics, articulation, tonal quality, and all the other dimensions that contribute to the energy or tension level of the music. Unlike these other dimensions, however, tempo relationships can easily be measured in an empirical and reasonably accurate manner.

As with the previous example, the intention here is not to raise the issues that are the concern of the original study, but simply to point out that the method is viable and useful, and permits a *kind* of discussion that would be hard or impossible to sustain without the empirical data that the method provides. One of Cook's main arguments in the original study is that Furtwängler makes use of relatively large-scale arch-shaped tempo profiles that allow him to use tempo for both structural and rhetorical purposes in performance. Without the tempo graphs which the "tap along" method provides, it would be impossible—or at the very least verbally cumbersome and far more open to dispute—to demonstrate the particular characteristics of performance that are used to argue both for the particular audible characteristics of Furtwängler's performances, and for the existence of a specific history and ideology of conducting that Cook traces back to Wagner and Bayreuth.

Evaluative and Qualitative Methods

Measuring the timing, dynamic, and even timbral properties of performances has produced a wealth of previously unknown information but, as has already been pointed out, it gives only a very partial view of what happens in performance. In particular, such an approach entirely misses the social dimension of performance (the interactions between performers, and between performers and others, discussed in Davidson, chapter 4, this volume). While it is possible to quantify some of these characteristics, there is much to be gained from adopting a qualitative approach.[8] A method which owes a lot to work in psychotherapy is to get performers to speak about their own performances, and then to analyze both what they say and what they do. As a research method this "talking analysis" is aimed at discovering the intentions, motivations, and evaluations of one or more performers in relation to their own (or another's) performance. The data for this kind of approach are usually of two kinds: first, a sound recording of one or more performances, and second, a sound recording of the *commentary* by one or more of the original performers, or another commentator. The commentary is often made by a person who listens to the original sound recording of the performance, stopping the recording as often as he or she likes to make whatever comments are appropriate, and possibly doing so on more than one occasion. In this way a detailed account can be built up outside the pressure of "real-time" performance. The subsequent treatment of the resulting commentary can take many forms (see Davidson, chapter 4, this volume; Robson 1993), usually concerned in one way or another with a content analysis.

An example of this approach is the work of Sansom (1997), who studied musical and personal interactions in free improvisation. The study involved a number of pairs of performers who improvised together, the participants being experienced improvisers who had played music with one another previously. Sansom recorded each improvising duo, and then on subsequent occasions asked each of the two players individually to listen to the recording and to stop it and comment on anything that occurred to them about what was happening or what they had been thinking about at the time. These commentaries were also recorded and then subjected to a content analysis. The following (Sansom 1997, ii: 9) is an extract from the comments provided by one of the members of a guitar and saxophone duo— two players who are very experienced improvisers and have frequently played together in the past:

> Sort of little funk chords come out there for some reason, it took me quite a lot by surprise. I quite like the sound, I reiterated them a few times . . . I never usually do . . . techniques so recognizable as that, very rarely. . . . Another thing from that, I don't really play on the beat, I play in the bits in between. . . . And often on playback it sounds a bit weird 'cos it's just like a little time gap between you—the same rhythm but not together on it. I was thinking about it there because the melodic thing isn't important, we were both skidding about anywhere. We both decided to play around with the rhythm and it sounded a bit messy but er . . .

I really enjoyed that bit . . . sort of juxtaposing really brutish behaviour with really small, er, considerate little things . . . I can't remember what comes next, I hope it's something very quiet—we'll see. . . .

Right. Mick didn't feel like stopping at the same time as I did . . . er . . . obviously a certain energy that I was feeling diminished. I thought it was a good time to stop. At a time when Mick was still on a high, so I started to listen to see what he would do. How far he would go on without me commenting. I'd a fair idea he would go on quite a distance . . . I'd no idea what he'd make it into. . . .

The analysis of this and similar passages provided by Sansom's participants focuses on both musical and interpersonal processes. As the extract demonstrates, the players' transcripts constitute a complex mix of recollection, current comments, awareness of musical materials, and awareness of interpersonal dynamics. Sansom's content analysis categorizes the remarks into themes that then form the basis for a discussion of creativity and interaction in ensemble improvisation. The advantage of a qualitative approach such as this is its potential to investigate an enormous diversity of phenomena that the quantitative methods discussed earlier are incapable of addressing, including issues of motivation, intention, reaction, and evaluation.

A difficulty, however, is the way in which empirical method is combined with interpretation. Every empirical method has an interpretative component, but in most quantitative methods the premises and boundaries of interpretation are usually fairly well recognized. Qualitative methods, however, have been accepted for a very much shorter time, and have not yet acquired the stability (it may simply be familiarity) of their quantitative counterparts. When a quantitative test gives a certain outcome, and subsequent discussion then interprets that result and places it in the context of other work, it is fairly clear (if one accepts the premises of the method) where the reporting of results stops and interpretation starts. This is much less clearly the case with a qualitative method such as that used by Sansom, where the assignment of verbal data to content categories is itself a strongly interpretative process. The objection leveled at qualitative research of this kind is that it is too speculative— that it sets itself up as empirical, and then goes about its business in a manner that looks more like literary criticism. This objection partly reflects the fact that the interpretative assumptions of most quantitative methods have simply become so deeply embedded as to be invisible, but it remains the case that qualitative methods have yet to attain the systematic and explicit character of empiricism in the eyes of many. Robson (1993) and Smith, Harré, and van Langenhove (1995) provide fuller accounts of this debate.

Analyzing Visual Components of Performance

Performance is not only a sonic event, and the visual component of performance offers a rich domain for empirical study. In a number of publications, Davidson (1993, 1994, 1995) showed how observers could make accurate judgments of the expressive properties of performances on the basis of video data. The participants in her studies watched and listened to a number of different types of material: normal video with or without sound, video with sound from a different performance overdubbed, and what are called "point-light displays." These last are video recordings made with the performer wearing small spots or strips of reflective material on the major joints (wrist, elbow, shoulder, hip, knee) and head in strong illumination, and then played back on a monitor with the contrast turned to maximum. The resulting image consists simply of spots of light, with the rest of the body and instrument invisible. Earlier work in psychology (e.g., Runeson and Frykholm 1983) showed that viewers are able to perceive significant attributes (such as gender, physical effort, and intention) from a point-light display, suggesting that this information is conveyed by the dynamics of the moving display. Davidson showed similarly that viewers were able to distinguish accurately between expressionless, normal, and exaggerated performances by a variety of instrumentalists on the basis of as little as two seconds of point-light video without sound. She also found that, when sound was present, nonmusicians tended to be less influenced by it than by the video image: for example, when a point-light video of an exaggerated performance was overdubbed with the sound of the same person playing in an expressionless manner, nonmusicians tended to rate the performance toward the exaggerated end of the scale—whereas their ratings were toward the expressionless end of the scale when the *image* was from the expressionless performance and the sound from the exaggerated condition.

Other studies by Davidson (e.g., Davidson 1994, 1995) used ordinary video images and were designed to investigate whether a performer made use of a fixed repertoire of expressive gestures in performance, and whether viewers could identify their meaning. The technique involved making video recordings, from a fixed position, of a performer (in this case a pianist) who played a mixture of repertoire. The video recordings were shown to viewers who were asked to identify specific types of movement gesture, and give some indication of what they thought these gestures "meant" in terms of their relationship with the music. A variant of this method was a study (Clarke and Davidson, 1998) that combined the type of MIDI data analysis described earlier in this chapter with a movement analysis taken from a video recording. In this case, the movement analysis involved the detailed tracking of a pianist's head movements using specialized video analysis equipment. The resulting continuous plot of head position was then compared with MIDI data from the piano in an analysis of the relationship between expressive movement, and expressive timing and dynamics.

At a still more detailed level, Sloboda, Clarke, Parncutt, and Raekallio (1998) used video to record the hand movements of pianists as part of a project on keyboard fingering. A camera was mounted directly above the keyboard of a MIDI instrument, with powerful sideways illumination to highlight (with light and shadow) which finger depressed which key. The video recording was then used to match the finger that depressed each key with the corresponding note in the MIDI output. There is also the potential to use rather more sophisticated and automated methods in analyzing movement in performance. A preliminary study by Winold, Thelen, and Ulrich (1994) investigated the bow-arm movements of cellists, using a method which employed an optoelectronic motion analysis system, in which the position in space of various specified points on the player and instrument (just the bow in this case) were continuously tracked by computer. The technique has the potential to provide data on the continuous movements of instrumentalists and conductors during performance, and offers the prospect of a much more diverse and detailed study of movement in performance than has so far been undertaken.

Example: The Detection of Expression in Point-Light Displays.

Having discovered that viewers can pick up the expressive intentions of performers from point-light displays, Davidson (1994) studied which parts, or combinations of parts, of the body are particularly "informative" in making expressive judgments. The design of this study was that a single performer (a pianist) played a short extract of music in three different performance manners (deadpan, expressive, exaggerated), and with seven different arrangements of point-light patches attached to his body:

1. All patches: head, right shoulder, right elbow, and both wrists
2. All patches except elbow
3. Head and wrists only
4. Wrists only
5. Head only
6. Elbow only
7. Shoulder only

This is clearly not an exhaustive list of all the possible combinations, but it represents the maximum that could be reasonably investigated given that the pianist had to play the music in each of these point-light arrangements, and in each of the performance manners, resulting in 21 (3 × 7) performances. Video recordings were made of all 21 performances, and were shown (without sound) in different random orders to a total of 15 observers (graduate music students) who were instructed to rate each performance on a seven-point scale of expressivity (from 1 = inexpressive to 7 = highly expressive).

The results showed that the observers were reliably able to identify the three different manners of performance; that the different point-light arrangements resulted in significantly different patterns of scores; and that the scores for the three versions were different for each point-light arrangement. From this somewhat complex pattern of findings, one simple discovery is that the head and wrists seem to convey most of the expressive information: the "head and wrists only" arrangement gave results that were essentially identical to those for the "all patches" condition, and even "head only" gave a pattern of scores that was close to that for "all patches". "Wrists alone," however, seemed to give very misleading information, with all three performance manners eliciting rather similar (and inappropriately high) expressivity ratings. Some of the observers' comments indicated that it was the level of *activity* in the wrists (largely a consequence of the movements necessary simply to play the piece) that led to consistently high ratings. As one subject put it (Davidson 1994: 297–298) "I suspect I'm rating this wrist performance as highly expressive just because there is plenty of action. When wrists are combined with other areas of the body, I look to the whole, and the emphasis on fast motion is reduced for I see an elegant arch of the back and a delicate hand lift and it is from the combined information that I am able to recognize the intention of the piece." The study, then, shows how relatively simple techniques can be used to investigate how different parts of the body are involved in communicating expression, and what relationship there might be between quantitative and more qualitative factors in this process. Since this empirical work was done, the available technology has developed enormously, and rather than asking the performer to play 21 times, with different point-light arrangements for each, it would now be possible simply to record three performances (deadpan, expressive, and exaggerated), each with the full array of point lights, and then use computer editing facilities to edit out individual point-lights, allowing all possible combinations to be investigated, and ensuring that each performance manner, of which each edit was a variant, really *was* constant.

Performance Models and Algorithms

The availability of powerful desktop computers and associated software has made new empirical methods possible, and has also facilitated the construction of models of musical performance. Artificial models of performance have played a significant part in the development of empirical approaches and have often been closely connected with empirical work. When research in the late 1970s demonstrated that musical performance possessed a variety of systematic features, it became an attractive proposition to see whether these features could be embodied in, and simulated by, an artificial model of some kind: Sundberg, Fryden, and Askenfelt (1983), Clynes (1983), and Todd (1985) represent some of the earlier examples of this kind of work. While the model developed by Sundberg and his coworkers was based on their own intuitions, and makes no claim to be derived from explicit empirical evidence, Todd's various models (Todd 1985, 1989, 1992) come from analyses of performance data, and have in turn motivated and directed subsequent empirical studies using one or other model as their starting point (e.g., Windsor and Clarke 1997).

The function and purpose of such models have been misunderstood by some—at times because of inappropriate claims made by their authors. As with the majority of work in artificial intelligence, the primary purpose of a model is as an explanatory device: the model embodies certain psychological principles, and the aim is to draw conclusions from its successes and failures about the principles on which it is based. The outputs are of comparatively little significance in themselves: a *model* of expressive performance, for example, has little value as a *source* of expressive performances, but has the potential to identify important issues in the theory on which it is based.

The purpose of this brief discussion is neither to explain in detail how any of the various models work, nor to chart their successes and failures, but simply to note some general characteristics of the approaches that they embody, and their implications for the empirical study of performance. The models in this field can be divided into those that approach the subject by means of a single explanatory principle (e.g., Todd 1985) and those which adopt a "multi-rule" approach (e.g., Sundberg, Friberg, and Fryden 1991; Juslin, Friberg, and Bresin 2001–2002). Todd (1985, 1989, 1992) has proposed a number of variants of a model of expressive timing and dynamics based on sensitivity to phrase structure, and implemented by means of an algorithm (a rule system) that uses tempo and dynamic curves based on pendular motion. The algorithm takes the pitches and rhythms of the score as its input, along with a hierarchical phrase structure analysis of the music, supplied by the user.[9] A tempo and dynamic curve is applied to each phrase unit at every level of structure, the result being a pattern of tempo and dynamics that directly reflects the hierarchical importance of every phrase boundary; the user can direct the model to work within more or less extreme limits of tempo and dynamic variation, and to pay more or less attention to different levels of the phrase structure. The output of the model is a file specifying the precise temporal and dynamic value (i.e., the "expressive" value) of each note from the original input file.

The model developed by Sundberg and his coworkers (see, e.g., Sundberg, Friberg, and Fryden 1991) is rather different in conception and operation. Rather than using a single principle that is responsive to hierarchical structure, it consists of a collection of separate and much more specific rules, some of which operate globally and have no sensitivity to structure, while others are responsive to local features of the music. An example of the former is the rule "the higher, the louder" which increases the dynamic level of a note in proportion to its pitch height; an example of the latter is the "melodic charge emphasis" rule, which increases the duration, dynamic, and degree of vibrato applied to a note according to the harmonic remoteness of the note from its local tonic.

Finally, Juslin, Friberg and Bresin (2001–2002) have proposed a model which combines four elements corresponding to the acronym GERM: a set of generative rules (G) that relate musical structure to performance expression; principles of emotional expression (E) in performance; a component that introduces deliberate random variability (R) in timing, intended to simulate the uncontrolled low-level variations that characterize the human motor system; and a component which is intended to capture the motion character (M) of expressive performance. The generative rules in the first element are essentially those developed by Sundberg and his coworkers, but the addition of the three other elements is an attempt to develop a model that is more inclusive than previous attempts, and that accounts for the influence of features other than structure alone in the shaping of performance expression. An initial empirical evaluation of the model, reported in the paper, suggests that the E element is actually the most powerful, but that the idea of four separate but interacting components is indeed a powerful way to model performance expression, leaving the authors to conclude that "by considering all four components of the GERM model together, we will be better able to understand the variability usually found in music performance data" (Juslin, Friberg and Bresin 2001–2002: 109).

From an empirical point of view, the value of such models lies in the definite predictions that they make, against which one can investigate the phenomena of real performance. They may represent a rather more interesting baseline for the measurement of expressive deviation than the idealized flat line of the score—a baseline that, after all, has no psychological reality (repeated studies have shown that it is impossible for a human performer to produce a completely deadpan, or expressionless, performance). In a similar manner, Parncutt, Sloboda, Clarke, Raekallio, and Desain (1997) offer an ergonomic model of piano fingering *not* as a plausible "solution" to the problem of how pianists decide on fingerings, but as a baseline of physical constraints against which to assess actual fingering choices - which arguably are influenced by much more than physical convenience. There has been relatively little empirical investigation of the available models of expression, with the possible exception of Clynes's work which, because of its controversial claims, has attracted rather more attention and investigation than others (e.g., Repp 1989, 1990b, Thompson 1989, Clynes 1990, 1995). Such empirical work as there is has generally aimed to test the models, assessing the success with which they simulate real performance. An alternative approach, however, is use the model as a tool, as a way of highlighting what it is that makes human performances interesting. This is the perspective taken by my final example.

Example: Schubert's Impromptu in G Flat Major

Windsor and Clarke (1997) use Todd's (1992) model in conjunction with an expert performance of the first 16 bars of Schubert's G flat major Impromptu in order to investigate different components of expressive timing and dynamics. After recording MIDI data (tempo and dynamics) from an expert performance on a Disklavier piano, Windsor and Clarke attempted to simulate the performance using Todd's model, with the only inputs being the pitches and rhythms of the score, and a phrase structure analysis. Different simulation attempts varied only in the "weight" given to each level of the phrase structure, on the assumption that if the model has any validity it should be able to approximate the expert performance if an appropriate pattern of weightings could be found. The output from each attempt was compared with the data from the expert performance using correlation analysis, trying with successive simulations to arrive at the best fit (i.e., the highest correlation) between the simulation and the data. The study found that the best fit for the timing data required weighting the lowest levels of the phrase structure (half-bars and bars) more heavily than the middle and high levels; this weighting, however, resulted in a rather poor fit for the dynamic data, which were modeled much better by weighting the middle and high levels more heavily than the lower ones. This has implications both for the principles and design of the model, and for an interpretation of what the performer might be doing. In terms of the model, it demonstrates that the assumption that timing and dynamics are rigidly and directly linked is too simplistic; and in terms of performance expression, it suggests that performers may be using timing and dynamics in different ways to project (or respond to) different aspects of structure. In this performance, timing seemed to operate in response to more local structures, and dynamics to middle-level structures.

The simulations, although approximating to the expert performance, captured its features in only a rather partial manner—and the study was equally concerned with those aspects of the performance that the model did *not* capture (it included a discussion of how these discrepancies might be explained). The advantage of the model, then, is that it highlights those features of the data that are not systematic, or that are systematic according to some different principle. Those same features might have emerged from a comparison with the "flat line" of the score, but they are thrown into much sharper relief when the data are analyzed against the background of an attempt to model the generic features of performance by systematic means. The paper concludes (Windsor and Clarke 1997: 149):

> In this paper, we have demonstrated the way in which a model of perform-
> ance may act as a tool in the analysis of performance data. Although the
> model fails to account for every aspect of a human performance, and could
> possibly be revised in the light of the data collected here, these failures are
> seen as positive because they highlight different aspects of musical expression.
> The model provides a baseline that is derived from a strong theoretical posi-
> tion, against which other expressive strategies can be assessed. In its clear and
> unambiguous modeling of continuous expressive strategies, the model allows
> one to factor out noncontinuous strategies in a manner not possible when a
> performance is analyzed in relation to an isochronous score.

Conclusions and Prospects

Since the late 1970s, when the "contemporary" period of empirical work on per-
formance began, there have been a number of significant achievements. A much more systematic description of a whole variety of phenomena that were previously only known in broad outline is now available, and as a result there is more extensive recognition of the importance of studying music as performance rather than in the score-
based manner that has up to now been the dominant mode. This interest in the de-
tailed characteristics of performance converges with a dramatically increased interest in the history of recorded performance. The confluence of these two lines of research raises the fascinating prospect of a much more serious and detailed examination of performance style and its historical changes, as well as a way of bridging the divide between the ways in which notated music and unnotated music are studied. If music is studied as performance, then whether it exists in a notated form or not becomes an issue that is separable from how (or whether) the music is studied at all.

There have been problems, however. Because of the sheer volume of data that comes from even a relatively short performance, there has been the danger of a lack of perspective. It is easy to become buried in the expressive minutiae of a four-bar phrase and to forget that performance is rather more than tempo curves and dynamic accents. A related problem is that the aims and types of explanation and dis-
cussion that are of interest to psychologists working in this field may be of less in-
terest to musicologists, and *vice versa*. Psychologists are, broadly speaking, more interested in general mechanisms (of motor control, perception, cognition) than in particular instances, while musicology tends to be primarily concerned with inves-
tigating phenomena that are more narrowly focused and more specifically located in terms of history, culture, or genre. This has at times meant that the two disciplines, which should have much in common, pass each other like ships in the night. Equally, the repertories that have been investigated have been limited (most of the psychology of music has been concerned with the tonal, metrical concert music characteristic of the period from about 1750 to 1850), and the data have often been

regarded in historically and culturally impoverished terms—though there has recently been something of a shift here, with Repp's work on large collections of commercially recorded performances spanning most of the twentieth century (e.g. Repp 1990a, 1992, 1998).

Finally, many of the empirical methods described in this chapter have led to a thoroughgoing reification of performance—to a view of performance that treats it as a thing rather than a process. This is an almost inevitable consequence of the way in which temporal phenomena are transformed into static representations of one sort or another (graphs, data lists, written descriptions). Some of the work described in this chapter retains the more dynamic character of performance as a process, but this has been the exception, and the more general tendency is to convert performance, in one way or another, into something that is disturbingly like a score—an irony given that one of the motivations for studying performance in the first place (as observed at the start of this chapter) was to get away from the tyranny of the score.

Various prospects for empirical work on performance can be envisaged. More automated methods for deriving data from commercial recordings seem inevitable (arriving on the back of digital signal processing technologies in studio recording and editing, and speech processing research), and these should enable much more extensive analyses of large bodies of recorded performance. This in turn will allow more diverse repertories to be tackled, and different questions to be explored. It will be interesting to see whether the emphasis then shifts from the concern with general mechanisms characteristic of existing published research toward more focused questions relating, for instance, to specific styles, performers, or pieces. Equally, the diversification of methods (the analysis of MIDI data and recorded performances now complemented by video and discourse analyses) promises a more integrated and complementary relationship between quantitative and qualitative approaches, and an overdue recognition of the kind of work that has gone on for many years within ethnomusicology (see Stock, chapter 2, this volume). This, and a greater awareness of social and developmental issues (see Davidson, chapter 4, this volume), signals an opportunity to move beyond the cognitive orientation of the last 20 years into a far more multidimensional approach to the study of musical performance.

Notes

1. There are additional features such as pitch bend and other so-called controller values, but these have never been studied in the literature discussed in this chapter.
2. Information about POCO, and instructions for using it via the Web, can be found at http://www.nici.kun.nl/mmm.
3. The issue of how a MIDI value based on the speed of a hammer, or a key depression, relates to the actual loudness of the corresponding note complicates things a little. But most synthesizers and Disklaviers implement an essentially linear relationship between MIDI values and decibels (a measure of loudness that takes into account the nonlinearity of the human auditory system in its response to the physical intensity of a sound source; see chapter 8, this volume).
4. Strictly speaking the transformation expresses each data point as its reciprocal value: value A in milliseconds is transformed into $1,000/A \times 60$, which converts it into tempo expressed in beats per minute (BPM).

5. The only exceptions are a one-bar break in the left hand at the midpoint of the piece, a similar one-bar break just before the three-chord cadence that concludes the piece, and the cadence itself (which consists of two minims and a semibreve).

6. For a discussion of auditory streaming see chapter 8, this volume.

7. The option of using independent judges is usually unrealistic, since in order to produce a good set of "tap along" data, a person has to get to know the music very well so as to be able to anticipate and track tempo fluctuations.

8. The distinction between quantitative and qualitative approaches can be simply expressed as the difference between phenomena that you can measure or give a value to (duration, dynamic, the number of occurrences of a word, the size of a movement, etc.), and those for which this is impossible (the semantic content of speech, the shape of a movement). Further discussion can be found in chapter 9, this volume.

9. There is no attempt within Todd's model to simulate, or model artificially, the process by which structure is assigned to a score.

References

Bengtsson, I., and Gabrielsson, A. (1977). "Rhythm research in Uppsala," in *Music, Room, Acoustics*. Stockholm: Royal Swedish Academy of Music, 17: 19–56.

Binet, A., and Courtier, J. (1895). "Recherches graphiques sur la musique." *L'Année Psychologique* 2: 201–222.

Bowen, J. A. (1996). "Tempo, duration, and flexibility: Techniques in the analysis of performance." *Journal of Musicological Research* 16: 111–156.

Clarke, E. F. (1993). "Imitating and evaluating real and transformed musical performances." *Music Perception* 10: 317–343.

Clarke, E. F. (1995). "Expression in performance: Generativity, perception and semiosis," in J. Rink (ed.), *The Practice of Performance*. Cambridge: Cambridge University Press, 21–54.

Clarke, E. F., and Davidson, J. W. (1998). "The body in performance," in W. Thomas (ed.), *Composition—Performance—Reception. Studies in the Creative Process in Music*. Aldershot: Ashgate Press, 74–92.

Clynes, M. (1983). "Expressive microstructure in music, linked to living qualities," in J. Sundberg (ed.), *Studies of Music Performance*, Stockholm: Royal Swedish Academy of Music, 39: 76–181.

Clynes, M. (1990). "Some guidelines for the synthesis and testing of pulse microstructure in relation to musical meaning." *Music Perception* 7: 403–422.

Clynes, M. (1995). "Microstructural musical linguistics—composers pulses are liked most by the best musicians." *Cognition* 55: 269–310.

Cook, N. (1995). "The conductor and the theorist: Furtwängler, Schenker and the first movement of Beethoven's Ninth Symphony," in J. Rink (ed.), *The Practice of Performance*. Cambridge: Cambridge University Press, 105–125.

Davidson, J. W. (1993). "Visual perception of performance manner in the movements of solo musicians." *Psychology of Music* 21: 103–113.

Davidson, J. W. (1994). "What type of information is conveyed in the body movements of solo musician performers?" *Journal of Human Movement Studies* 26: 279–301.

Davidson, J. W. (1995). "What does the visual information contained in music performances offer the observer? Some preliminary thoughts," in R. Steinberg (ed.), *Music and the Mind Machine: The Psychophysiology and Psychopathology of the Sense of Music*. Berlin: Springer Verlag, 105–113.

Day, T. (2000). *A Century of Recorded Music: Listening to Musical History*. New Haven: Yale University Press.

Gabrielsson, A. (1999). "The performance of music," in D. Deutsch (ed.), *The Psychology of Music*, 2nd ed. San Diego, Calif.: Academic Press, 501–602.

Honing, H. (1990). "POCO: An environment for analysing, modifying, and generating expression in music." *Proceedings of the 1990 International Computer Music Conference*, 364–368. San Francisco: Computer Music Association.

Juslin, P. N., Friberg, A., and Bresin, R. (2001–2002). "Towards a computational model of expression in music performance: The GERM model." *Musicae Scientiae*, special issue on Current Trends in the Study of Music and Emotion: 63–122.

Manning, P. (1993). *Electronic and Computer Music*, 2nd ed. Oxford: Oxford University Press.

Martin, S. (2002). "The case of compensating rubato." *Journal of the Royal Musical Association* 127: 95–129.

Palmer, C. (1996). "Anatomy of a performance: Sources of musical expression." *Music Perception* 13: 433–454.

Palmer, C. (1997). "Music performance." *Annual Review of Psychology* 48, 115–138.

Parncutt, R., and McPherson, G. E. (eds., 2002). *The Science and Psychology of Music Performance. Creative Strategies for Teaching and Learning*. Oxford: Oxford University Press.

Parncutt, R., Sloboda, J. A., Clarke, E. F., Raekallio, M., and Desain, P. "An ergonomic model of keyboard fingering for melodic fragments." *Music Perception* 14: 341–382.

Penfold, R. A. (1990). *Practical MIDI Handbook*, 2nd ed. Tonbridge: PC Publishing.

Povel, D-J. (1977). "Temporal structure of performed music. Some preliminary observations." *Acta Psychologica* 41: 309–320.

Repp, B. H. (1989): "Expressive microstructure in music: A preliminary perceptual assessment of four composers' 'pulses'." *Music Perception* 6: 243–274.

Repp, B. H. (1990a). "Patterns of expressive timing in performances of a Beethoven minuet by nineteen famous pianists." *Journal of the Acoustical Society of America* 88: 622–641.

Repp, B. H. (1990b). "Further perceptual evaluations of pulse microstructure in computer performances of classical piano music." *Music Perception* 8: 1–33.

Repp, B. H. (1992). "Diversity and commonality in music performance: An analysis of timing microstructure in Schumann's *Träumerei*." *Journal of the Acoustical Society of America* 92: 2546–2568.

Repp, B. H. (1998). "A microcosm of musical expression: I. Quantitative analysis of pianists' timing in the initial measures of Chopin's Etude in E major." *Journal of the Acoustical Society of America* 104: 1085–1100.

Repp, B. H. (1999). "A microcosm of musical expression: II. Quantitative analysis of pianists' dynamics in the initial measures of Chopin's Etude in E major." *Journal of the Acoustical Society of America* 105: 1972–1988.

Rink, J. (ed., 1995). *The Practice of Performance. Studies in Musical Interpretation*. Cambridge: Cambridge University Press.

Rink, J. (ed. 2002). *Musical Performance. A Guide to Understanding*. Cambridge: Cambridge University Press.

Robson, C. (1993). *Real World Research. A Resource for Social Scientists and Practitioner-Researchers*. Oxford: Blackwell Publishers.

Runeson, S., and Frykholm, G. (1983). "Kinematic specification of dynamics as an informational basis for person-and-action perception: Expectations, gender, recognition, and deceptive intention." *Journal of Experimental Psychology: General* 112: 585–615.

Sansom, M. J. (1997). "Musical Meaning: A Qualitative Investigation of Free Improvisation." Unpublished Ph.D. thesis, University of Sheffield.

Seashore, C. E. [1967 (1938)]. *The Psychology of Music*. McGraw-Hill. (Republished by Dover Books, New York, 1967.).

Shaffer, L. H. (1981). "Performances of Chopin, Bach and Bartók: Studies in motor programming." *Cognitive Psychology* 13: 326–376.

Sloboda, J. A., Clarke, E. F., Parncutt, R., and Raekallio, M. (1998). "Determinants of fingering choice in piano sight-reading." *Journal of Experimental Psychology: Human Perception and Performance* 24: 185–203.

Smith, J. A., Harré, R., and van Langenhove, L. (eds., 1995). *Rethinking Methods in Psychology*. London: Sage.

Sundberg, J., Fryden, L., and Askenfelt, A. (1983). "What tells you the player is musical? An analysis-by-synthesis study of music performance," in J. Sundberg (ed.), *Studies of Music Performance*, Stockholm: Royal Swedish Academy of Music 39: 61–75.

Sundberg, J., Friberg, A. and Fryden, L. (1991). "Common secrets of musicians and listeners: An analysis-by-synthesis study of musical performance," in P. Howell, R. West, and I. Cross (eds.), *Representing Musical Structure*. New York and London: Academic Press, 161–197.

Thompson, W. F. (1989). "Composer-specific aspects of musical performance: An evaluation of Clynes's theory of pulse for performances of Mozart and Beethoven." *Music Perception* 7: 15–42.

Todd, N. P. (1985). "A model of expressive timing in tonal music." *Music Perception* 3: 33–58.

Todd, N. P. (1989). "A computational model of rubato." *Contemporary Music Review* 3: 69–89.

Todd, N. P. (1992). "The dynamics of dynamics: A model of musical expression." *Journal of the Acoustical Society of America* 91: 3540–3550.

Widmer, G. (2002). "Machine discoveries: A few simple, robust local expression principles." *Journal of New Music Research* 31: 37–50.

Windsor, W. L., and Clarke, E. F. (1997). "Expressive timing and dynamics in real and artificial musical performances: Using an algorithm as an analytical tool." *Music Perception* 15: 127–152.

Winold, H., Thelen, E., and Ulrich, B. D. (1994). "Coordination and control in the bow arm movements of highly skilled cellists." *Ecological Psychology* 6: 1–31.

CHAPTER 6

Computational and Comparative Musicology

Nicholas Cook

Introduction

The middle of the twentieth century saw a strong reaction against the comparative methods that played so large a part in the disciplines of the humanities and social sciences in the first half of the century, and musicology was no exception. The term "comparative musicology" was supplanted by "ethnomusicology," reflecting a new belief that cultural practices could only be understood in relation to the particular societies that gave rise to them: it was simply misleading to compare practices across different societies, the ethnomusicologists believed, and so the comparative musicologist was replaced by specialists in particular musical cultures. A similar reaction took place in theory and analysis: earlier style-analytical approaches (largely modeled on turn-of-the-century art history) gave way to a new emphasis on the particular structural patterns of individual musical works. Perversely, this meant that the possibility of computational approaches to the study of music arose just as the idea of comparing large bodies of musical data—the kind of work to which computers are ideally suited—became intellectually unfashionable. As a result, computational methods have up to now played a more or less marginal role in the development of the discipline.

In this chapter I suggest that recent developments in computational musicology present a significant opportunity for disciplinary renewal: in the terms introduced in chapter 1, there is potential for musicology to be pursued as a more data-rich discipline than has generally been the case up to now, and this in turn entails a re-evaluation of the comparative method. Central to any computational approach, however, are the means by which data are represented for analysis, and so I begin with some examples of "objective" data representations before introducing the issue of comparison. (The examples I discuss are graphic, but the same points could have been made in terms of numerical representations.) This is followed by an extended case study of an important current software package for musicological research, the Humdrum Toolkit, and the chapter concludes with a brief consideration of the prospects for computational methods in musicology.

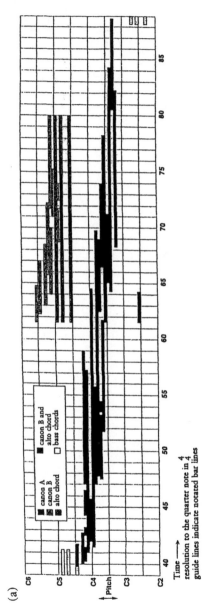

(a)

Time ⟶
resolution to the quarter note in 4
guide lines indicate notated bar lines

Range Graph, *Lux aeterna*, Section 2

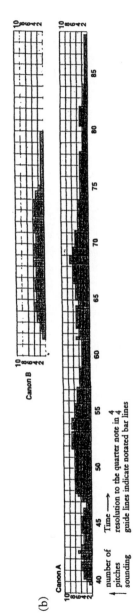

(b)

Time ⟶
resolution to the quarter note in 4
guide lines indicate notated bar lines

Pitch Count Graph, *Lux aeterna*, Section 2

(c)

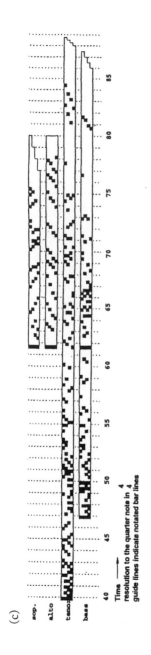

Entrance Graph, *Lux aeterna*, Section 2

(d)

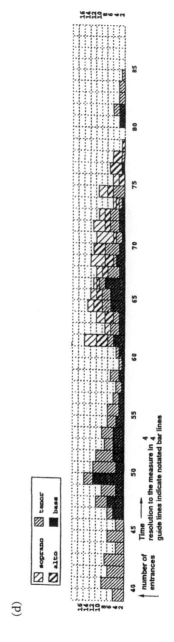

Entrance Graph Summary, *Lux aeterna*, Section 2

Figure 6.1.   Graphic analyses of Ligeti, *Lux aeterna*, section 2 (from Clendenning 1995: 948–49).

Issues of Representation

A picture, as everyone knows, is worth a thousand words. Each of the graphs in Figure 6.1 (from Clendenning 1995: 248–249) represents a different aspect of the same section from Ligeti's *Lux aeterna*: (a) charts pitch against time, giving an immediate impression of the music's registral profile, (b) shows how many different pitches (not pitch classes) are present at any given point, and (c) highlights voice entries, with each separate voice (four each of soprano, alto, tenor, bass) having a separate horizontal line which is shaded whenever the voice enters, while (d) shows essentially the same information as (c), only in terms of the total number of entries at any given point. These graphs are "objective" in the sense that, once you have agreed how a graph is to be laid out, everyone should end up with the same result; the information is all there in the score, so that the analysis becomes, in effect, a matter of reformatting. But the decisions about how to lay them out are not necessarily self-evident. For example, in (a) to (c) the minimum values on the time axis are quavers, whereas in (d) they are whole bars; other values would have been possible, and the decision to use these particular values represents a judgment by the analyst that they will be the most informative in this context. There is also a degree of analytical judgment in the separate identification of the canons in (a) and (b).

That said, however, it is obvious that there is scope for automation in graphs like this—and not just in drawing them up (the graphs in Figure 6.1 were generated by a computer drawing package) but in the processing of the data. The graphs in Figure 6.2 (from Brinkman and Mesiti 1991: 5, 6, 13, 17) were automatically generated from a machine representation of the score.[1] Again, each graph represents a different way of extracting and viewing the information in a score, this time bars 1 to 26 of the first movement from Bartók's String Quartet no. 4: (a) corresponds to Figure 6.1 (a), (b) shows each instrumental part separately with the vertical lines providing an impression of the linear movement from one pitch to another, and (c) charts the first appearance of each pitch, while (d) represents the dynamic level of each instrument (based on whether it is playing and on notated dynamic value) and of the whole (in effect a summation of the dynamic graphs of each instrument).

But what are we to make of such representations? What do they enable us to see that we can't hear, and in any case, what is the point of *seeing* music at all? It is a commonplace to describe Ligeti's texture-oriented works as "visual," and Brinkman and Mesiti (who in their article offer a case study of Webern's *Symphonie* Op. 21) emphasize the spatial symmetry of Webern's serial structures, commenting that "the graphs allow us to view all parts together in their spatial environment. [This] is especially helpful since the pitch symmetry that is essential to the musical structure of this work is somewhat obscured by the notated score" (Brinkman and Mesiti 1991: 21). The question then is the extent to which this problem of obscuring applies to other repertories, in other words how valuable this kind of visualization is for music in general. Yet this question is in some ways misguided: there is no such thing as a good or bad representation of music *per se*, there are good and bad—or at least better and worse—representations *for particular purposes*. To say that visual representations are more appropriate for twentieth-century than for other repertories, or for answering certain kinds of questions about the music than others, is simply to define their usefulness, not to criticize them.

Nevertheless Brinkman and Mesiti produced some interesting results for music that one wouldn't normally think of as particularly "visual," including some strikingly different representations of music by Bach and Mozart as well as by Bartók, Schoenberg, Wolpe, and Berio. At the very least, such comparisons serve to underline the variety of textures found in different composers or styles—and texture is at the same time one of the most important aspects of music in terms of how we experience it, and one of the hardest to say anything useful about. It is not hard to imagine how Brinkman and Mesiti's software could be used within a variety of pedagogical contexts, enabling students to literally and instantaneously "see" different pieces of music in a variety of different ways—and the ability to switch easily and quickly from one representation of music to another is a crucial element of practical musicianship. That this has not happened, and that the potential of the approach has not been fully realized, reflects the cost of translating academic research projects into software products for the real world, and illustrates an all-too-familiar pattern in musicological software: a sustained burst of initial enthusiasm is followed by running out of money, resulting in software that is sometimes less than fully functional, often less than fully documented, rarely properly supported, and usually soon obsolete.

But my principal answer to the question "what are we to make of such representations?" is a different one. Brinkman and Mesiti (1991: 7) emphasize the particular usefulness of their graphs "as a device for comparing different pieces"; Matt Hughes, whose quantitative analysis of Schubert's Op. 94 no. 1 was discussed in chapter 1, similarly claimed of his method that it was "a tool for organizing data so that one may more discernibly view tendencies and interassociations," adding that it was "best utilized when viewing groups of compositions or sections of a composition rather than a single work" (Hughes 1977: 145, 150). And there is a general point to be made here: the more objective an analytical approach is, the more its musicological value is likely to be realized through making comparisons between different pieces—and sometimes large numbers of them. For example, when you carry out a Schenkerian analysis, you are in a sense making a comparison between the piece in question and the norms of common-practice voice leading, as systematized in the Schenkerian background and middleground. But the value of the analysis consists primarily in the lengthy process of making it, deciding which notes go with which, which are more important than others, and so forth; the process is lengthy because it involves a vast number of interpretive judgments, requiring you to weigh up different factors in relation to one another. At the end of it, you have a knowledge of the music—you might call it an intimacy—that you did not have at the outset, and there is a sense in which the final graph is significant mainly as a record of this learning process. With any kind of computational approach, by contrast, all of this happens automatically, and in some cases almost instantaneously; the only output is the graphic or numerical representation of the music that results. And such representations rarely tell you anything very useful by themselves: they may well be vulnerable to the cheap but telling jibe that they either show you what you hear anyhow (in which case they are redundant), or else they don't (in which case there are

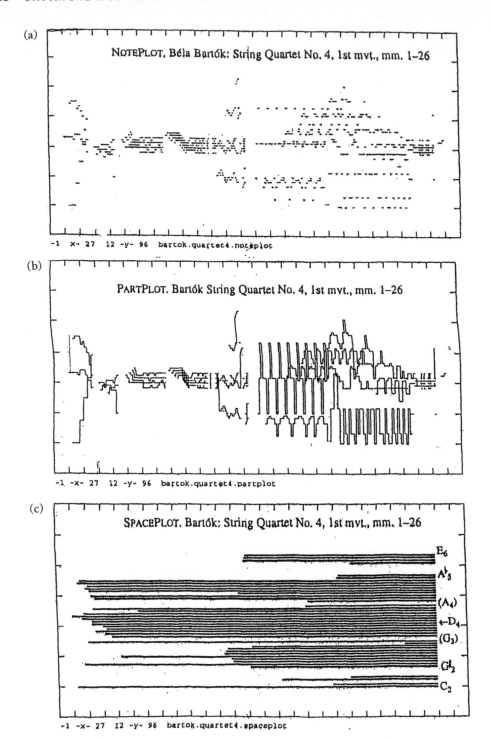

(a) NOTEPLOT, Béla Bartók: String Quartet No. 4, 1st mvt., mm. 1–26

-1 x- 27 12 -y- 96 bartok.quartet4.noteplot

(b) PARTPLOT, Bartók String Quartet No. 4, 1st mvt., mm. 1–26

-1 -x- 27 12 -y- 96 bartok.quartet4.partplot

(c) SPACEPLOT, Bartók: String Quartet No. 4, 1st mvt., mm. 1–26

-1 -x- 27 12 -y- 96 bartok.quartet4.spaceplot

(d)   DYNPLOT. Bartók: String Quartet No. 4, 1st mvt., mm. 1–26

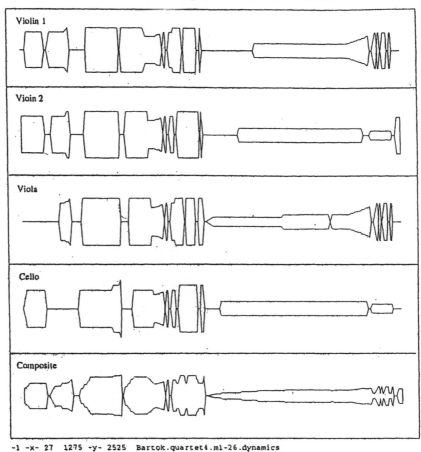

-1 -x- 27 1275 -y- 2525 Bartok.quartet4.ml-26.dynamics

Figure 6.2.   Graphic analyses of Bartók, String Quartet No. 4, I, bars 1–26 (from Brinkman and Mesiti 1991: 5, 6, 13, 17).

irrelevant). It is when you compare representations of different pieces that useful information may emerge.

The value of objective representations of music, in short, lies principally in the possibility of comparing them and so identifying significant features, and of using computational techniques to carry out such comparisons speedily and accurately. At this point, however, the issue of reduction (already broached in chapter 1, this volume) has to be confronted. This can conveniently be explored in relation to the analysis of folksongs, since a large of proportion of early work in computational analysis was based on such material: there were substantial existing collections of folksongs to work on, and the music was monophonic and scalar, hence could be coded very compactly—a vital consideration in the days when computer memory was a scarce and expensive commodity. But of course, if you code folksongs as a series of pitches, or scale degrees, then you are leaving out all the variables of into-

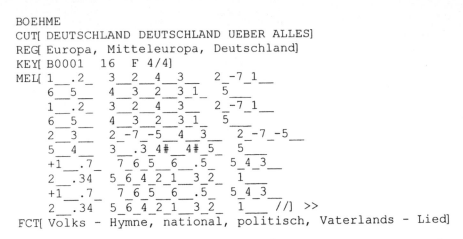

BOEHME
CUT[DEUTSCHLAND DEUTSCHLAND UEBER ALLES]
REG[Europa, Mitteleuropa, Deutschland]
KEY[B0001   16   F 4/4]
MEL[1__.2_ 3__2__4__3__   2_-7_1__
     6__5__ 4__3__2__3_1_   5__
     1__.2_ 3__2__4__3__   2_-7_1__
     6__5__ 4__3__2__3_1_   5__
     2__3__ 2_-7_-5_ 4__3__ 2_-7_-5__
     5__4__ 3__.3_4#__4#_5_ 5__
     +1__.7_ 7_6_5_ 6__.5_ 5_4_3__
     2__.34 5_6_4_2_1_ 3_2_ 1__
     +1__.7_ 7_6_5_ 6__.5_ 5_4_3__
     2__.34 5_6_4_2_1_ 3_2_ 1___ //] >>
FCT[Volks - Hymne, national, politisch, Vaterlands - Lied]

Figure 6.3   *EsAC* code for "Deutschland über alles" (Helmut Schaffrath, *Essen Musical Data Package*)

nation, ornamentation, timbre, and other aspects of singing style, not to mention the original contexts of use and cultural connotations of the songs. And that obviously limits what you can conclude from comparing them.

At this point a concrete example may be helpful, and Figure 6.3 is taken from the Essen Musical Data Package, a series of databases of popular and traditional vocal repertories together with tools for encoding and analysis.[2] Coordinated until his death in 1994 by Helmut Schaffrath, the Essen databases consisted by the following year of some 10,000 songs, mainly European (and largely German), but with some representation of other traditions, particularly Chinese; they are still being added to, though development has been transferred from Essen to Warsaw (Selfridge-Field 1995). Figure 6.3 shows "Deutschland über alles" in the custom code used by the package, *EsAC* (the Essen Associative Code), and several of the data fields are self-explanatory: BOEHME is the name of the database in which this song is located, CUT contains the title, REG is the region from which it comes, and FCT is the functional category of the song, while KEY contains not only its key (F) but also the numbering of the song in the database (B0001), the value of the smallest note value (16, a sixteenth or semi-quaver), and the time signature (4/4). The tune itself is contained in the field MEL, using a simple code based on the scale degree (with # for sharp and b for flat degrees), + and − to indicate shifts to a higher or lower register, respectively, and a rhythmic notation based on the shortest value (semi-quaver), with a dot prolonging the value by 50 percent, a single underline character (_) by 100 percent, and a double underline character (__) by 200 percent. That should suffice for the tune to be read; the only other information contained in the MEL field is // (for the end of the melody), the use of spaces to indicate bar lines (the melody has been notated across the bar lines), and the splitting up of the melody into separate lines, each of which represents a phrase (this represents a judgment on the part of the transcriber, and as such is a rather unusual feature of the *EsAC* code).

What can be done using this information? The distributed version of the Essen database comes with a simple analytical utility (ANA), which takes a complete database as its input, and generates as its output an annotated version of the file in which up to 12 different kinds of analytical information are added for each song. These include straightforward statistical information such as the distribution of ascending and descending intervals (how many ascending minor seconds?), the distribution of durations (how many crotchets, quavers, semi-quavers?), and distribution of scale degrees (how often does the fifth scale degree appear in the lower register?); there are also some derived measures such as the percentage of ascending steps and leaps. They also include some less obvious information, including the pattern of phrase repetitions in pitch and duration, a coding of the contour of each phrase, the melodic spine (based on the notes at metrically stressed beats), and the final notes of each phrase (this is where the coding of phrases comes in).[3] A limitation of the ANA software is that it provides data for each song separately, whereas the statistical information would be more useful if it were provided across the database as a whole, but there is a reason for this: the package was intended for use with a commercial relational database package, which would facilitate this kind of analysis. Needless to say, the original package is no longer obtainable.[4]

But what can be *done* using this information? Schaffrath himself published a number of studies based on his datasets, in which he used this kind of analytical information to support broad stylistic generalizations, for example as between different traditions: "German folk songs," he concluded from one such study (1992: 107), "generally skip more often up than down; in the Chinese pool the opposite applies. . . . German songs use the interval of a fourth 51% more often than Chinese songs do. This might be explained by the preference for pentatonic scales." But there is also a different way in which such information can be used, which is for purposes of searching, identification, and classification. A database of 10,000 folksongs is not unlike a bibliographic database, and to locate individual items or groups of related items you search for particular features, combining them so as to narrow the search down to a manageable number of hits. In some contexts all you need to search a bibliographic database is the author's name; in other cases you need to combine an author name, two title keywords, and year to locate the article you need. In the same way, you might try to locate a particular song by searching for its first few notes or incipit; this is the way that traditional dictionaries of themes operate (for instance, Barlow and Morgenstern 1983), and it works well with "art" music, where there are fixed scores. But it is not such a good way to search for folksongs, which typically exist in a large number of variants, often involving variation or the interpolation of notes. That is why ANA includes a routine to derive the final notes of each phrase: as Schaffrath (1997: 349) explains, "although variants may contain different numbers of notes or melodic contours, they tend to retain underlying harmonic structures." Or you could combine such a search with a particular melodic spine and/or pattern of phrase repetition. And whereas I have described the use of such features in terms of simply locating items, the same processes can be used to group together songs or repertories in ways that might reflect, for example, historical development, linguistic associations, or conditions of use. In such ways the automated analysis of musical style can become a means of generating or verifying musicological hypotheses.

Or at least that is the aspiration. In practice, *EsAC* and ANA suffer from obvious limitations, ranging from the pragmatic (the output of ANA is only marginally more user-friendly than machine code) to those of principle. *EsAC* can cope with only a narrow range of music (monophonic, restricted to three octaves, and so on), and is well adapted for only a narrow range of applications. ANA extracts a limited number of features, each of which represents a radical reduction of the music and is intended for a particular purpose (such as statistical generalization or pattern matching); moreover, the usefulness of these reductions depends on a number of quite specific assumptions, such as that the final-note patterns of phrases vary less than incipits. All this makes sense in terms of what the Essen package is designed for; it is, to adopt outdated software jargon, a "turnkey" solution to folksong analysis, or at least to a certain sort of folksong analysis. And it would be possible to imagine trying to develop the code, and the analytical software, in such a way as to be more flexible — to cope with music of any desired degree of complexity and variety, and to extract from it every feature that could be of any possible interest under any possible circumstances. That would be like the approach of business software developers in the 1980s, who aimed at prepackaged solutions in which every eventuality had been foreseen and the appropriate feature bolted on somewhere, if only you could find it.

In musicology, as perhaps also in the office, this represents a basic misapprehension — in terms not only of the unlimited variety of musical materials, but also of the variety of purposes for which people will want to represent them; as Huron (1992: 11) puts it, "The types of goals to which music representations may serve are legion and unpredictable." Complexity is not the solution. There are, after all, much more complicated codes than *EsAC* which fulfill certain purposes extremely well while being very poorly adapted for others. MIDI code has transformed entire sectors of the music industry, but because it tries to understand all music on the model of keyboard music its handling of microtonal inflection is inelegant, to say the least; it also doesn't distinguish enharmonic equivalents, and has to be drastically reconfigured if useful analytical information is to be extracted from it — even something as simple as locating a C major triad.[5] Again, DARMS[6] is an extremely powerful code designed for purposes of printing and publication (it is the basis of all A-R Edition scores), and accordingly it understands music as a kind of graphics; it doesn't think of an e^1 but of a notehead on the bottom line of a stave that has an F clef on it. As a result, it too needs drastic reconfiguration if analytically useful information is to be extracted from it (Brinkman 1986). And though the problems of multiple codes are alleviated by the existence of interchange utilities (e.g., to turn DARMS into MIDI), there are limitations to what is possible: since MIDI does not distinguish between C♯ and D♭, the information is simply not there to translate into DARMS, which does make the distinction.

As with business software, the solution to this problem of multiple requirements is not the creation of ever more complex and unwieldy integrated solutions, but a modular approach involving an unlimited number of individual software tools designed to serve individual purposes; that way, when you want to do something new, you simply design a new tool to do it. Modular approaches like this, however, need some kind of framework within which to work — in essence, a set of rules for the representation of data in machine-readable files, and for the transfer of information between different software tools. Humdrum is an example of just such a framework.

A Case Study: The Humdrum Toolkit

Developed by David Huron in the early 1990s, Humdrum[7] consists of two distinct elements: in the first place a syntax—the set of rules I referred to—and in the second, a "toolkit" consisting at present of something over 70 separate software routines for manipulating the data in different ways for different purposes. It runs in a UNIX environment,[8] and its modular approach is much more readily understood by those who have experience of UNIX than those who do not. Like Humdrum, UNIX can be thought of as a set of rules plus a set of tools: individual UNIX commands (which have names like *grep*, *sort*, and *cat*) do simple things like searching files for a particular string and extracting, deleting, or altering it, or rearranging data within or between files. The power and flexibility of the system comes not from these individual tools but from the possibility of "pipelining" them so that the output of one tool becomes the input of the next, forming chains of commands of unlimited length. The Humdrum toolkit is simply a set of additional UNIX tools designed specifically for manipulating music-related data. It is this open and modular philosophy, which always allows for an additional tool to be added when required, that explains why— as Huron (1997: 375) puts it—"Humdrum is especially helpful in music research environments where new and unforeseen goals arise." Unfortunately, as we shall see, it also means that the user has to have a detailed understanding of the way the data are encoded and manipulated. Humdrum, in short, has a steep learning curve.

All this may sound very abstract, so Figure 6.4 shows the first two phrases of "Deutschland über alles" in *kern* code, the normal Humdrum format for representing notated music (only two phrases because when printed out—though not in terms of internal storage—*kern* is much less compact than *EsAC*).[9] This is a direct translation into *kern* of Figure 6.3, so the same information may be found in the data fields preceded by !!! (the exclamation marks identify them as comments); only the information concerning Schaffrath, the copyright statement, and the !!!ARL line (which gives latitudinal and longitudinal coordinates) are new. As for the other lines, **kern means that what follows is in *kern* (the double asterisk means that this label defines the data that follows), and the lines preceded by a single asterisk define the instrument category and instrument (in each case "vox" or voice), meter (4/4), key signature (B♭, the "flat" being designated by "−"—the sign for sharp is "+"), and key (F).[10] The tune itself begins on the following line, preceded by a curly bracket (this indicates the phrases, while the lines beginning with "=" are bar lines). "4.f" means that the first note is the F above middle C (if it were an octave lower it would be F, if an octave higher ff, if an octave higher than *that* fff, and so on); the "4" means that it is a quarter note (crotchet), and the " . ", unsurprisingly, that it is dotted. It should now be possible to read the melody quite straightforwardly. (The apparently simplistic reciprocal notation for durations is unexpectedly flexible, coping with most things short of Ferneyhough; triplet quavers, for instance, work out as 6, quintuplet semi-quavers as 20). That explains everything in Figure 6.4, except the " *− ", which marks the end of the record. It should also explain everything in Figure 6.5, which shows the same phrases (with the comments omitted), as set in G major by Haydn in the second movement of his String Quartet Op. 76 no. 3: instead of the single column (or *spine*) of Figure 6.4, there are now four, one for each line of the

```
!!!OTL: DEUTSCHLAND DEUTSCHLAND UEBER ALLES
!!!ARE: Europa, Mitteleuropa, Deutschland
!!!ARD: Europa%Mitteleuropa%Deutschland@
!!!ARL: 51.5/10.5@
!!!SCT: B0001
!!!YEM: Copyright 1995, estate of Helmut Schaffrath.
**kern
*ICvox
*Ivox
*M4/4
*k[ b-]
*F:
{ 4.f
8g
=1
4a
4g
4b-
4a
=2
8g
8e
4f}
{ 4dd
4cc
=3
4b-
4a
4g
8a
8f
=4
2cc}
*-
```

Figure 6.4   *Kern* code for first two phrases of "Deutschland über alles."

music. It is helpful to think of this as being laid out like staff notation, only rotated by 90 degrees.

Kern is not as easy to read as *EsAC* (which, apparently, was designed to be sight read). And it would seem to be better adapted for linear textures than, say keyboard music—though in fact there is no limitation in this respect, partly because you can put more than one note on a single line within any one spine, and also because you can collapse spines into one another or create new ones at any point. It is also more flexible than it looks. In the first place, you don't have to specify everything in Figures 6.4 or 6.5; there is no need to encode phrases, or bar lines, or durations, or pitches (in fact the *only* mandatory lines are "**kern" and "*—"). In the second place, there is a large number of further codes and interpretations built into *kern*, al-

```
**kern        **kern        **kern        **kern
*k[ f#]       *k[ f#]       *k[ f#]       *k[ f#]
*G:           *G:           *G:           *G:
*clefF        *clefF        *clefC3       *clefF4
*M4/4         *M4/4         *M4/4         *M4/4
*tb24         *tb24         *tb24         *tb24
=0-           =0-           =0-           =0-
2r            2r            2r            2r
4.g           4.B           4G            4G
.             .             4r            4r
8a            8d            .             .
=1            =1            =1            =1
4b            4g            2r            2r
4a            4f#           .             .
4cc           4a            4d            4F#
4b            4g            4d            4G
=2            =2            =2            =2
8a            4c            8F#           4D
8f#           .             8A            .
4g            4B            4G            4GG
4ee           4cc           2r            2r
4dd           4b            .             .
=3            =3            =3            =3
4cc           4f#           4A            4D
4b            4g            4B            4G
4a            2e            4e            4C
8b            .             4G            4C#
8g            .             .             .
=4            =4            =4            =4
2dd           2d            2F#           2D
*-            *-            *-            *-
```

Figure 6.5   *Kern* code for Haydn, String Quartet Op. 76, no. 3, II, bars 1–4

lowing you for instance to include symbols for articulation or ornamentation, clefs, stem direction, or the number of staff lines, if any (and whether they should be colored or dotted). But more than that, **kern spines can be mixed with others, including, for example, such predefined representations as **text (for lyrics) or **IPA (lyrics, but now notated using the International Phonetic Alphabet), or new representations defined by the user: you might, for example, create spines labeled **bowing, to show how a given pattern is (or might be) bowed, or **timing, to encode the rhythmic nuances in a particular performance, or **heartbeat, to record listeners' physiological responses to hearing the music. Then again, you might not use **kern at all, but an alternative representation for pitch; predefined representations include **pitch (using the International Standards Organization format), **deg (scale degrees, as in *EsAC*), **solfg (French fixed-do solfège), **freq (frequency expressed in cycles per second), or the self-explanatory **midi; any of these representations can be automatically translated to any other, provided of course that the relevant information is there to be translated (recall the problem with MIDI and enharmonic equivalents). There is also a particularly well-developed **fret representation, which turns pitch notation into tablature notation based on any specified number of strings and tuning, or of course you might always invent a new representation for some particular repertory or purpose.

And what does all this enable you to do? For a start, you can replicate the functions of ANA: to extract the melodic spine of Figure 6.4, for instance, you locate the downbeat of each bar (search for lines beginning "=" and then skip to the next line), skip over the duration figures, and extract the pitch symbol(s) to a new file. Or you could just as easily search an entire "BOEHME" database for melodic motions from ^4 to ^5 and establish how frequently they occur by comparison with the reverse motion (you would translate the database into **deg records in order to do this, and search for adjacent lines containing 4 and 5, skipping over irrelevant symbols like durations, and finally counting the number found). Or you could search all of Bach's chorales (the Riemenschneider collection is available in *kern* code) in order to establish how often the melodic leading-notes are approached from beneath, as against from above: to do this, you extract the spines containing the melodies, turn them into **deg records, and count the occurrences of "^7" as against "v7."[11] (This particular task is easier than it sounds, because **deg automatically codes the direction in which a given scale degree was approached, though not the size of the interval involved). Then again, shifting to a different level of complexity, you could analyze the relationship between a particular succession of vowels in song texts and the melodic or rhythmic contexts within which they occur. You could establish how far particular harmonic formations are correlated with specific metrical locations (and analyze the results by composer, period, or geographical origin). Or you could classify different melodic, harmonic, or structural contexts in Chopin's complete mazurkas, and use this as the basis for analyzing timing information extracted from a large number of recordings.

But the best way to see what Humdrum is capable of is to examine published studies that have used it, of which the majority (though by no means all) are by Huron and his coworkers; I shall briefly describe five. An article on the melodic arch in folksongs (Huron 1996) is based on the Essen collection and provides a direct comparison with Schaffrath's own work. Its purpose is to test systematically the frequent, but inadequately supported, claim that "arch" contours are prevalent throughout Western folksongs, and Huron points out the dangers of "unintentional bias" (1996: 3) when such generalizations are supported by a small number of possibly handpicked examples: they can be firmly established only through the analysis of data sets large enough to allow the drawing of statistically significant conclusions. He puts forward two basic ways in which folksongs might be said to exhibit arch-shaped contours—within each phrase, and overall—and systematically analyzes the Essen collection for each. For the first test, individual phrases throughout the collection were sorted according to the number of notes in them, and the average contour for each phrase-length computed; for the second, the average pitch of each phrase of each song was computed, and the resultant contour classified. The overall conclusion was that there is a strong tendency toward arch-shaped contours on both measures (though a third approach, based on the nesting of arches within one another, was not supported).

A project like this might be described as regulative: it takes an existing musicological claim and tests it rigorously against a large body of relevant data, adopting criteria of significance and certainty that may be unfamiliar in musicology but are normal in data-rich disciplines. Two further studies illustrate the range of musicological claims that can be tested in this manner. A study carried out in collaboration with Paul von Hippel (Hippel and Huron 2000) focused on the "gap-fill" model of melody, according to which listeners expect melodic leaps to be followed by a change of direction; this is an important element of Narmour's "implication-realization" theory, which seeks to explain how listeners experience music on the basis of whether or not implications set up by the music are realized in what follows. What is at issue is not whether or not melodic leaps are usually followed by a change of direction, which is undoubtedly the case; it is whether or not this happens (as Krumhansl has concluded on the basis of experimental studies)[12] because of listener expectations. The alternative is that it is a trivial consequence of the limited registral range of vocal music, a possibility which von Hippel and Huron (2000: 63) explain by comparison with

> a simplified melody that is confined to a range of three adjacent pitches— for example, A, B, and C. In such a melody, the only skip available is between A and C. Upward, this skip must land at the top of the range; downward, it must land at the bottom. After a skip, therefore, there is no way for a melody to continue moving in the same direction. On the contrary, two of the three available pitches can be reached only by a reversal. Although most melodies have a wider range, they are subject to the same basic argument.

If this second possibility is the case, then gap-fill patterns will be no more common in real folksongs than in randomly generated melodies with otherwise comparable characteristics—and, to cut a long story short, this is exactly what von Hippel and Huron found. If their argument (which I have grossly simplified) is accepted, then it provides a striking instance of how studies based on large data sets can raise questions about conclusions derived even from experiments as meticulously controlled as Krumhansl's.[13]

A third study (Huron 2001) makes a similar kind of point in relation to "art" music. It reassesses Allen Forte's (1983) set-theoretical analysis of the first movement of Brahms's String Quartet Op. 51, no. 1—an application to high Romantic music of an approach originally developed for twentieth-century music, bringing with it an appearance of objectivity and rigor in stark contrast to conventional motivic descriptions of such music. (In other words, Forte's article is a late expression of the postwar culture of objectivity described in chapter 1, this volume.) Whereas a "motive" is simply a characteristic melodic figure that recurs prominently throughout a piece, Forte's "alpha" ic (interval class) pattern can be defined much more precisely: it is a particular intervallic configuration that may occur in any of the standard transforms of set theory (prime, inversion, retrograde, retrograde inversion), in any rhythmic configuration, and at any metrical point. So Huron proceeds to search systematically for Forte's "alpha" pattern, not only in the first movement of Op. 51, no.1 but also in the first movements of Brahms's other quartets—a comparable repertory in which the "alpha" pattern, if it is really characteristic of Op. 51, no. 1, should be significantly less common. First, he demonstrates that, as defined by Forte, the "alpha" pattern is common in Op. 51, no. 1, but no more so than in the other quartets. However, if you restrict the search to instances of the pattern that begin on metrically strong beats and come at the beginning of slurs, then it is more prevalent in Op. 51, no. 1 than in the others. This is particularly the case if you look for the pattern only in its prime form, and even more so if you consider only those cases where the pattern coincides with a long-short-long rhythmic pattern. So the prevalence of Forte's "alpha" pattern is confirmed—but only under precisely those conditions that are captured by the conventional idea of a motive! The conclusion must be that the appearance of rigor in Forte's analysis as against traditional analytical descriptions is just that, an appearance.

Important and indeed salutary as this regulative function may be, it would be wrong to give the impression that computational analysis is good only for testing the validity of existing theoretical or analytical claims. It can also be used to undertake work that could hardly be achieved in any other way. A spectacular example is the correlation of musical features with geography, a project once again based on the Essen database (Aarden and Huron 2001). Recall that the Essen records include information concerning the geographical origins of the songs contained in them—sometimes down to the level of an individual town or village—and that the *kern* version of "Deutschland über alles" added longitudinal and latitudinal coordinates in the !!!ARL field (a new field defined specifically for Aarden and Huron's project). Standard Humdrum commands can be used to extract records from the database and output their coordinates; these are then used as input to a mapping program. By way of example, Figure 6.6 shows the distribution of major- and minor-mode songs within the Essen database; these maps were generated using the GEO-Music site (http://www.music-cog.ohio-state.edu/cgi-bin/Mapping/map.pl, not accessible at publication time), established as part of the project. It is hard to know what conclusions might be drawn from this comparison (other than that the major mode is considerably more widespread than the minor); the southward skewing of the major-mode data as against the minor simply reflects the three occurrences in Italy—hardly a basis for robust generalization—while the concentration in Germany and central Europe evident in both cases reflects the bias of the Essen database. A fully fledged musicological research project would no doubt involve dealing with more features at a greater level of detail. Nevertheless this example does indicate the potential for computational methods to draw together quite diverse kinds of information; it also illustrates the value of graphic presentation of the complex data generated by work in comparative musicology.

A final study (Huron and Berec, forthcoming) is perhaps even more suggestive in terms of possible musicological applications. Like Hofstetter's attempt (mentioned in chapter 1) to turn a claim about the "spirit of nationalism" into an empirically testable proposition, Huron's and Berec's starting point is a woolly, common-language concept: idiomaticism. How might you set about defining what is idiomatic on, say, the trumpet in such a way that a computer could make evaluations of just how idiomatic a particular piece of music is? In the first place, Huron and Berec say, idiomaticism is not the same as difficulty: a piece of trumpet music can be difficult but idio-

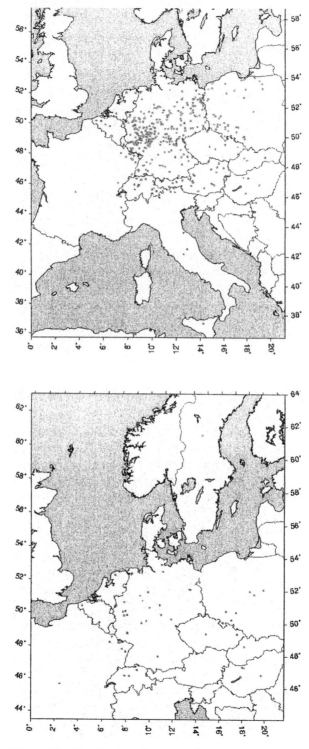

Figure 6.6   Distribution of major- and minor-mode songs
(generated using the Geo-Music site)

119

matic, or easy and unidiomatic. It is rather a matter of achieving the desired musical effect in the easiest possible manner. For example, a piece will be idiomatic if it is significantly easier to play as written than when transposed up or down by say a semitone; this is "transposition idiomaticism." So Huron and Berec evaluated the difficulty of a number of pieces when played in all transpositions from an octave below the original to an octave above, and in several cases the original proved to be significantly easier to play than most or all of the transposed versions. (They also ran a parallel test based on how much more difficult the music was when played at a different tempo from the notated one, with similar results.) But there was also a further finding: the pieces had been selected so as to include examples by both trumpet virtuosi and nontrumpeters, and the conclusion in respect of both transposition and tempo idiomaticism was the same—that expert trumpeters compose more idiomatically than composers who cannot play the instrument.

That conclusion might be considered predictable, not to say obvious (just as in the case of Hofstetter's discovery that there are differences between national styles). And it would have been of limited interest if Huron and Berec had simply asked trumpeters to play the pieces at different transpositions and at different tempos, and to say how difficult they were, an approach that would not have required Humdrum, of course. But instead—and this is the real point of their study—they attempted something much more challenging: what they refer to as "the design and implementation of a computer model of a trumpet performer." Their model takes a *kern* file as its input, and evaluates the difficulty of performance along a variety of different dimensions: in terms of the valve transitions between successive notes; in terms of register, particularly in the case of sustained notes; in terms of dynamics; and in terms of tonguing at different speeds. (The information on which they based the model included performer assessments in the case of valve transitions, tests of performance in the case of tonguing, and physiological data concerning lung capacity and diaphragm support in the case of sustained notes.) The model was tested using a series of trumpet studies set for different grades by the Royal Conservatory of Music of Toronto; there was a generally fairly high correlation between its estimates of their difficulty and the Royal Conservatory's. But of course the main test was the evaluation of idiomaticism, and the fact that the model come up with what everybody knows confirms the extent to which it actually works. That is the real conclusion to be drawn from the study.

Do musicologists really *need* a computer model of a trumpet performer? One answer to this is that the approach could be readily generalized to other instruments: to the recorder (where finger transitions would be of particular importance, owing to the complexity of cross-fingerings), to the piano (the model might propose the best fingering, which could be tested against those specified by editors or used by performers), or to the guitar (in effect a modeling of the dance of the fingers on the fretboard). But the more substantial answer lies behind this. One of the chronic problems with analyzing music is the tendency toward abstraction: the more sophisticated our analytical models, the more divorced the object of analysis seems to become from the experience of music, and especially from the sense of physical engagement in which much if not all music has its source. It is conventional to deplore this, but to do nothing about it. In this context a computer model of the electric guitarist's left hand could become, perhaps paradoxically, a means of thinking the body back into musical analysis: you could, to give just one example, chart the interaction of the dancing fingers with the ear—of the imperatives of the fretboard with those of "purely musical" implication and realization—in rock guitar improvisation. In this way computational musicology holds out the promise not only of providing more robust answers to questions that have already been asked, but also of making it possible to ask new questions.

Conclusion: Brave New World?

Promises, promises . . . and it must be admitted that computational software has a hardly better record of delivering on its promises than dot com companies. Let's stick with Humdrum as the most likely current candidate for a powerful, general-purpose computational aid for musicology, and explore some of the practicalities of doing musicology with it.

Q. Is it easy to get hold of?

A. Yes, at the time of writing you can download it for free, or you can buy it for the cost of the materials from the Center for Computer Assisted Research in the Humanities at Stanford.[14]

Q. Will it actually run on my computer? Don't I have to be using a UNIX machine?

A. You can run it on a PC or a Mac, but you will need to install a UNIX toolkit. You can probably get that for free, too.[15]

Q. But will I be able to find the music I want to work on in *kern* code?

A. That depends what you want to work on. The Essen package is available in *kern*, and so is some of the Densmore collection of Native American music, so if you are interested in folk music you can start work right away. As for Western "art" music, there is quite a lot out there: not only Bach's chorales but also most of his cantatas, as well as the *Well-Tempered Clavier*; substantial amounts of Corelli, Vivaldi, Handel, and Telemann; chamber and orchestral music by Haydn and Mozart; and most of the Beethoven symphonies.[16] The hope, of course, is that as more musicologists use Humdrum, so more music will be encoded, encouraging more musicologists to use Humdrum—and in this way you get a virtuous circle. (The same applies to the development of the tools themselves.)

Q. And if I can't find what I want?

A. If it exists in some other code you may be able to translate it into *kern*. Translation routines exist for the *MuseData* code used by the Center for Computer Assisted Research in the Humanities (CCARH), the Plaine and Easie Code used for RISM (*Répertoire international des sources musicales*), and *MUSTRAN*, as well as the code used by Leland Smith's music notation program SCORE, and the "Enigma" code used by Finale. Not all of these translators are readily available or unproblematic, but if you still can't find what you want you can of course encode your own. Rather than doing it by typing in the code, you can use an encoding routine that enables you to enter the music on a MIDI keyboard—rather like step-time entry in a sequencer package. There are also utilities for playing *kern* code (via MIDI), for displaying music notation on screen, or for outputting it as a PostScript file (though not all of these are available if you are running Humdrum on a PC or a Mac). You can turn *kern* files into *Finale* ones for printing, too.

Unfortunately, none of this addresses the real difficulties of integrating Humdrum into everyday musicological life. The fact is that not everybody is happy with a UNIX command-line environment, or finds it easy to remember the different commands with their multiple (and often complex) options; people who use UNIX (or Humdrum) on a daily basis can operate it much more quickly than a graphic environment (like Windows, with its drop-down menus and mouse control), but if Humdrum is to become part of everyday musicological life then what matters is its accessibility to the *occasional* user. Michael Taylor (1996) has developed a graphical user interface (GUI) for Humdrum, though it is not publicly distributed at the time of writing,[17] and this makes life considerably easier for the occasional user: there are drop-down menus listing the various Humdrum commands and dialog boxes where you set the associated options, and you can even select musical elements using ordinary language ("any bar line," "at least one flat," or "C major chord," for instance).[18] For nonspecialist users such an interface—if generally available and supported—would surely represent a substantial step in the right direction: it not only looks familiar but also constantly reminds you of the commands and options that are available, without significantly compromising Humdrum's functionality and flexibility.

But such an approach can only go so far. This is because, to use Humdrum at all, you need quite a detailed knowledge of its representations (*kern* and the rest); a great deal of Humdrum usage has to do with things like extracting the spine you are interested in, merging spines, or stripping out information that is not wanted for any particular operation—and even ordinary-language definitions cannot protect you from the need to understand what is going on in the code. For this reason Andreas Kornstädt (1996) advocates a different approach: instead of "a *Humdrum* 'command center' with lots of buttons and gadgets with names like **yank** and **MIDI | smf**," as he puts it (1996: 119), he has developed an analytical environment into which different GUI modules can be slotted for different applications. Each module can be thought of as a "browser" that let users view just those musical elements that they are interested in, and no others; for instance, Kornstädt has created such a system for leitmotivic analysis, in which users can define leitmotifs and locate their occurrence in a score on the basis of on-screen notation and intuitive commands. This, again, is not publicly available, but another of Kornstädt's customized applications of Humdrum is: an on-line thematic dictionary, called Themefinder.[19] You type in some pitches from the tune you want to find (or alternatively you can type in the scale degrees, or the intervals between the notes, or even just its contour), and the software finds all the matches in its database and displays them on screen in musical notation. There are no Humdrum commands; you don't even need to know it is Humdrum that is doing the work—and what makes this possible is that Themefinder is designed to do one thing and one thing only. It is hard at the present time to tell how far Kornstädt's approach—the development of specialized systems for different analytical purposes—will prove to be compatible with the flexibility and unpredictability of real-world musicological research, or whether it represents a particularly sophisticated way of falling into the same traps as 1980s office software. There is also the question of how the substantial costs of developing and updating a comprehensive system of this kind are to be found.

Maybe, in the coming years, the combination of user-friendly interfaces for Humdrum and a developing body of musicological work using it will provide the necessary momentum for it to become more generally used, so that in time it will become just one of those skills that musicologists have to acquire (like using notation software, for example). Or maybe that is just not going to happen; in that case, computational software like Humdrum might still become part of the wider musicological scene, but as a specialist professional service, rather than a skill you acquire for yourself (rather like note processing was a decade or so ago). In other words, if you had a project in which computational approaches could play an important part—in generating or testing hypotheses on the basis of a large body of data, for instance—then you would call in the services of a specialist computational musicologist, who would arrange for any necessary encoding of data, carry out the analysis, and provide advice on the interpretation of the results. What the ordinary musicologist would need to know, then, would be not how to extract or collapse Humdrum spines, but how to formulate a research question in such a way that advantage can be taken of computational methods to answer it more securely than is possible using the methods traditional in data-poor fields. Whether anyone could make a decent living as a specialist computational musicologist is another matter.

Using computers for musicology is like using computers for anything else: you need to have reasonable expectations about what they can do. However open and flexible its design, any musicological software is a tool, and like any tool it is good for some things and not for others. The articles by Huron and his coworkers that I have described in this chapter might be characterized as finding musicological uses to which computational tools can be put; in essence, they illustrate the software's potential, and they do so in a manner that owes more to social-scientific discourse than to traditional humanities writing, with their explicit hypotheses, control groups, quantification of significance, and formulation in what Huron (1999b) has termed the "boilerplate language" of scientific inquiry. Perhaps that is only to underline the distinction between "cognitive" or "systematic" musicology, as such work is sometimes called, and the close attention to context and what might be termed epistemological pluralism of the traditional discipline. But what I am suggesting is that musicology in the broadest sense can take advantage of computational methods and transform itself into a data-rich discipline, without giving up on its humanist values. Understood that way, scientific discourse is unlikely to offer a general model for the musicology of the future: it is up to musicologists to develop such a model. And that does not mean trying to find musicological uses to which computational tools can be put, but the reverse: discovering the tools that are most appropriate to a particular musicological purpose, and taking full advantage of them. At present we hardly have such a thing as a model of how sophisticated computational approaches might be integrated within a sustained, musicologically driven project. Yet the tools are ready and waiting.[20]

Notes

1. The routines used to create these graphs, which took advantage of the NeXT computer's Postscript display, have not to date been disseminated, but the principles underlying them were described in chapter 20 of Brinkman 1990.
2. Helmut Schaffrath, *Essen Musical Data Package* (Menlo Park, Calif.: Center for Computer Assisted Research in the Humanities [CCARH], 1995) [data and analytical software on four floppy discs for MS-DOS]); 6,225 folksongs were included in this release. Both data and software are now available at www.esac-data.org. (All URLs were correct at press time, but Web resources change rapidly. Search engines may provide a better means of access to the resources listed in this chapter.)
3. A full listing of the analytical output for "Deutschland über alles," reformatted and annotated for clarity, may be found in Selfridge-Field 1995; see also Schaffrath 1992, 1997.
4. Since *EsAC* consists entirely of ASCII characters, it is possible to import the records into modern databases. However researchers now generally prefer to access the *kern* version of the databases and process them using Humdrum (see note 7 below).
5. Hence the need for translation programs such as POCO (see chapters 5 and 8, this volume).
6. Digital Alternate Representation of Musical Scores; for details see Selfridge-Field 1997, chapters 11–15.
7. David Huron, *The Humdrum Toolkit: Software for Music Researchers* (Stanford, Calif.: Center for Computer Assisted Research in the Humanities, 1993 [three floppy discs and 16-page installation guide]). A wide range of information may be accessed from the Humdrum Toolkit home page (http://dactyl.som.ohio-state.edu/Humdrum; links to on-line resources are at http://dactyl.som.ohio-state.edu/Humdrum/resources.html).
8. UNIX is an operating system, like MS-DOS or Windows, but includes a large number of general-purpose tools and thus fulfils many of the functions of a programming environment as well. Developed in the late 1960s, it remains the environment of choice for many professional software developers and researchers.
9. For a summary of *kern* see Huron 1997; for detailed descriptions see Huron 1995, 1999a.
10. Lines beginning with asterisks are known as "interpretation records," those with two asterisks being *inclusive* interpretations (something is either in *kern* or it isn't), and those with one asterisk being *tandem* interpretations (of which you can have any number).
11. In a review of the Humdrum Toolkit, Jonathan Wild (1996) includes what is essentially a tutorial on this precise task; assuming that the chorales have been concatenated into one file, the entire analysis consists of seven commands pipelined to another—in other words, it can be executed with a single command line. Further analytical applications of Humdrum are discussed in Huron 2002, which appeared after this chapter had gone into production.
12. See this volume, pp. 7–8.
13. A follow-up study (Hippel 2000) reanalyzed the experimental data on the basis of which Burton Rosner and Leonard Meyer had claimed that gap-fill patterns reflect listener expectations; von Hippel concludes that that the apparent effects of gap-fill expectations were an artifact of experimental design (specifically, effects of training). Of course listeners may have such expectations, but von Hippel's and Huron's point is that these are the result of melodic patterns and not the other way around.

14. See the Humdrum download page at http://dactyl.som.ohio-state.edu/ HumdrumDownload/downloading.html. Additional tools developed by Craig Sapp can be downloaded from http://www.ccarh.org/software/humdrum/museinfo.

15. UWIN (free to educational/research users) is accessible through the Humdrum download page (see n. 14). Commercial alternatives are available from Morton Kern Systems (MKS Toolkit, like UWIN for Windows) or from Tenon Intersystems (for Mac). There is a further alternative: a number of Humdrum commands can be run online at http://musedata.stanford.edu/software/humdrum/online; you select the command you want, supply the input data (by pasting it into a window, uploading a file, or supplying its URL), set the options, and receive the output as plain text or in HTML. Twenty of the 70 or more Humdrum commands are currently available in this way, with an emphasis on data translation and conversion. (Not accessible at publication time.)

16. There are two principal sources for such material (from both of which they may be obtained free): the KernScores site at http://kern.humdrum.net, and CCARH's MuseData site (http://www.musedata.org).

17. "Humdrum Toolkit GUI" currently exists only in a 16-bit version, but further development (and eventual distribution) is planned by the Sonic Arts Centre at Queen's University, Belfast.

18. Only a few of these "regular expressions," as they are known in UNIX jargon, are built into the interface, but you can add your own, along with new interpretations; this is where you would define **timing or **heartbeat.

19. Accessible at http://www.themefinder.org; for a brief description see Kornstädt 1998.

20. My grateful thanks to David Huron, who has influenced this chapter in many ways, not least through making it possible for me to work with him in 2000 as a visiting scholar at the Cognitive Musicology Laboratory, Ohio State University, Columbus.

References

Aarden, B., and Huron, D. (2001). "Mapping European folksong: Geographical localization of musical features," in Walter B. Hewlett and Eleanor Selfridge Field (eds.), *The Virnal Score: Representation, Retrieval, Restoration* (Computing in Musicology 12). Cambridge, Mass.: MIT Press, 169–183.

Barlow, H., and Morgenstern, S. (1983). *A Dictionary of Musical Themes*, rev. ed. London: Faber.

Brinkman, A. R. (1986). "Representing musical scores for computer analysis." *Journal of Music Theory* 30: 225–275.

Brinkman, A. R. (1990). *Pascal Programming for Music Research*. Chicago: Chicago University Press.

Brinkman, A. R., and Mesiti, M. R. (1991). "Graphic modeling of musical structure." *Computers in Music Research* 3: 1–42.

Clendenning, J. P. (1995). "Structural factors in the microcanonic compositions of György Ligeti," in E. W. Marvin and R. Hermann (eds.), *Concert Music, Rock, and Jazz since 1945: Essays and Analytical Studies*. Rochester, N.Y.: University of Rochester Press, 229–256.

Forte, A. (1983). "Motivic design and structural level in the First Movement of Brahms's String Quartet in C Minor." *Musical Quarterly* 69: 471–502.

Hippel, P. von (2000). "Questioning a melodic archetype: Do listeners use gap–fill to classify melodies?" *Music Perception* 18: 139–153.

Hippel, P. von, and Huron, D. (2000). "Why do skips precede melodic reversals? The effect of tessitura on melodic structure." *Music Perception* 18: 59–85.

Hughes, M. (1977). "[Schubert, Op. 94 No. 1:] a quantitative approach," in M. Yeston (ed.), *Readings in Schenker Analysis and Other Approaches.* New Haven: Yale University Press, 144–164.

Huron, D. (1992). "Design principles in computer-based music representation," in A. Marsden and A. Pople (eds.), *Computer Representations and Models in Music.* London: Academic Press, 5–39.

Huron, D. (1995). *The Humdrum Toolkit: Reference Manual.* Menlo Park, Calif.: Center for Computer Assisted Research in the Humanities [accessible online at http://dactyl .som.ohio-state.edu/Humdrum/commands.toc.html].

Huron, D. (1996). "The melodic arch in Western folksongs." *Computing in Musicology* 10: 3–23.

Huron, D. (1997). "*Humdrum* and *Kern*: Selective feature encoding," in E. Selfridge-Field (ed.), *Beyond MIDI: The Handbook of Musical Codes.* Cambridge, Mass.: MIT Press, 375–401.

Huron, D. (1999a), *Music Research Using Humdrum: A User's Guide.* Stanford, Calif.: Center for Computer Assisted Research in the Humanities [accessible online at http://dactyl.som.ohio-state.edu/Humdrum/guide.toc.html].

Huron, D. (1999b). "Methodology: On Finding Field-Appropriate Methodologies at the Intersection of the Humanities and the Social Sciences." 1999 Ernest Bloch lectures, University of California at Berkeley, #3 [accessible online at http://dactyl.som .ohio-state.edu/Music220/Bloch.lectures/3.Methodology.html].

Huron, D. (2001). "What is a musical feature? Forte's analysis of Brahms's Opus 51, No. 1, Revisited." *Music Theory Online* 7.4.

Huron, D. (2002). "Music information processing using the Humdrum Toolkit: Concepts, examples, and lessons." *Computer Music Journal* 26/2: 11–26.

Huron, D., and J. Berec (forthcoming). "Characterizing idiomatic organization in music: A theory and case study." *Journal of New Music Research.*

Kornstädt, A. (1996). "SCORE-to-Humdrum: A graphical environment for musicological analysis." *Computing in Musicology* 10: 105–122.

Kornstädt, A. (1998). "*Themefinder:* A web-based melodic search tool." in Walter B. Hewlett and Eleanor Selfridge-Field (eds.), *Melodic Similarity: Concepts, Procedures, and Applications* (Computing in Musicology, 11). Cambridge, Mass.: MIT Press, 231–236.

Schaffrath, H. (1992). "The retrieval of monophonic melodies and their variants: Concepts and strategies for computer-aided analysis," in A. Marsden and A. Pople (eds.), *Computer Representations and Models in Music.* London: Academic Press, 95–109.

Schaffrath, H. (1997). "The *Essen Associative Code,*" in Eleanor Selfridge-Field (ed.), *Beyond MIDI: The Handbook of Musical Codes.* Cambridge, Mass.: MIT Press, 343–361.

Selfridge-Field, E. (1995). *Essen Musical Data Package* (CCARH Technical Report No. 1), Menlo Park, Calif.: Center for Computer Assisted Research in the Humanities [distributed with the *Essen Musical Data Package*].

Selfridge-Field, E. (1997). *Beyond MIDI: The Handbook of Musical Codes.* Cambridge, Mass.: MIT Press.

Taylor, W. M. (1966). "*Humdrum* Graphical User Interface." M.A. dissertation., Music Technology program, Queen's University of Belfast.

Wild, J. (1996). "A review of the Humdrum Toolkit: UNIX tools for music research, created by David Huron." *Music Theory Online* 2.7.

CHAPTER 7

Modeling Musical Structure

Anthony Pople

More than 20 years ago, music analysis was famously described by Ian Bent as "that part of the study of music which takes as its starting-point the music itself, rather than external factors" (Bent 1980: 341). Indeed, analysis is generally motivated by a desire to encounter a piece of music more closely, to submit to it at length, and to be deeply engaged by it, in the hope of thereby understanding more fully how it makes its effect. It is perhaps not surprising, then, that if you were to take a look at the kinds of writing that have at one time or another been thought of as music analysis, the variety would be immense. To a large extent this is because of the personal element in analysis: a piece of analytical writing is almost always the work of one person, and is founded in that person's own experience of an individual work. But even in this regard music analysis is significantly different from music criticism, or indeed literary criticism, because analysts generally try to play down the fact that their analyses are dependent on a personal viewpoint. Although music analysis certainly does have a critical dimension as one of its characteristic attributes (see Pople 1994), a writer of music analysis will in general try to present his or her observations as representing a musical experience that can be shared, and will address the reader as a kindred spirit eager to inquire about the piece in the same terms as the author has done.

This balance between the personal point of view and the potential for capturing shared experience makes music analysis a domain that is not only by its very nature empirical, but also one on which formal empirical methods can be brought to bear. However, the fact that one can say this in relation to analysis as the term is understood today is very much a consequence of the prevailing close relationship between music analysis and music theory.

As Nicholas Cook has pointed out, there is a broad historical distinction between music theory—which studies musical works in order to deduce "more general principles of musical structure"—and music analysis, in which the interest is focused on individual pieces of music (Cook 1987: 7). Since about 1970, without contradicting this distinction, a symbiotic relationship has arisen between theory and analysis: theory has developed by using analysis as a kind of test-bed, while professional analysts have by and large conscientiously used the language of contemporary theory to express their insights. This scenario is sufficiently close to the scientific model of hypothesis and experiment to have aroused antagonism from some humanities scholars (see, for example, Snarrenberg 1994: 50–55). But it has also allowed other scholars from disciplines that are more committed to formal methodologies, including cognitive psychologists and computer scientists, to see music analysis as a potentially fruitful domain of research. Some of what has been achieved is remarkable, but from a music analyst's point of view the question is: can it engage the reader's musical interest as deeply as can analytical writing based on expert human contemplation?

It is important to bear this in mind if one is to weigh up the value of differing approaches in which the empirical quality so fundamental to analysis is treated more formally. I have written elsewhere that "when people read something called 'music analysis' they assume that they will be 'told something about the piece'," and that in this respect there are specifically two types of failure that can occur if the analysis fails to engage sufficiently with the personal, empirical, critical and didactic aspects of analysis:

> The kind of . . . writing that remains tangled up in its own high-level assumptions, and so deals with musical detail in an anecdotal fashion . . . certainly "tells us something"; but, to those who expect the strategic sweep of analysis to range constructively through to the personal/empirical, what it tells us may not seem to be "about the piece." Conversely, work that is excessively bottom-up . . . may remain tangled in the empirical and fail to cross other than trivially into the critical/didactic domain; it is certainly "about the piece," but may "tell us" little or nothing. (Pople 1994: 121)

As Cook points out, good analysis does not merely reflect and describe experience, but also has the ability to make us hear the music differently (Cook 1987: 228–229). Together, these observations constitute a set of linked criteria that should be borne in mind as we examine in detail such issues as the place of rigorous technical language in music theory, the quasi-scientific approach to the relationship between theory and analysis, and the modeling of music analysis from interdisciplinary perspectives.

Formal Theory, Informal Analysis

Take, for example, the development of a rigorous terminology for the description of serial music at Princeton University in the 1960s, under the influence of the mathematically trained composer and theorist Milton Babbitt. In an article on "Twelve-Tone Rhythmic Structure and the Electronic Medium" published in the inaugural issue of the journal *Perspectives of New Music*, Babbitt outlined a theory of serial rhythm using language that mathematicians would regard as informal, but which to classically trained musicians might seem mathematical:

> [As] a means of informally evaluating the temporal constraints imposed by the formation of a twelve-tone set, I shall assume on purely empirical grounds that there are eleven qualitatively significant temporal relationships which can hold between two musical (say, pitch) events. Let x and y designate these events, and let a left parenthesis signify the time point initiation of the event and a right parenthesis signify the time point termination . . .

1. x) < (y. [that is, the termination of x precedes the initiation of y]
2. (x < (y; x) < y); but x) <| (y. [that is, the initiation of x precedes that of y; the termination of x precedes that of y; but the termination of x does not precede the initiation of y]
3. (x < (y; x) <| y); y) <| x).
4. (x < (y; y) < x).

[etc.] (Babbitt 1962: 52–53)

As Babbitt points out, what he writes is derived from empirical analysis of musical events, but his observations have been transmuted into abstract terms that can subsequently be treated as theory. (This is in line with the distinction between theory and analysis described by Cook.) But although Babbitt's process can in turn be reversed, by using the abstract terms as a method for analysis, this way of working has never caught on among analysts—most likely because, although one can look for concrete examples of Babbitt's equations, this isn't going to succeed, other than in a trivial way, in helping us to hear the music differently.

A second example, as interesting for its similarities to the Babbitt case as its differences—and far more productive analytically—is the set-class theory of Allen Forte, the principal concepts of which were outlined in his book *The Structure of Atonal Music* (Forte 1973). Forte's theory aimed to provide a system that would enable the analysis of atonal music to achieve two important objectives: (1) to avoid all vestiges of tonal terminology (e.g., convolutions such as "minor seventh chord with the fifth omitted but with both raised and lowered elevenths"); and (2) to enable absolutely any configuration of notes to be given a label for purposes of discussion and comparison. These two objectives were met simultaneously by presenting a means for all pitch configurations to be labeled in an entirely new way making no reference to any tonal categories.

The labeling system depends on three basic concepts: pitch-class, pitch-class set, and set-class. (Unfortunately, the distinction between the second and third of these concepts was initially obscured by Forte's presentation, though it has been clarified in the work of later writers.) As the prevalence of the word "class" indicates, the underlying principle is one of classification. To understand what a pitch-class is, ask yourself what is the tonic of a piece in C major: the answer, naturally enough, is "C," but not any particular C—rather it is a category that stands for all the notes C, irrespective of further considerations like which register the C is in, whether it is a crotchet or a quaver, whether the tempo is fast or slow, whether it is played loudly or softly, or by whichever instrument. And since Forte is concerned with the totally chromatic world of atonal music he doesn't distinguish between C and its enharmonic equivalents B♯ and D♭♭, he simply labels the keys on the keyboard with integers starting with 0 for the keys that play B♯, C, or D♭♭ and working upward to 11 for the keys that play B natural (or A♯♯ or C♭). A pitch-class set, naturally enough, is a set of pitch-classes, such as [0, 3, 4, 6]: these are, if you like, C, E♭, E, and F♯ (or their enharmonic equivalents), but it doesn't matter what order they are heard in, or whether they are played at the same time, or anything of that kind—it is simply a collection of the four pitch-classes, taken in the abstract.

Finally a set-class is a classification of pitch-class sets, so that the vast number of possibilities can be reduced to manageable proportions (in the case of Forte's system, about 200 set-classes in all). Pitch-class sets (abbreviated to pc sets) are reckoned to belong to the same class if they are related by transposition of all their constituent pitch classes by the same interval, and/or inversion of the intervals between the constituent pcs. This can be expressed numerically: two of the pc sets that belong in the same class as our set [0, 3, 4, 6] are [1, 4, 5, 7]—transposing each pc up a semitone—and [0, 2, 3, 6], which though it's harder to see at first is simply the original set turned upside down. Forte gives this set-class the composite label 4–12, because it has four pcs in it and is 12th in his list of the four-note set-classes, organized according to the intervals they contain.

That, in a nutshell, is the theory, but what of analysis? Taken on its own, Forte's labeling system is as lacking in operational specifics as are Babbitt's equations. But the prospect of turning the theory around, and looking for examples of pc sets in musical scores, turned out to be far more appealing in Forte's case. Inspired by the analytical examples that accompanied Forte's exposition of his theory in *The Structure of Atonal Music*, many analysts took up his approach and found in it a new and productive way of approaching previously intractable scores by composers such as Schoenberg, Webern, Berg, Ives, Bartók, and Stravinsky. What demands our attention here is the fact that, while Forte's labeling system involves the rigorous application of a few easily grasped principles, the analytical application of the theory has evolved over time as a constellation of customs and practices. We should look at this in more detail.

To find pc sets in a musical score you have to divide it up into groups of notes, a process known as segmentation. For example, Bryan Simms's segmentation of bars 20–21 of the last of Berg's Four Songs Op. 2 (Figure 7.1) interprets the piano part as a sequence of chords (shown by enclosing the notes in rectangular boxes), and ignores the voice part altogether.

Looking at the piano part in this way allows Simms to identify the chords as examples, alternately, of set-classes 4–Z29 and 4–Z15 (Simms 1993). Another analyst, John Doerksen, finds these set-classes too, but decides in addition that it is worth identifying the set-classes 3–8 and 6–Z13 by segmenting the vocal line after the first note in bar 21 (Doerksen 1998; see Figure 7.2). He also identifies the larger

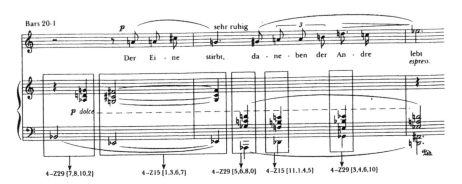

Figure 7.1.   Segmentation and set-class analysis by Bryan Simms of Berg, "Warm die Lüfte," bars 20–21 (from Simms 1993: 124).

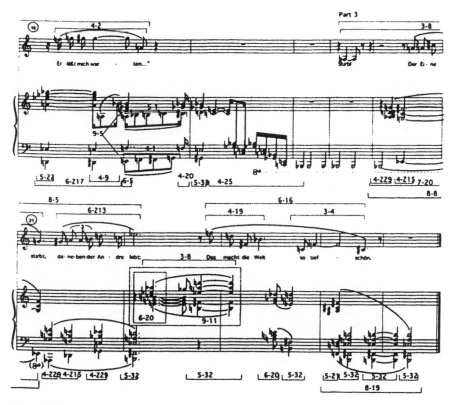

Figure 7.2.   Segmentation and set-class analysis by John Doerksen of Berg, "Warm die Lüfte," bars 19–21 (from Doerksen 1998: 199).

set-class 8–5 that is formed by these two segments taken together, and in a similar way he groups two of the adjacent piano chords to form 7–20, while adding the notes of the vocal line at this point gives him 8–8.

The next stage is to take stock of the set-classes and to find relationships between them. Forte's theory offers various relationships "off-the-shelf," as it were, such as the "Z" relationship that holds between 4–Z15 and 4–Z29 – meaning that the same distribution of intervals is to be found in these two classes. (For further theory concerning set-class relationships see Forte 1973, Rahn 1980, and the excellent summary in Castrén 1994.)

To summarize: the theory of set-classes is written in formal terms, and represents a fixed point in the constellation of theory and methods, whereas the associated methods of analysis are varied, and even the most fundamental process – that of segmentation – depends largely on personal habits of working at an analysis. As a result, although many computer programs have been written that make it easy to find the set-class designation that corresponds to a list of pitch names, and to determine relationships among the set-classes found in an analysis, these all function rather like a pocket calculator; they can save time, but they don't engage directly with the business of analysis, and so the empirical engagement with the score remains entirely the responsibility of the analyst. At best, however, the time-saving capability of computer-based tools can speed up the process of trying out an analytical hunch to see whether it "works," then modifying it if it doesn't, then trying again, and so on. This back-and-forth motion between the musical imagination and the evidence of the score itself is highly characteristic of analysis. To the extent that there is often a corresponding circularity of reasoning involved in set-class analysis— equating relative "success" with a segmentation that results in a smaller, more tightly related list of set-classes—it may be argued that using a computer program to find out how small and tightly related one's list of set-classes is, offers a genuine enhancement of the overall analytical process.

Quasi-Formalized Analysis

Several authors have moved beyond the scenario described above and have attempted to capture something of the analytical process itself in quasi-formal terms. Some of this endeavor has been pedagogical: in textbooks, the need to convey how analysis is done tends to lead to stage-by-stage descriptions (see Forte and Gilbert 1982, Cook 1987, Dunsby and Whittall 1988). Under the rubric *Models of Musical Analysis* (Everist 1992, Dunsby 1993), a number of writers have gone further in providing specific, fully worked, examples of analytical practice. Since these are intended to stand as models for analyses of works other than those used by way of example, their broad aim is to capture, albeit in particular musical contexts, the conceptual and operational processes that analysis entails.

Something similar may be said of the generative theory of tonal music developed by Fred Lerdahl and Ray Jackendoff in the late 1970s and early 1980s (Lerdahl and Jackendoff 1983), an approach developed further since that time in a number of publications by Lerdahl (notably Lerdahl 2001). Their system of formal (and in some cases informal) rules aims to reproduce the kinds of judgment that human musicians make about tonal music of the common-practice period. As they put it, "We take the goal of a theory of music to be a *formal description of the musical intuitions of a listener who is experienced in a musical idiom*" (1983: 1; emphasis in the original). This statement tells us that Lerdahl and Jackendoff are making a psychological claim about the accuracy of their theory with respect to human intelligent behavior. In other words, they aim not merely to come up with a description of the music that in some way matches a description that a listener might make, but also to describe the way in which the listener might make it—to shed light on the psychological processes that the listener might employ, even though to the listener those processes might remain no more than felt or tacitly understood.

Although Lerdahl and Jackendoff's belief that rule-systems can capture the psychological processes of an experienced listener should be evaluated primarily on its own terms, practical considerations demand that their rules produce tangible output that can be compared with the sorts of description of a musical score that might be made by a human being. And since the tangible descriptions made by humans are, de facto, music analyses, it follows that Lerdahl and Jackendoff's rules produce music analyses as well. Importantly, however, their system does not replicate existing kinds of analytical output—otherwise they would merely be claiming to show the psychological processes that produce, for example, a Schenkerian analysis. Instead, their theory introduces new analytical concepts of its own, but because they recognize that various established methods of analysis do express something of the musical intuitions of an experienced listener, they appropriate a number of ideas that are familiar to analysts.

Lerdahl and Jackendoff's theory is set out in four sets of "well-formedness rules" which model different types of musical thought. These four limbs of the theory are: (1) "Grouping Structure," which describes how the mind articulates a chronological stream of musical events by associating events into groups that seem to belong together in some way; (2) "Metrical Structure," which they describe as "the regular, hierarchical pattern of beats to which the listener relates musical events" (1983: 17; see Cooper and Meyer 1960); (3) "Time-Span Reduction," which is based on the grouping and metrical structures but is expressed reductively, that is, by selecting within each articulated time-span an event that is considered the most important; and (4) "Prolongational Reduction," which is based on Schenkerian principles. To give a flavor of the theory, the following are the first and last Grouping Structure well-formedness rules:

GWFR 1
Any contiguous sequence of pitch-events, drum beats, or the like can constitute a group, and only contiguous sequences can constitute a group. (Lerdahl and Jackendoff, 1983: 345)

GWFR 5
If a group G1 contains a smaller group G2, then G1 must be exhaustively partitioned into smaller groups. (Lerdahl and Jackendoff, 1983: 345)

And the following are the first and second Prolongational Reduction well-formedness rules:

PRWFR 1
There is a single event in the underlying grouping structure of every piece that functions as prolongational head.

PRWFR 2
An event e_i can be a direct elaboration of another event e_j in any of the following ways:

a. e_i is a *strong prolongation* of e_j if the roots, bass notes, and melodic notes of the two events are identical.
b. e_i is a *weak prolongation* of e_j if the roots of the two events are identical but the bass and/or melodic notes differ.
c. e_i is a *progression to or from* e_j if the harmonic roots of the two events are different.

(Lerdahl and Jackendoff, 1983: 351)

In addition, there is for each of these four systems an accompanying set of "preference rules" which describe how any conflicts within, or between, these four types of judgment might be resolved. These rules are expressed rather differently from the "well-formedness rules," because they don't presume to operate the same way in every musical situation: their application is not automatic, but depends on a judgment of the musical context. For example, the first of the preference rules relating to Grouping Structure is expressed as follows:

GSPR 1 Avoid analyses with very small groups—the smaller the less preferable (Lerdahl and Jackendoff 1983: 345)

Notice how this rule talks of "analyses"! It does not take the form "Intuitions about Grouping Structures prefer . . .," despite the authors' overall intention to describe musical intuitions. Of course, it might be possible to rephrase all the preference rules in the second way, but that is not the point I want to make. It is rather that the distinction between well-formedness rules and preference rules corresponds to a distinction one can make about the application of music theory in practical analysis: the well-formedness rules describe those overlearned psychological routines that are applied intuitively, whereas the preference rules describe the areas of judgment that a self-aware analyst will handle explicitly through conscious thought. One might argue about exactly where the line is drawn—indeed, it may depend very much on the individual analyst's capacity to avoid making unwarranted assumptions—but the line is there to be drawn nonetheless.

What does all this mean in practice? Figure 7.3 shows a composite analysis by Lerdahl and Jackendoff of the opening of Mozart's 40th Symphony, shown in reduced score with bar numbers (Lerdahl and Jackendoff 1983: 259). The metrical structure is shown directly below the score notation by combinations of dots placed under the main beats: the more dots there are under a beat, the greater its metrical stress. The horizontal brackets underneath the dots show the grouping structure. Note how the groups are organized hierarchically in layers of brackets: for example, the lowest bracket at level (a) extends notionally well beyond the extract analyzed here, and at the next largest level (b) the time-span covers all the music up to the point where the opening material recurs; the two time-spans at level (c) lie exactly within (b), and so forth. The tree-diagram above the score and the notational systems below the grouping brackets together express the time-span reduction. The prolongational reduction (Figure 7.4; Lerdahl and Jackendoff 1983: 260) is derived in a further stage of analysis.

Lerdahl and Jackendoff's system charts a process leading from the score as an uninterpreted input through to the production of a structural description. This description both expresses an interpretation of the score and traces the process through which the interpretation comes into being. All of this arises not through psychological experiment or automated data processing of the score, but by contemplation and working-out: what emerges, then, is an acutely self-aware form of analysis. And just as is the case with set-class analysis, the empirical aspects are explicitly separated from the rational (i.e., logically consistent) aspects. Lerdahl and Jackendoff themselves address this issue in terms of a distinction between necessary and sufficient conditions:

For example, there are no necessary and sufficient conditions for a portion of the musical surface to be judged a group. The grouping well-formedness conditions are necessary conditions on groups, but not sufficient. Each preference rule is an attribute that creates family resemblances among grouping structures, but since every preference rule can be overridden by the proper confluence of circumstances, it is a sufficient condition only in the absence of conflicting evidence. Where preference rules come into conflict, dubious judgments of grouping result; where a great number of preference rules reinforce each other, a stereotypical grouping structure results. (1983: 313)

In other words, the rational, logically consistent part of their theory says a great deal about groups but cannot, of itself, find them in the music.

The similarity between this state of affairs and the status of segmentation in the set-class theory/analysis mix suggests that it might be possible to go beyond the apparently ad hoc nature of set-class analytical practices by framing some preference rules, in Lerdahl and Jackendoff's sense, that describe how set-class analysis is done. To do this, we might look at the kinds of criteria that various writers on set-class-based analysis have come up with, and rephrase them as preference rules. The first of these paraphrase Forte's own criteria:

1. Prefer segments that have a beginning and an end, both of which are determined in some way, for example, by an instrumental attack or a rest. (cf. Forte, 1973: 84)
2. Prefer segments that correspond to sets identical with or related to those of other segments. (cf. Forte 1973: 85–88, 91–92 and passim)
3. Prefer to designate a configuration that is isolated as a unit by conventional means, such as: (a) a rhythmically distinct figure; (b) something indicated by a notational feature, such as a rest or a beam; (c) a chord; (d) an ostinato pattern. (1973: 83)
4. Prefer vertical groupings through the entire texture. (cf. Forte 1973: 89)
5. Prefer to form composite segments from subsegments that are contiguous or linked in some other way. (cf. Forte 1973: 84)
6. Prefer composite segments that do not extend across a rest in all parts. (cf. Forte 1973: 90)
7. Prefer a segmentation based on knowledge of a particular composer's way of composing. (cf. Forte 1973: 92; and Forte 1972)

From Joel Lester (1989: 89–90):

8. Prefer groupings of pitches that are important to the sound of the passage.
9. Prefer segments that enhance our hearing and understanding of the piece.
10. Prefer segments formed of pitches that appear together: (a) consecutively as a melody; (b) simultaneously as a harmony; (c) associated texturally or timbrally, as in the accompaniment to a melody; (d) related in some other way.

And from Bryan Simms (1993: 127):

11. Prefer segmentations created by rhythm and meter.
12. Prefer segmentations created by the presentation of notes as chords.
13. Prefer segmentations created by the placement of rests.

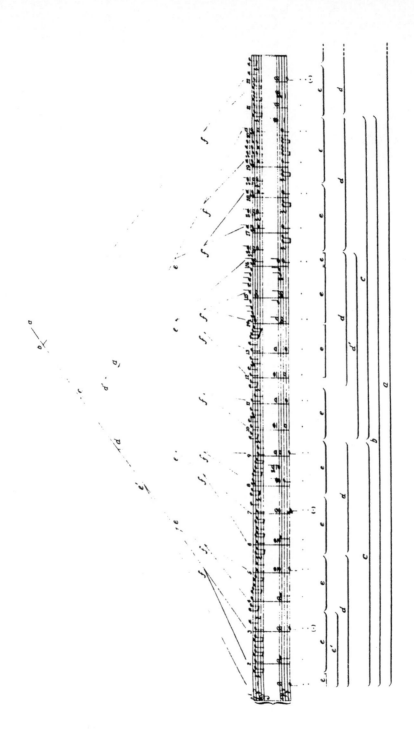

Figure 7.3. Grouping structure, metrical structure, and time-span reduction of Mozart, Symphony No. 40 in G minor, bars 1–22 (from Lerdahl and Jackendoff 1983: 259).

137

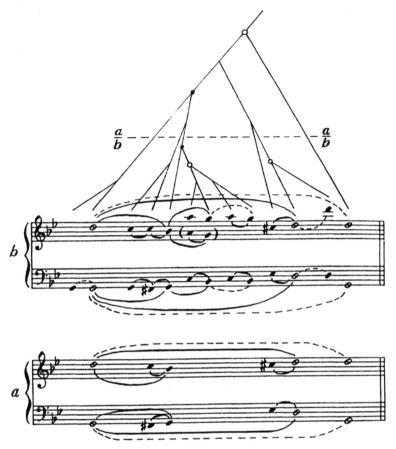

Figure 7.4. Prolongational reduction of Mozart, Symphony No. 40 in
G minor, bars 1–22 (from Lerdahl and Jackendoff 1983: 260).

14. Prefer segmentations created by groupings of notes under a slur or phrase
    mark.
15. Prefer segmentations created by motivic elements.
16. Prefer segmentations created by disjunctions in register or color.

These formulations are generally less specific than are Lerdahl and Jackendoff's
for tonal music, but in substantive terms there is a great deal of common ground
among these three (and other) authors. And, like the Lerdahl/Jackendoff rules, these
rules do not simply take, as their inputs, the results of well-formedness rules operating in another part of a broader musical system, while passing on nothing in return. Instead, they form part of a network, feeding their own results into preferen-
tial judgments being made elsewhere. To put this another way: the things that Forte's
theory of set-classification leaves out—rhythm, register, dynamics, instrumentation, the words in a vocal piece, and so forth—still feed into pc set analysis through
the practical business of segmentation.

Modeling Analytical Practice with Formal Systems

So far, we have examined ways of working, and complexes of ideas, in which there is a clear methodological gap between the uninterpreted contents of a musical score (something we might think of as "data") and the application of rules in relation to an interpretative process that we call "analysis"—which in its classic form is undertaken through musical contemplation. We have seen examples of formally expressed music theory, and of the quasi-formal description of how an analyst engages with the score, but we have not yet considered any work that attempts to capture the processes of music analysis themselves in terms of genuinely formal rules. It is perhaps not surprising to find that the discipline that initially pushed hardest to achieve this was artificial intelligence (AI) research, for in this field the idea that a musical score might be treated as data, and that empirical processing of it might be accomplished automatically, was akin to the way researchers conceived the classic domains of AI: natural language, visual recognition, and complex gaming (such as chess).

One of the most notable attempts to use the early digital computer for music analysis was undertaken by Terry Winograd (1968). Winograd, whose reputation was made in the field of artificial visual intelligence, took the classic AI approach of modeling: that is to say, his computer program was not designed to produce a new kind of music analysis, but to produce by artificially intelligent means the kinds of analysis that human beings could already make. In common with a great deal of later similar research in the same vein, Winograd's work was based on a grammatical framework, in his case the "systemic linguistics" of M. A. K. Halliday:

> Systemic grammar is based on the fact that any sentence in a language will
> exhibit a number of features which the speaker has selected from a limited
> and tightly organized set available in that language. What is important
> in the understanding of a language is the way in which these features are de-
> pendent on each other. . . . A feature T1 may be conditional on a feature T2,
> in that the presence of T1 implies the presence of T2 . . . [or] may on the
> other hand preclude the possibility of T2. Thus, "interrogative" and "declara-
> tive," or "triad" and "7th" are incompatible pairs. . . . Further, a set of mutu-
> ally exclusive features may exhaust the possibilities for an obligatory property
> of the sentence. . . . Such sets are called systems and form a key part of the
> theory. . . . The diatonic note system in music has seven terms (A, B, . . . G)
> while the Linearity system used in this grammar has six: (passing, anticipa-
> tion, suspension, auxiliary, contained in adjacent chord, and nil). (Winograd
> 1968: 9)

In other words, one component of the grammar embodies a rule that a note, if it is implicated in a linear relationship, must do so in one and only one of the six ways listed.

Winograd organized his grammar into five "ranks": Composition, Tonality, Chord Group, Chord, and Note. His diagram of the "network" of systems at the rank of Chord is shown in Figure 7.5. The program, written in LISP, operated by parsing the music in retrograde motion, a procedure chosen because the function of a chord in tonal music is very often governed by the chord that precedes it.

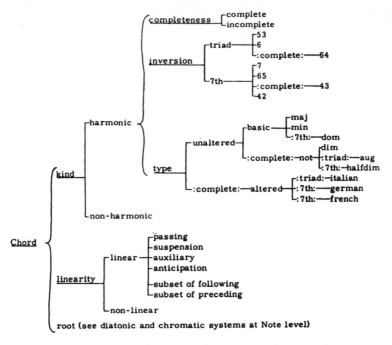

Figure 7.5.   Systemic chord grammar (from Winograd 1968: 17).

A journey through the music in chronological sequence "from left to right" raises a number of possible expectations at many given moments (see Meyer 1956, 1973; Narmour 1977, 1990, 1992), all of which would have had to be kept track of by Winograd's program, whereas going through the music "from right to left" meant that the program had fewer possible paths to calculate because it had parsed the resolution of a given harmony before coming to the harmony itself. (We should note, incidentally, that presenting the musical data to the program as a sequence of chords may involve an act of segmentation on the part of the researcher.) The program produced impressive results, comparable with analyses that might have been produced by human analysts (see Figure 7.6). The fact that it did so, despite operating in a counter-intuitive "right to left" manner, illustrates how the modeling approach is concerned fundamentally with the plausibility of the end product as an imitation, rather than with replicating psychological processes (at least those of listeners).

Winograd's pioneering example established that the modeling approach is viable for simple tonal analysis. What are the prospects for applying this approach to set-class analysis? As we have seen, in this case it is the business of segmentation that is the obstacle, because it seems amenable only to semiformal description at best. To show this, it is instructive to look at the shortcomings of a more ambitious attempt to automate the segmentation process, the rule-based system developed by James Tenney (1980). Among the pieces he worked on were two for solo flute: Debussy's *Syrinx* (1912) and Varèse's *Density 21.5* (1936). The monophonic nature of these pieces immediately reduced the complexity of the segmentation process: in effect the

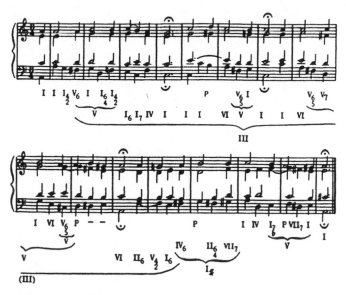

Figure 7.6.   Analysis of "Puer natus in Bethlehem" generated by
Winograd's grammar (from Winograd 1968: 41).

segmentation needed only to be "vertical"—as it also was in the case of Winograd's
chord parsing program—and the complexities of atonal contrapuntal texture were
thus avoided. Tenney's approach, then, addressed some but not all of the issues focused in the preference rules for atonal segmentation listed earlier in this chapter.

Tenney's vertical segmentation divided the music into time-spans—which he
termed temporal gestalt-units (TGs)—by giving specific weighting to quantifiable
factors, such as rests, dynamics, and large intervals. His model produced hierarchical segmentations that reflected the grouping of groups, the grouping of groups of
groups, and so forth. A fundamental principle he applied was that "The perceptual
formation of TGs at any hierarchical level is determined by a number of factors of
cohesion and segregation, the most important of which are proximity and similarity; their effects may be described as follows: relative temporal proximity [and] relative similarities of TGs at a given hierarchical level will tend to group them, perceptually, into a TG at the next higher level. Conversely, relative temporal separation
and/or differences between TGs will segregate them into separate TGs at the next
higher level." (1980: 208)

Tenney went on to develop measures of proximity in four domains: duration,
pitch, intensity, and timbre. These measures were then assigned weightings—so
that, for example, it could be determined whether a boundary existed between two
notes that were close in temporal terms but distant in terms of pitch, or whether a
sudden fortissimo would create a segment boundary even when there was little difference between the notes concerned in terms of, say, pitch and timbre. Thus the system of weights operated in lieu of an array of preference rules. In fact, Tenney used

different weighting factors in different analyses, adjusting the computer implementation (which was written by Larry Polansky) so as to produce the "best" (i.e., preferred) results in each case (1980: 219–220).

The beginning of Tenney's segmentation of Varèse's *Density 21.5* is shown above the flute stave in Figure 7.7. This may profitably be compared with a segmentation of the same piece by Jean-Jacques Nattiez, originally published in French in 1975 (see Nattiez 1982), which Tenney shows below the stave. Nattiez was an important figure in the semiology of music (see Nattiez 1975, 1990), and his segmentation was undertaken as a preliminary stage in a grand comparative study of analyses of the work. The idea was that the initial segmentation could be undertaken without prejudice as to musical signification, so that by comparing other analyses with this segmentation their underlying priorities of interpretation could be exposed. The major flaw in this argument, of course, is that segmentation simply can't be done in such a "neutral" way by an experienced musician. For example, the fact that Nattiez could read music meant that he was bound to make some kinds of judgment about musical signification on the basis of the notation—indeed, perhaps the best he could hope for was to suspend some kinds of judgment and hope that people would trust him. Still, such relativism is something that circumstances impose on semiology as a whole, and it doesn't invalidate that discipline any more than Einsteinian relativism invalidates physics.

Tenney's discussion of the difference between their two analyses hinges on a concern that the weightings between parameters may need further adjustment: "discrepancies . . . remain which suggest that our weightings may not be quite 'optimum' after all, or that they are simply different from those unconsciously assumed by Nattiez. . . . Finally, however, I must say that I think our segmentation represents the perceptual 'facts' here more accurately than Nattiez's at certain points" (Tenney 1980: 221).

For the English translation of his analysis, Nattiez prepared a rebuttal of Tenney's points, largely in order to defend his own segmentation (Nattiez 1982: 324–329). But, from the point of view of anyone wanting to refine Tenney's approach to modeling segmentation, the most telling point that Nattiez makes is that the balance of weightings between parameters should be flexible not merely from one piece to another but also within the boundaries of the individual piece. This is tantamount to saying that the system of weightings is not sufficiently complex, or perhaps not sufficiently multileveled, to model the kinds of perceptual judgment that actually take place within specific contexts. Given my argument that the weightings in Tenney's system actually fulfill the same function as a complex of preference rules, the question arises as to whether either approach (or a combination of them) is an adequate basis for automated replication of the complexities of musical segmentation.

However, there is a significant alternative to both of these. The use of neural networks (or "nets") as a tool for AI modeling of pattern matching quickly gained the reputation of being a stronger way of producing artificially intelligent machines than rule-based systems. The term "neural network" refers to the intention to make such a system akin to the brain in terms of its underlying organization, but without claiming that the way in which an artificial neural network behaves in performing a par-

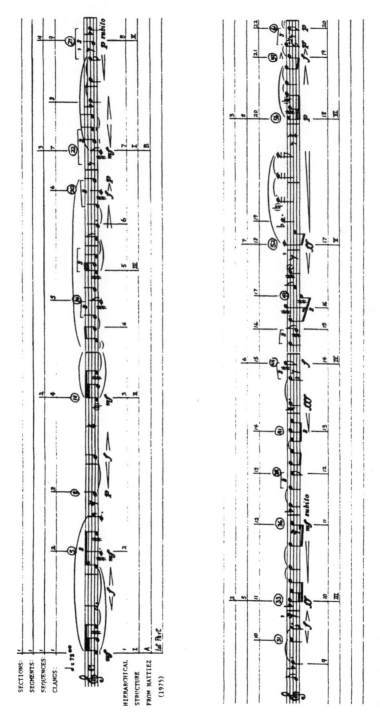

Figure 7.7. Segmentations by James Tenney and Jean-Jacques Nattiez of Varèse, *Density 21.5* (from Tenney 1980: 222).

143

ticular task is, at the level of its quasi-neuronal "circuitry," the same as the behavior of an organic brain accomplishing the same task. Motivating this approach—which was developed more or less independently by researchers in the United States, Europe, and Japan in the 1970s—was the desire to make machines that could learn. In its most basic form—actually, too basic to be useful except as an introductory description—a neural network comprises a group of input nodes connected to a group of output modes. For a simple musical application, there might be 12 input nodes corresponding to the 12 pitch classes, and a number of output nodes representing common chords. A dataset, for instance a chorale harmonization, could be used as input material to this: the likely imbalance among the pitch-classes—since chorales tend not to be made up of 12-tone rows!—would mean that some input nodes were "stimulated" more than others. As a result, the strength (measured by a variable numerical value) of the connections between those nodes and the corresponding output nodes would be enhanced and others reduced. Overall, then, the network would in some sense have "learned" through its "experience" of the data. This outline description only hints at the practical complexities of neural networks used by researchers, for example, in terms of "hidden" layers of nodes, nodes that inhibit as well as those that excite, and the classic "back-propagation" method that is intended to improve the performance of the system as a whole.

One of the questions that has bedeviled research using neural networks is: When the network learns, just what does it learn? The question arises because the learning is not set out explicitly in terms of rulelike descriptions of responses to certain types of input ("if you give it an X, then the network does such and such"); instead, the network's learning is embedded in its changed patterns of connection. Although methods exist to unravel the network patterns so that they can be usefully examined, there remains a difference in kind between these declarative and procedural descriptions of intelligent behavior. Since music theory is almost exclusively expressed in rule-based, declarative terms that encapsulate overt knowledge, the procedural learning that is accomplishable by neural networks might seem comparatively unpromising in this field. Rather, one might expect to use neural networks to model the kind of high-level musical processes that experts seem to find easier to do than to explain: musical composition, for example, or interactive performance between human musicians and computers (Rowe 1993: 229–237). Alternatively, in line with the classic use of neural networks in artificial visual intelligence, we could see their musical niche in modeling low-level psychoacoustic phenomena. Marc Leman embraces this idea, and discusses the distinction that it implies between symbolic and subsymbolic mental processing: "The subsymbolic representation assumes that there is more to mental representation than just symbols. For example, when we imagine a chord we do not recall the symbols, but we hear it internally. . . . Since there is no consensus on how a musical image can be described in a nonsymbolic way, the definition of subsymbolic representation is diffuse from the beginning. Initially, we would define it as the level between the acoustical and the symbolic representation . . . ." (Leman 1993: 132; see also Leman 1992)

The trouble is, Leman is clearly trying to define something that, properly speaking, is indefinable—and indeed this difficulty signals a major issue that emerges in the attempts of various writers to assess how neural networks can, or should, be applied to musical research. One characteristic of a neural network is that it remains to some extent inscrutable: but does this imply that neural network modeling should be restricted to musical phenomena that are also more or less inscrutable? Or would this simply amount to a confusion of the ends with the means? The music psychologist Jamshed Bharucha has adopted a median position, by using used neural networks to model the kinds of chord and key recognition that one finds in basic music theory, and he helpfully contrasts neural network models with symbolic grammars: "I suspect . . . that although highly trained musicians may use formal symbolic processes together with a host of other processes, the passive processing of music by most listeners is minimally symbolic. What then does one make of rule-based theories of music, such as that of Lerdahl and Jackendoff (1983)? These can be construed as formalizations of constraints on neural processing of music. In other words, either neural nets are implementations of grammars, or grammars are formal descriptions of neural nets." (Bharucha 1999: 436)

A harder line, however, is taken by John Rahn (1994), who—presumably on the basis that present-day computers cannot avoid using symbolic data—has argued that even a neural network that models the perception of pitch from acoustic data "does nothing but process representations." Rahn maintains that, despite the inscrutability of such a network as compared with a formal description of symbolic relations—and despite the fact that the network is modeling something that lies in the realm of subconscious mental processing—"this net is doing symbolic processing, and no processing model could do otherwise" (Rahn 1994: 232). Indeed, as Rahn goes on to indicate, the work of Robert Gjerdingen (1990) shows that neural networks can with advantage be put to work on musical data that are unambiguously symbolic.

Beyond Modeling?

Gjerdingen's work differs from the modeling approach in that, while the focus remains the end product, it is a product that—at last, one might say!—has the potential to "tell us something about the piece," or at least about a style. In line with his larger research interest into the usage of specific pitch schemata (small-scale patterns) in the classical style (see Gjerdingen 1988), Gjerdingen set up a self-organizing neural network that would take as its input some simple keyboard pieces in this style, written by Mozart as a child, and to give as its outputs 25 (as yet unforeseen) schemata. The input data were organized on an event-by-event basis, and included representations of the pitches and contours of the melody, bass, and inner voices, together with simulated short-term memory traces of recently preceding events: "After the pieces had been taught to the network 12 times . . . and after [it] had had a chance to make nearly 10,000 successful categorizations, a stable category structure emerged. . . . When learning began [the output layer] was inchoate. Then it slowly organized itself, by itself, as it encountered [input-layer] patterns that bore family resemblances to each other" (Gjerdingen 1990: 357).

Gjerdingen's interpretations of these stable output categories is shown in Figure 7.8, in which he translates the numerical data into musical notation. The patterns do not match high-level music theory concepts such as cadence types, although they did encourage him to suggest with confidence a small amendment to the New Mozart Edition. Adding two further levels to the network, however, enabled it to recognize cadence types (1990: 365–366). The results of this incremental approach are interesting with respect to our criteria on music analysis: the emergence of "cadence detectors" at the fourth level validates the expanded network as a model, which is reassuring but "tells us" little that we didn't already know about the music; the unfamiliar concepts that emerge from the simpler two-level network, on the other hand, usefully reveal aspects of the music that are unfamiliar in terms of explicit theory.

The question of complexity versus simplicity in music theory is particularly relevant to Eugene Narmour's "implication-realization" theory of melodic structure (1990, 1992). His approach is through feature analysis, and the complexity of his approach can be gauged by the fact that so many categories are invoked that the mnemonics referring to them are continually repeated for the reader's convenience at the foot of the page in his two books on the subject. In fact, through empirical testing and statistical analysis, Glenn Schellenberg (1997) found that the five underlying principles of Narmour's theory could be satisfactorily reduced to two, pitch proximity and pitch reversal; each applies to a third note following what is termed an implicative interval. The pitch proximity principle "states that when listeners hear an implicative interval in a melody, they expect the next tone to be proximate in pitch to the second tone" (1997: 309); the pitch reversal principle applies more strongly to large implicative intervals than to small ones, and predicts that "listeners often expect the [third] tone . . . to be proximate to the first tone of the implicative interval" as well as to the second (1997: 312). In other words: listeners expect that melodies will be generally conjunct, that leaps will tend to be small, and that a larger leap will generally be followed by a smaller interval in the opposite direction[1] — findings that are very much in line with the results of Knud Jeppesen's pioneering study of Palestrina's style (1927), which is itself a classic example of empirical musicology. All this seems at first sight to undermine Narmour's work considerably, both by characterizing it as overdetermined and, though Schellenberg doesn't explicitly make this point, by showing that it has merely the predictive power of a model rather than the enlightening potential of good analysis. In the light of Gjerdingen's work, however, one might wonder whether the very over-determination of Narmour's theory could put it into the same category as Gjerdingen's initial, two-layer network, so that the fact that its categories are at a lower level than those of Schellenberg's revision might actually make them more interesting to use in the analysis of specific melodies. This is likely to depend on whether it turns out that Narmour has in fact made explicit some useful concepts that conventional, high-level melodic theory normally glosses over. Time will tell: an alternative possibility is that they will be thought no more worthwhile than Babbitt's equations about serial rhythm.

Encouraging though Gjerdingen's work is, it is still—to follow Cook's distinction—an approach that looks at individual pieces in order to deduce "more general principles of musical structure": in other words, a tool for theory-building rather than analysis. A recent line of research that is genuinely analytical in orientation,

Figure 7.8.   Pitch/contour schemata recognized in early Mozart by Robert O. Gjerdingen's *ART pour l'art* neural network (from Gjerdingen 1990: 360; "The largest noteheads indicate the strongest pitch traces, arrows signify traces of contour, 'd' means the trace of a contrapuntal dissonance, and 'ΤΤ' signifies a harmonic tritone."

however, and that also reduces the "gap" between uninterpreted score data and the input to a formalized empirical system, is David Temperley's work in the field of automated harmonic analysis (Temperley 1997). The system produced by Temperley and his coworker, Daniel Sleator, is intended to be capable of analyzing common-practice tonal music in terms of triadic harmonies and seventh chords (its analysis of the melody "Yankee Doodle" is reproduced in Figure 7.9).

In doing so, it does not rely on human judgments about segmentation, but can judge for itself where each new harmony begins, based on five preference rules:

> **Pitch Variance Rule**: Try to label nearby pitches so that they are close together on the line of fifths. . .
>
> **Compatibility Rule**: In choosing roots for chord spans, prefer certain . . . root relationships over others. Prefer them in the following order: 1, 5, 3, b3, b7, ornamental. (An ornamental relationship is any relationship besides these five.) . . .
>
> **Strong-Beat Rule**: Prefer chord spans that start on strong beats of the meter. . . .
>
> **Harmonic Variance Rule**: Prefer roots that are close to the roots of nearby segments on the line of fifths. . . .
>
> **Ornamental Dissonance Rule**: An event is an ornamental dissonance if it does not have a chord-tone relationship to the chosen root. Prefer ornamental dissonances that are closely followed by an event a step [whole tone] or half-step [semitone] away in pitch height. (Temperley 1997: 49–54)

The system is presented as being explicitly algorithmic: Temperley does not make psychological claims for it, beyond noting that "much evidence exists that harmonic analysis is performed by trained and untrained listeners during listening" (1997: 31). He also draws attention to the fact that, in waiting until the entire piece has been processed before assigning an analysis to it, the algorithm is "clearly unsatisfactory as a model of listening" (1997: 58). But then, to produce a model of listening was not his intention.

The more important question is: is this a model of analysis? Or does it actually analyze, in the sense of satisfying our earlier criteria? The fact that the system processes the entire piece before committing itself does not disqualify it from being a model of analysis—far from it. Indeed, its assignment of chord roots and judgments of segmentation seem exactly designed to model basic analytical processes. In particular, by accomplishing segmentation in an automated way—and far more convincingly than Tenney did—Temperley and Sleator have made an important contribution. (We should note that metrical data still have to be supplied to the program, though this is often in itself an automatic process of transcription.) However, there is then the question of what these analyses "tell us about the piece": do they have the power to change how we hear the music? In this regard I think there is less cause for enthusiasm, for the system is severely limited both in stylistic terms and in terms of the analytical results it presents. What is more, as Temperley candidly points out, when the system's judgments differ from those that he himself might make, these are not really intriguing new interpretations but, instead, "questionable

Figure 7.9.   Harmonic analysis of "Yankee Doodle" produced by
Temperley's preference rules as implemented in Sleator's program
(from Temperley 1997: 63).

choices," a "definite mistake," "problematic," or even "completely wrong" (1997: 63–4). This system nonetheless has great potential for further development (see Temperley and Sleator 1999, Temperley 2001): what it perhaps most needs is to encompass a greater range and complexity of musical judgment while retaining the most admirable of its present features.

Some recent work by the present author can claim at least to meet the first of these desiderata. The "Tonalities" project (Pople forthcoming) is focused on the so-called "breakdown" of tonality around 1900: in contrast to this traditional view, it claims that "tonality" should not be viewed as a more or less fixed system, but means something different in, say, middle-period Debussy than in late Wagner—and different again in late Mahler, early Schoenberg, Rachmaninoff, Sibelius, Busoni, Strauss, Vaughan Williams, Ives, Gershwin, and so forth. I argue that even where such music is regarded as tonal, but with exceptional features that require comment, treating these different musics as special cases endangers the working link between theory and analysis—so that one might ask whether it is tonal analysis, rather than tonality, that is breaking down.

The system provides the capability for handling a wide diversity of tonal systems by means of a theoretical framework that uses explicit theoretical definitions and analytical procedures, but is also highly configurable: not all features are necessarily active for every analysis, and some features can be fine-tuned to provide further flexibility within well-defined constraints. This work draws on a range of tonal theories, including neo-Riemannian theory (Cohn 1995, 1997, 1998; Krumhansl 1998), and also uses some aspects of set-class theory. Although focused on the diversity of tonalities around 1900, it can handle both Bach chorales and "atonal" music that is texturally similar to tonal models. The complexity of the theory is such, however, that its analytical application is only practicable using a computer: thus a large degree of automation is involved. The essence of the system in practice is that the analyst defines a tonal system by selecting from a range of detailed options (Language Settings); then, taking as its input a simplified score representation of the music, the computer software follows through the analytical implications of these choices, using a raft of analytical procedures—themselves numerous and complex—designed to produce communicable output that may lead the analyst to refine the choice of Language Settings. This process of exchange between human and machine typically continues until the analyst is satisfied both that the analysis produced by the software satisfactorily matches his or her detailed judgments about the specific piece or extract being analyzed, and that the Language Settings satisfactorily match his or her conception of the music at a stylistic level: in a sense, the determination of the most appropriate Language Settings constitutes the most important outcome of the analytical process. At the same time, and importantly in the present context, this iterative process is liable to include phases where the software introduces possibilities that the analyst may not have considered, but which nonetheless appear on reflection highly plausible. In this sense, the Tonalities system has the potential to satisfy our basic criteria on analysis, because it can change the way the analyst hears and thinks about the piece, as well as helping to make explicit the criteria underlying apparently intuitive judgments.

The program is implemented in the form of an extensive Visual Basic "plug-in" for Microsoft Excel, with the simplified score representation taking the form of a spreadsheet: pitch data are supplemented by indications of metrical stress (as in Temperley's system), and by a "vertical" segmentation into harmonic areas. (In the latter respect, the Tonalities system leaves a wider "gap" between the uninterpreted score and the input data than Temperley's does; in compensation, its stylistic range and complexity of analytical judgment are considerably greater.) An analysis of a striking but harmonically complex passage from Schoenberg's tone poem *Pelleas und Melisande* is shown in Figures 7.10–11: the repeated two-bar figure is segmented at the half-bar level, and the analysis consists of reports on each of the four segments, followed by a summary. The segments are analyzed by the software in chronological order, with diminishing memory traces of earlier segments being maintained (as in Gjerdingen's work), but without looking ahead beyond the immediate segment boundary. As Tonalities works through the segments, the immediately preceding segment may be re-evaluated in retrospect, but this would only be done in order better to "understand" the segment currently being analyzed—the report on that earlier segment, once issued, is not revised.

The Tonalities software comes with a large library of built-in gamuts (scales, modes and the like) and chords, and it is possible to customize it by adding new ones. When the software analyzes a segment, it matches the pitches and texture of the segment to as many as possible of the chords and gamuts selected in the Language Settings. It assigns a rating to each of these, then pairs each possible chord with each possible gamut—a chord/gamut pair is at this stage termed a prolongation—and assigns a composite rating to each of these pairs. Next, it filters the list of possible prolongations by applying a range of tests, comparisons, and preferences, until there emerges a single best prolongation (or a few equal-best prolongations), which it reports: in the text of the segment reports (see Figure 7.11), the *prolonged chord* and the *prolonging gamut* are the components of the reportable chord/gamut pair. It is important to note that the prolonging gamut is not an identification of "key," but applies only within the segment, reflecting the motions between chord notes and nonchord notes. Similarly, the *Chord function within segment* is, as the name implies, a within-segment relationship, rather than a judgment in relation to some sort of "key" that applies in a notional larger context. In order to reinforce the point that many of the system's judgments are based on criteria such as set membership, inclusion and exclusion, the *Pitch-class content* of the segment is reported, using set-class names and pc integer notation. Next comes a report on the *dissonance* analysis that Tonalities undertakes as a focal stage of the process of prolongation *filtering*: this part of the report serves to relate every nonchord note to one or more chord notes.

From the second segment onward, the analytical reports include information about how the segment-to-segment transition has been analyzed. Two lines are added to the report, showing the link between the two chords in terms of a *connective gamut* and either a *chord progression, root movement, trichord distance*, or a count of *common tones*. (As with the prolonging gamut, the *connective gamut* should not be confused with conventional judgments of key, because it has a specific meaning here: it is a gamut that encompasses salient subsets of the two chords.) Tonalities reports the link from one chord to the next as a chord progression only if the connective gamut and both chords are functional: otherwise, it tries to report the root movement in relation to the prolonging gamut from one or other of the segments, if necessary invoking the functional association(s) of a nonfunctional gamut (e.g., the association of the octatonic collection with dominant-quality chords, as in the report on segment 4 in Figure 7.11). If the appropriate conditions apply, it will report the motion as a trichord distance in terms of the group-cycles established by Neo-Riemannian theory, as again shown in the report on segment 4. Alternatively, if it cannot do any of these things, it reports the number of common tones held between the salient subsets of the two chords (see the reports on segments 2 and 3). As the report on segment 3 shows, Tonalities is prepared to look for diminished-fifth substitutions—and indeed other more extreme examples of function substitution—depending on how far the Language Settings depart from the default "common-practice" configuration.

It is an important aspect of the system that chord types and gamut types can be selected or deselected from the Language Settings, and certain of their properties changed, as the user thinks fit. For example, if the "major triad" chord type is deselected then the software won't recognize any major triads. When it starts an analysis the software makes a summary assessment of the user's choice of Language Settings, and this affects much of its decision making, particularly during the process of prolongation filtering. In effect, the system amplifies the analyst's hunches about the piece and allows them to be successively evaluated and refined. Among early users of the system (Nicholas Cook, Jonathan Dunsby, and Michael Russ), a point of debate concerned the extent to which one has to understand the inner workings of the software to get the best from it in terms of this dialogue. At the time of writing, the best answer to this question seems to be that the software implements an explicit body of music theory, so that (as with any other theory) expertise will reap rewards; but at the same time the operational component of the theory is of such complexity that probably no user (and this includes the author) can expect always to second-guess the analysis that will emerge from challenging musical situations. And since the empirical motivation for analysis constantly drives one to understand just such challenging music, the Tonalities system can be said to have the potential to participate, albeit as the junior partner, in an expert-to-expert dialogue about the analysis of specific pieces.[2]

Figure 7.10.   Schoenberg, *Pelleas und Melisande*, rehearsal no. 59, bars 1–4.

Prospects

At the beginning of this chapter I observed the importance of individual thought and judgment in analyzing music—this despite the fact that analytical writing addresses a community on the basis of shared perceptions and musical thought processes. One of the many corollaries of this dualism is that reading analysis is an individual matter too, just as writing analysis is. Habitual readers of analysis will also have in mind their own individual interpretations of the works they're interested in from this point of view—probably not written down, perhaps not even fully thought through, but sufficient to subject the analyses they read to certain criteria of usefulness. In short: analysis must provide new insights, and written analyses are the currency in which these insights are traded.

Schoenberg, Pelleas und Melisande, final section
Segment 1 (verticals 1 to 8)
Prolonged chord: minor-major seventh on Eb [Eb Gb Bb D / F Ab C]
Prolonging gamut: Eb melodic minor scale [Eb F Gb Ab Bb C D]
Chord function within segment: I
Pitch-class content: 7-34 (t=2) [0 2 3 5 6 8 10]
F4 [6, 4] as P between Eb4 [6, 3] and Gb4 [6, 5]
C7 [1, 5] as N after D7 [1, 1]
Ab6 [2, 5] as N after Bb6 [2, 1]
C6 [3, 5] as N after D6 [3, 1]
Ab5 [4, 5] as N after Bb5 [4, 1]
F3 [12, 7] as N after Eb3 [12, 1]
F4 [8, 8] as N after Eb4 [8, 7]
Segment 2 (verticals 9 to 16)
Prolonged chord: whole-tone dominant (b5) on Bb [Bb D Fb Gb Ab / F] with pedal Eb
Prolonging gamut: Eb harmonic minor scale [Eb F Gb Ab Bb D / Fb]
Chord function within segment: V
Connective gamut: chromatic [D Eb Fb Gb Bb]
Common tones: 1
Root movement: I-V in terms of prolonging gamut (Eb harmonic minor)
Pitch-class content: 7-9A (t=2) [2 3 4 5 6 8 10]
F4 [7, 4] as N before Gb4 [7, 5]
Segment 3 (verticals 17 to 24)
Prolonged chord: dominant seventh on E [E G# B D / F# G A Cb] with double pedal Eb/Bb
Prolonging gamut: A melodic minor scale [A B D E F# G# / Bb Cb Eb G]
Chord function within segment: V
Connective gamut: octatonic collection 1 [D E G# Bb B]
Common tones: 1
Root movement: V-bII[Vdim5] in terms of previous prolonging gamut (Eb harmonic minor)
Pitch-class content: 9-4B (t=2) [2 3 4 6 7 8 9 10 11]
Cb4 [10, 1] as enharmonic chord note
Cb3 [11, 1] as enharmonic chord note
A6 [1, 5] as N after B6 [1, 1]
F#6 [2, 5] as N after G#6 [2, 1]
A5 [3, 5] as N after B5 [3, 1]
F#5 [4, 5] as N after G#5 [4, 1]
F#4 [6, 5] and G4 [6, 8] as chained adjacencies after E4 [6, 4]
Segment 4 (verticals 25 to 32)
Prolonged chord: dominant minor ninth with suspended fourth on Bb [Bb Cb Eb F Ab / D E G A]
Prolonging gamut: octatonic scale on Bb [Bb Cb D E F G Ab / Eb A]
Connective gamut: octatonic collection 1 [D E F Ab Bb Cb]
Trichord distance: 4
Root movement: bII-V by association with prolonging gamut (Bb octatonic)
Pitch-class content: 9-5B (t=2) [2 3 4 5 7 8 9 10 11]
Eb1 [16, 1] as tonic note under dominant harmony
Eb2 [14, 1] as tonic note under dominant harmony
G6 [1, 1] as N before F6 [1, 5]
G5 [3, 1] as N before F5 [3, 5]
A4 [6, 1] as chromatic N before Ab4 [6, 5]
D4 [7, 3] and E4 [7, 4] as chained adjacencies before F4 [7, 5]
G4 [8, 4] as P between F4 [8, 1] and Ab4 [8, 5]
Summary of analysis (4 segments)
Chord types prolonged
dominant seventh: 25.0% (1)
dominant minor ninth: 25.0% (1)
whole-tone dominant (b5): 25.0% (1)
minor-major seventh: 25.0% (1)
[15 other common-practice chord types active but unused]
[3 other standard chord types active but unused]
[1 custom chord type active but unused]
Prolonging gamuts
Eb minor: harmonic 25.0% (1); melodic 25.0% (1)
A minor: melodic 25.0% (1)
octatonic 1: 25.0% (1)
[3 other gamut types active but unused]
Connective gamuts
octatonic 1: 66.7% (2)
chromatic: 33.3% (1)
[5 other selectable connective gamut types active but unused]

Figure 7.11.   Analysis by Pople's *Tonalities* software of Schoenberg *Pelleas und Melisande*, rehearsal no. 59, bars 1–4.

All of this sits uneasily with the perceived limitations of formally empirical enquiry. As we have seen, impressive results have been gained by a variety of means in modeling some of the outputs of traditional analysis, but this just hasn't been good enough for the analysts themselves. In recent years, however, ways have been found to use formal methods to produce analyses that can, on occasion, offer the kinds of insight that analysts want, while also modeling traditional, contemplative analysis convincingly enough to buy into the trade in such insights that has up to now been dominated by written analysis. There is thus a genuine prospect that empirical musicology, as outlined in this book, will be able in future to participate in the development of music analysis, though not—I think—to change its fundamental nature as an exercise of the musical imagination.

Notes

1. See this volume, p. 117, for discussion of von Hippel's and Huron's critique of the pitch reversal (gap fill) concept.
2. While Anthony Pople's untimely death has halted development of the "Tonalities" project, the software can be obtained in fully functional form on the "Tonalities" web site (http://www.nottingham.ac.uk/music/tonalities), where further details can be found. [Eds.]

References

Babbitt, M. (1962). "Twelve-tone rhythmic structure and the electronic medium." *Perspectives of New Music* 1/i: 49–79.

Bent, I. (1980). "Analysis," in Stanley Sadie (ed.), *The New Grove Dictionary of Music and Musicians*, I: 340–388. London: Macmillan.

Bharucha, J. (1999). "Neural nets, temporal composites, and tonality," in D. Deutsch (ed.), *The Psychology of Music*, 2nd ed. San Diego, Calif.: Academic Press), 184.

Castrén, M. (1994). RECREL: *A Similarity Measure for Set-Classes*. Helsinki: Sibelius Academy.

Cohn, R. (1995). "Maximally smooth cycles, hexatonic systems, and the analysis of late-romantic triadic progressions." *Music Analysis* 15: 9–40.

Cohn, R. (1997). "Neo-Riemannian operations, parsimonious trichords, and their Tonnetz representations." *Journal of Music Theory* 41: 1–66.

Cohn, R. (1998). "Introduction to Neo-Riemannian theory: A survey and historical perspective." *Journal of Music Theory* 42: 167–180.

Cook, N. (1987). *A Guide to Musical Analysis*. London: Dent.

Cooper, G., and Meyer, L. B. (1960). *The Rhythmic Structure of Music*. Chicago: University of Chicago Press.

Doerksen, J. (1998). "Set-class salience and Forte's theory of genera." *Music Analysis* 17: 195–205.

Dunsby, J., and Whittall, A. (1988). *Music Analysis in Theory and Practice*. London: Faber.

Dunsby, J. (ed. 1993). *Models of Musical Analysis: Early Twentieth-Century Music*. Oxford: Blackwell.

Everist, M. (ed. 1992). *Models of Musical Analysis: Music Before 1600*. Oxford: Blackwell.

Forte, A. (1972). "Sets and nonsets in Schoenberg's atonal music." *Perspectives of New Music* 11/1: 43–64.

Forte, A. (1973). *The Structure of Atonal Music.* New Haven: Yale University Press.

Forte, A., and Gilbert, S. (1982). *Introduction to Schenkerian Analysis.* New York: Norton.

Gjerdingen, R. (1988). *A Classic Turn of Phrase: Music and the Psychology of Convention.* Philadelphia: University of Pennsylvania Press.

Gjerdingen, R. (1990). "Categorization of musical patterns by self-organizing neuronlike networks." *Music Perception* 7: 339–369.

Jeppesen, K. (1927). *The Style of Palestrina and the Dissonance.* London: Oxford University Press.

Krumhansl, C. (1998). "Perceived triad distance: Evidence supporting the psychological reality of neo-Riemannian transformations." *Journal of Music Theory* 42: 265–281.

Leman, M. (1992). "Artificial neural networks in music research," in A. Pople and A. Marsden (eds.), *Computer Representations and Models in Music.* London: Academic Press, 265–301.

Leman, M. (1993). "Symbolic and subsymbolic description of music," in G. Haus (ed.), *Music Processing.* Oxford: Oxford University Press, 119–164.

Lerdahl, F. (2001). *Tonal Pitch Space.* New York: Oxford University Press.

Lerdahl, F., and Jackendoff, R. (1983). *A Generative Theory of Tonal Music.* Cambridge, Mass.: MIT Press.

Lester, J. (1989). *Analytic Approaches to Twentieth-Century Music.* New York: Norton.

Meyer, L. B. (1956). *Emotion and Meaning in Music.* Chicago: University of Chicago Press.

Meyer, L. B. (1973). *Explaining Music: Essays and Explorations.* Chicago: University of Chicago Press.

Narmour, E. (1977). *Beyond Schenkerism: The Need for Alternatives in Music Analysis.* Chicago: University of Chicago Press.

Narmour, E. (1990). *The Analysis and Cognition of Basic Melodic Structures: The Implication-Realization Model.* Chicago: University of Chicago Press.

Narmour, E. (1992). *The Analysis and Cognition of Melodic Complexity: The Implication-Realization Model.* Chicago: University of Chicago Press.

Nattiez, J.-J. (1975). *Fondements d'une sémiologie de la musique.* Paris: Union générale d'éditions.

Nattiez, J.-J. (1982). "Varèse's 'Density 21.5': A study in semiological analysis." *Music Analysis* 1: 243–340.

Nattiez, J.-J. (1990). *Music and Discourse: Toward a Semiology of Music.* Princeton, N.J.: Princeton University Press.

Pople, A. (1994). "Systems and strategies: Functions and limits of analysis," in A. Pople (ed.), *Theory, Analysis and Meaning in Music.* Cambridge: Cambridge University Press, 108–123.

Pople, A. (forthcoming). "Using complex set theory for tonal analysis: An introduction to the Tonalities project." *Music Analysis* forthcoming.

Rahn, J. (1980). *Basic Atonal Theory.* New York: Longman.

Rahn, J. (1994). "Some remarks on network models of music," in R. Atlas and M. Chelan (eds.), *Musical Transformation and Musical Intuition: Eleven Essays in Honour of David Lewin.* Roxbury, Mass.: Ovenbird Press, 225–235.

Rowe, R. (1993). *Interactive Music Systems: Machine Listening and Composing.* Cambridge, Mass.: MIT Press.

Schellenberg, E. (1997). "Simplifying the implication-realization model of melodic expectancy." *Music Perception* 14: 295–318.

Simms, B. (1993). "The theory of pitch-class sets,." in J. Dunsby (ed.), *Models of Musical Analysis: Early Twentieth-Century Music*. Oxford: Blackwell, 114–131.

Snarrenberg, R. (1994). "Competing myths: The American abandonment of Schenker's organicism," in A. Pople (ed.), *Theory, Analysis and Meaning in Music*. Cambridge: Cambridge University Press, 29–56.

Temperley, D. (1997). "An algorithm for harmonic analysis." *Music Perception* 15: 31–68.

Temperley, D. (2001). *The Cognition of Basic Musical Structures*. Cambridge, Mass.: MIT Press.

Temperley, D., and Sleator, D. (1999). "Modeling meter and harmony: A preference rule approach." *Computer Music Journal* 23: 10–27.

Tenney, J. (1980). "Temporal Gestalt perception in music." *Journal of Music Theory* 24: 205–241.

Winograd, T. (1968). "Linguistics and the computer analysis of tonal harmony." *Journal of Music Theory* 12: 2–49.

CHAPTER 8

Analyzing Musical Sound

Stephen McAdams, Philippe Depalle, and Eric Clarke

Introduction

Musicologists have several starting points for their work, of which the two most prominent are text and sound documents (i.e., scores and recordings). One aim of this chapter is to show that there are important properties of sound that cannot be gleaned directly from the score but that may be inferred if the reader can bring to bear knowledge of the acoustic properties of sounds on the one hand, and of the processes by which they are perceptually organized on the other. Another aim is to provide the musicologist interested in the analysis of sound documents (music recorded from oral or improvising traditions, or electroacoustic works) with tools for the systematic analysis of unnotated—and in many cases, unnotatable—musics.

In order to get a sense of what this approach can bring to the study of musical objects, let us consider a few examples. Imagine Ravel's *Boléro*. This piece is structurally rather simple, alternating between two themes in a repetitive AABB form. However, the melodies are played successively by different instruments at the beginning, and by increasing numbers of instruments playing in parallel on different pitches as the piece progresses, finishing with a dramatic, full orchestral version. There is also a progressive crescendo from beginning to end, giving the piece a single, unified trajectory. It is not evident from the score that, if played in a particular way, the parallel instrumental melodies will fuse together into a single, new, composite timbre; and what might be called the "timbral trajectory" is also difficult to characterize from the score. What other representation might be useful in explaining, or simply describing, what happens perceptually?

Figure 8.1 shows spectrographic representations (also called *spectrograms*) of the first 11 notes of the A melody from *Boléro*, in three orchestrations from different sections of the piece: (a) section 2, where it is played by one clarinet; (b) section 9, played in parallel intervals by a French horn, two piccolos, and celesta; and (c) section 14, played in parallel by most of the orchestra including the strings. We will come back to more detailed aspects of these representations later, but note that two kinds of structures are immediately visible: a series of horizontal lines that represent the frequencies of the instruments playing the melody, and a series of vertical bars that represent the rhythmic accompaniment. Note too that the density, intensity (represented by the blackness of the lines), and spectral extent (expansion toward the higher frequencies) can be seen to increase from section 2 through section 9 to section 14, reflecting the increasing number, dynamic level, and registral spread of instruments involved.

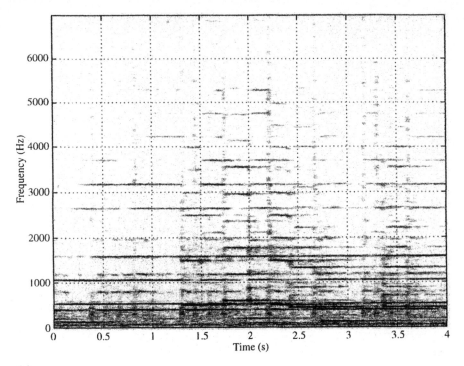

(a)

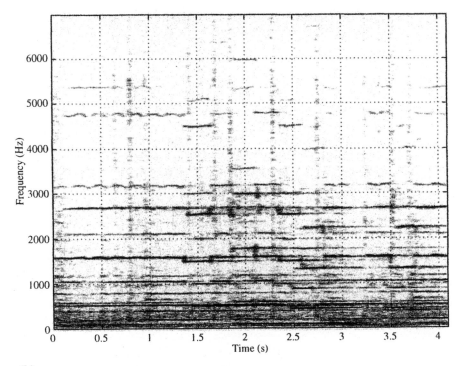

(b)

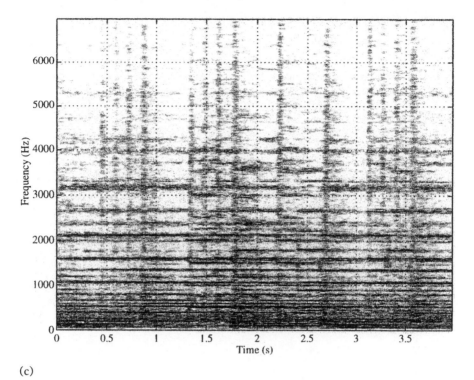

(c)

Figure 8.1   a. Spectrogram of the first 11 notes of the A melody from *Boléro* by Ravel (section 2). In this example, horizontal lines below 1,000 Hz represent notes, horizontal lines above 1,000 Hz their harmonic components. Percussive sounds appear as vertical bars (0.4 seconds, 0.8 seconds, 1.3 seconds, etc.). b. Spectrogram of the first 11 notes of the A melody from *Boléro* by Ravel (section 9). Notice the presence of instruments with higher pitches (higher frequencies). c. Spectrogram of the first 11 notes of the A melody from *Boléro* by Ravel (section 14). Notice the increase of intensity represented by increased blackness.

Now consider an example of electronic music produced with synthesizers: an excerpt from *Die Roboten*, by the electronic rock group Kraftwerk (Figure 8.2). First, note the relatively clean lines of the spectrographic representation, with little of the fuzziness found in the previous example. This is primarily due to the absence of the noise components and random fluctuations that are characteristic of natural sounds resulting from the complex onsets of notes, breath sounds, rattling snares, and the like. Several features of Figure 8.2 will be used in the following discussion, but it is interesting to note that most of the perceptual qualities of these sounds are not notatable in a score and can only be identified by concentrated listening or by visually examining acoustic analyses such as the spectrogram: for example, the opening sound, which at the beginning has many frequency components (horizontal lines extending from the bottom [low frequencies] to the top [high frequencies]), slowly dies down to a point (at about 1.4 seconds) where only the lower frequencies are

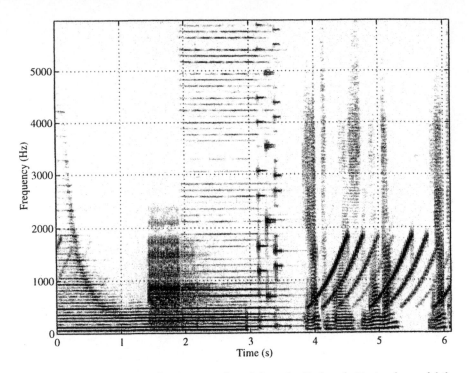

Figure 8.2. Spectrogram of an excerpt of *Die Roboten* by Kraftwerk. Notice the readability of the spectrographic representation that makes explicit continuous timbre, amplitude, and frequency variations.

present. This progressive filtering of the sound has a clear perceptual result that is directly discernible from this representation.

A spectrographic approach is also useful in the case of cultures in which music is transmitted by oral tradition rather than through notation. A telling example is the *Inanga chuchoté* from Burundi, in which the singer whispers (*chuchoter* is French for "to whisper") and accompanies himself on a low-pitched lute (Figure 8.3). This musical genre presents an interesting problem, in that the language of this people is tonal: the same syllable can have a different meaning with a rising or falling pitch contour. The fact that contour conveys meaning places a constraint on song production, since the melodic line must to some extent adhere to the pitch contour that corresponds to the intended meaning. But this is not possible with whispering, which has no specific pitch contour. The spectrogram reveals what is happening: the lute carries the melodic contour, reinforced by slight adjustments in the sound quality of the whispering (it is brighter when the pitch is higher, and duller when it is lower). There is a kind of perceptual fusion of the two sources, due to their temporal synchronization and spectral overlap, so that the pitch of the lute becomes "attached to" the voice.

In light of these examples, we can see how an approach involving acoustical analysis and interpretation based on perceptual principles can be useful in analyzing recorded sound. The spectrogram is just one possible means of representing

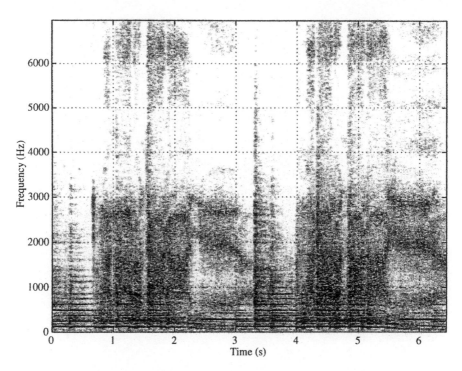

Figure 8.3. Spectrogram of an excerpt of *Inanga chuchoté* from Burundi. Notice the movements of shaded zones, within the range 500 to 3,000 Hz, that represent timbral variations of the whispered sounds. The onsets of the lute notes and plosive consonants produced by the voice are indicated by the vertical lines in the representation.

sounds: others bring out different aspects of the sound, and it is characteristic of all such representations that different features can be brought out according to the settings that are used in creating them. (This is similar to the way in which the correct setting of a camera depends on what one wants to bring out in the photograph.) The goal of this chapter is therefore to introduce some of these ways of representing sound, and to provide a relatively nontechnical account of how such representations work and how they are to be interpreted. The chapter is organized in three main sections, the first dealing with basic characteristics and representations of sound, the second with acoustical analysis, and the third with perceptual analysis; the two analytical sections conclude with brief case studies taken from the literature.

Basic Characteristics and Representations of Sound

Sound is a wave that propagates between a source and a receiver through a medium. (The source can be an instrument, a whole orchestra or loudspeakers; the receiver can be the ears of a listener or a microphone; the medium is usually air.) It can also be considered as a signal that conveys information from an instrument or loudspeaker to the ears of a listener, who decodes the information by hearing the time evolution of the acoustic wave, and recognizes instruments, notes played, a piece of music, a specific performer, a conductor, and so on. Using machines to analyze sound signals involves structuring the information in a way that is similar to what the ear does; such analyses usually provide symbolic information or—as in this chapter— graphical representations.

The analysis of a sound, then, starts with a microphone that captures variations in air pressure (produced by a flute, for example) and transduces them into an electrical signal. This signal can be represented as a mathematical function of *time*, and is therefore called a *temporal representation* of the sound. A graphical display of such a temporal representation is an intuitive way to begin to analyze it, and in the case of a solo flute note we might get the temporal representation in Figure 8.4, with time on the horizontal axis and the amplitude of the signal on the vertical axis. The figure reveals the way the sound starts (the attack), the sustained part with a slight oscillation of the level, and the release of the flute sound at the end. However, it fails to help us in determining the nature of the instrument and the note played, and in the case of more complex sounds—say an excerpt of an orchestral composition— very little is likely to emerge beyond a rough impression of dynamic level. That means that we need to find alternative representations based on mathematical transformations of the simple temporal representation. The most important of these transformations involve the idea of periodicity, since this is intimately linked to the perception of pitch—a primary feature of most musical sounds.

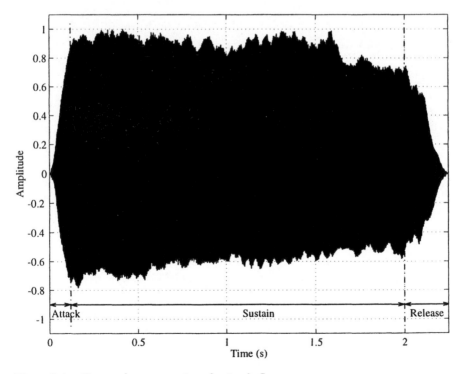

Figure 8.4.   Temporal representation of a simple flute note.

Figure 8.5 is a simple temporal representation, like Figure 8.4, but the temporal profile is shown at a much higher level of magnification. We can now begin to see the repeated patterns that define periodic sounds: the term *period* refers to the duration of the cycle, and the number of times the cycle repeats itself per second is called the *frequency* (or fundamental frequency). Thus, the frequency is the reciprocal of the period, and its unit is the Hertz (Hz). It can be seen from Figure 5 that six periods are a little shorter than seven divisions of the time axis (which are hundredths of a second), so that the fundamental frequency is 87.2 Hz—which is the F at the bottom of the bass clef.

While frequency determines the pitch of the clarinet sound in Figure 8.5, the particular shape of the wave is related to factors that determine its timbral properties. How might it be possible to classify or model the range of different shapes that sound waves can take? A *spectral representation* (or spectrum) attempts to model sounds through the superimposition of any number of waves of different frequencies, with each individual wave taking the form of a "sinusoid": this is a function that endlessly oscillates at a given frequency, and which can be approximated by the sustained part of the sound of a struck tuning-fork. Figure 8.6a shows a few sinusoidal oscillations at a frequency of 440 Hz (the standard tuning fork A). Now if, instead of showing amplitude against time as in Figure 8.6a, we were to show it against frequency, we would see a single vertical line corresponding to 440 Hz: this is shown in Figure 8.6b, a much more condensed and exhaustive representation of the signal by

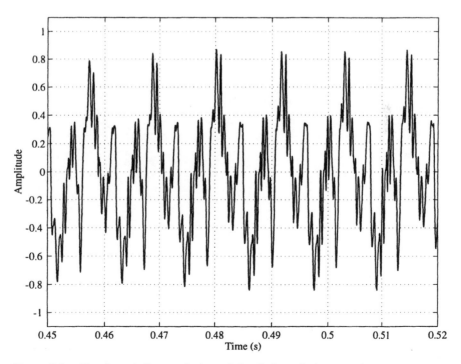

Figure 8.5.   Simple periodic sound: six periods of a bass clarinet sound.

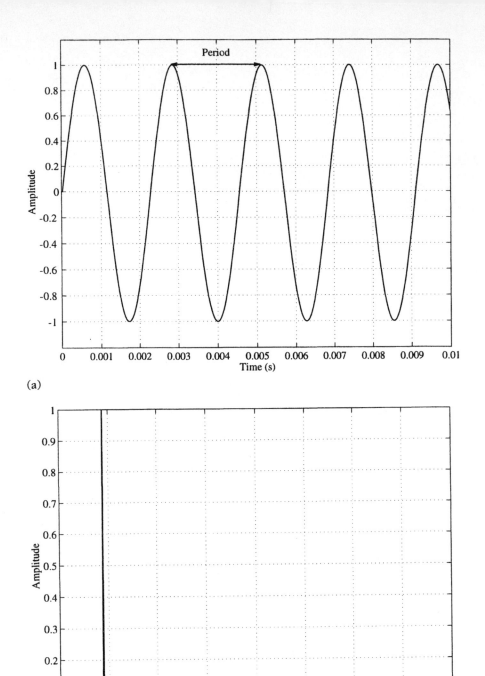

(a)

(b)

Figure 8.6   a. Sinusoidal sound (frequency = 440 Hz, amplitude = 1.0): temporal representation with a single period indicated. b. Sinusoidal sound (frequency = 440 Hz, amplitude = 1.0): spectral representation.

its *spectral content*, than by its temporal representation. The same representation can obviously show any number of different spectral components—different sinusoids—at different levels of amplitude: Figure 8.7a shows a temporal representation of a mix of three sinusoids at different amplitudes, and Figure 8.7b the resulting spectrum. While the number, frequency, or amplitude of the individual components are difficult to estimate from Figure 8.7a, all are immediately apparent from Figure 8.7b.

As there are only three sinusoids in Figures 8.7a and 8.7b, all in the central auditory range and at relatively similar dynamic levels, each will be heard as a separate pitch: in fact, since their frequencies are 440, 550, and 660 Hz, the percept will be an A major chord. A different set of sinusoids, by contrast, might produce the effect of a single pitch with a distinctive timbre. Because it represents only the acoustical qualities of the signal, not its perceptual correlates, the difference cannot be directly seen in a spectral representation.

The principle of decomposing a complex waveform into separate elements can be taken a good deal further than this. The mathematician Joseph Fourier demonstrated that a periodic signal, whatever the shape of its waveform, can always be analyzed into a set of harmonically related sinusoids ("harmonically," meaning that the frequencies of these sinusoids are multiples of the fundamental frequency—as, for instance, 440, 880, 1320 Hz, and so on are integer multiples of 440 Hz). The collection of these harmonics constitutes the *Fourier series* of the signal, and is an important property since it roughly corresponds to the way sounds are analyzed by the auditory system. In practice, then, analyzing a periodic or harmonic signal consists of determining the fundamental frequency and the amplitude of each harmonic component. Figure 8.8 compares waveforms and Fourier analyses of two simple signals often used in commercial synthesizers. (Note that in the Fourier representations in Figures 8.8a2 and 8.8b2 the frequency axis shows values as multiples of 10^4 Hz: thus "1" represents 10,000 Hz or 10 kHz.) The equidistant vertical lines represent the different harmonics of the fundamental frequency, which is again 440 Hz. Comparison of the sawtooth waveform (Figure 8.8a2) with a square wave (Figure 8.8b2) shows that the latter lacks even-numbered harmonics. Figure 8.8c, by contrast, shows the spectrum of the clarinet sound from Figure 8.5, which—while it exhibits vertical harmonic peaks—does not look as clean as the synthesized examples.

In addition to harmonic signals, there are *inharmonic* signals such as the sounds of bells (Figure 8.9a) or tympani (Figure 8.9b): these are not periodic, but can still be described as a series of superimposed sinusoids—although the sinusoids are no longer harmonically related. (They are therefore called *partials* rather than harmonics, and can take any frequency value.) Inharmonic sounds do not have a precise overall pitch, though they may have a pitch that corresponds to the dominant partial, or even several pitches. The bell sound in Figure 8.9a includes a series of near-harmonic components (a "fundamental frequency" at 103 Hz (G♯), a second harmonic at 206 Hz, a ninth one at 927 Hz, a thirteenth one at 1,339 Hz, and so on) but also other inharmonic components; these components give the sound a chord-like quality. The tympani spectrum in Figure 8.9b is similarly inharmonic, with some partials conforming to a nearly harmonic relationship with a fundamental frequency at 66 Hz (C). Indeed there are many sounds that we think of as clearly pitched but which are slightly inharmonic: Figure 8.9c shows the spectrum of a piano note

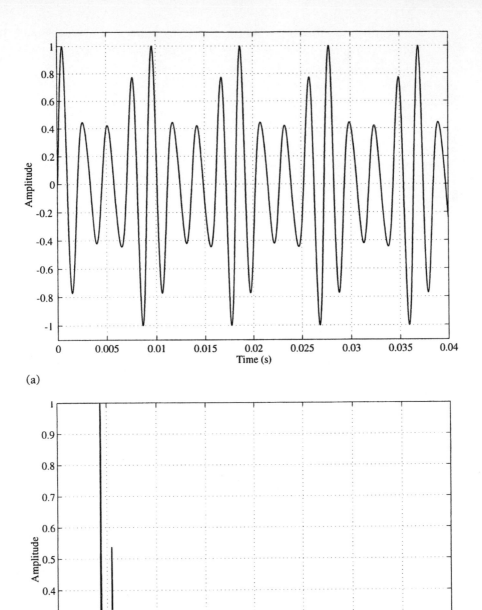

(a)

(b)

Figure 8.7   a. Mix of three sinusoids (frequencies are 440, 550, and 660 Hz; amplitudes are 1.0, 0.5, and 0.25, respectively): a. Temporal representation. b. Spectral representation

whose partial components are near-harmonics of the fundamental frequency 831 Hz (g#″), and one can see that the inharmonicity—represented by the difference between the positions of the actual partials and the theoretical positions shown by dashed lines—increases with frequency. (The cluster of low-frequency components, below the fundamental up to around 2,500 Hz, is produced not by the vibration of the piano strings, but by the soundboard.) Here the deviation from harmonicity at frequencies below about 5 kHz is sufficiently small that the listener perceives a precise pitch.

For the sound characterization to be complete, the category of *noisy* sounds has to be considered. By definition, these have a random temporal representation (such as the whispered sound between 2.2 and 3.2 seconds in Figure 8.3). Few instrumental sounds are completely noisy, but most of them include a certain amount of noise (the player's breath in the case of wind instruments, impact noise for percussion, and so on), and as we shall later see, this noisy part is nearly always very important for the perception of timbre. The sounds of wind and surf, replicated by electronic noise generators, are by contrast completely noisy. Such sounds are composed of a random mix of all possible frequencies, and their spectral representation is the statistical average of the spectral components. For example, white noise has a random waveform (Figure 8.10a). Although it has a spectrum that is theoretically flat, with all frequencies appearing at the same level, in practice the spectrum revealed by Fourier analysis is far from being perfectly flat (Figure 8.10b), and exhibits variations that are due to the lack of averaging of the random fluctuations in level of the different frequencies. These fluctuations can be reduced by taking the average of several spectra computed on successive time-limited samples of the noisy sound.

Now that the basic characteristics of sounds have been described, it is important to mention one major aspect of "natural" sound signals: their characteristics (frequency, amplitude, waveform, inharmonicity, or noise content) always vary over time. Sounds with perfectly stable characteristics (such as the sinusoids in Figure 8.6, or the stable low-frequency sound in *Die Roboten*, between 2 and 3 seconds in Figure 8.2) sound "unnatural" or "synthetic." These time-varying characteristics are called *modulations* and can take various forms. Amplitude modulations range from uncontrolled random fluctuations, such as in the flute note in Figure 8.4, to the tremolo on the low sustained note in *Die Roboten* (between 1.5 and 2 seconds in Figure 8.2); frequency modulations can include vibrato (the undulating horizontal lines produced by the piccolo during the first 1.5 seconds of Figure 8.1b) or pitch glides (the upward sweeping "chirp" sound in *Die Roboten* between 3.8 and 4.5 seconds, Figure 8.2). Apart from their impact on the character of individual sounds, the presence and synchronization of modulations are very important for the perception of fused sounds, and will be discussed in the final section of this chapter.

This means that there is a significant element of approximation or idealization in all but the simplest representations of sound which we have been discussing. Most obviously, spectral representations (Fourier or otherwise) relate amplitude and frequency: they represent values averaged over a discrete temporal "window" or "frame," and therefore tell us nothing about changes in the sound during that period of time. (One could represent the changes by showing a series of spectral representations one after another, in the manner of an animation, but even then each frame

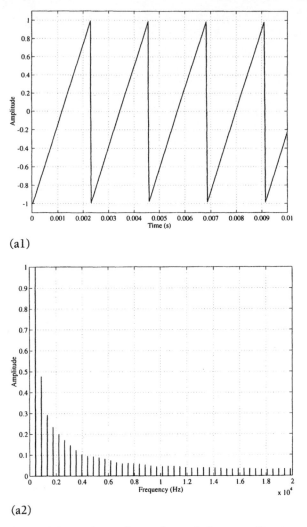

(a1)

(a2)

Figure 8.8   a1. Sawtooth waveform. a2. Spectrum (Fourier series) of a sawtooth waveform. b1. (next page) Square waveform. b2. Spectrum (Fourier series) of a square waveform. c. Spectrum (Fourier series) of a clarinet waveform.

would represent the average over a given time span.) There is also a similar point in relation to periodicity. While from a mathematical point of view a periodic signal reproduces exactly the same cycle indefinitely, in the real world any sound has a beginning and an end: for this reason alone, musical sounds are not mathematically periodic. Moreover, they nearly always show slight differences from one period to the next (as can be seen from the waveform of the clarinet sound in Figure 8.5). In practice, a sound is perceived as having a definite pitch as soon as there is a sufficient degree of periodicity, not when it is mathematically periodic, and we therefore need an analytical tool that will identify degrees of periodicity on a local basis, show-

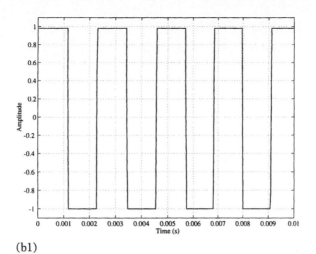

(b1)

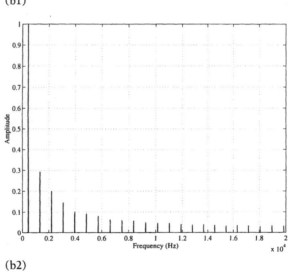

(b2)

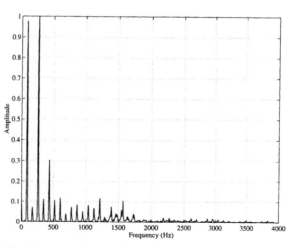

(c)

169

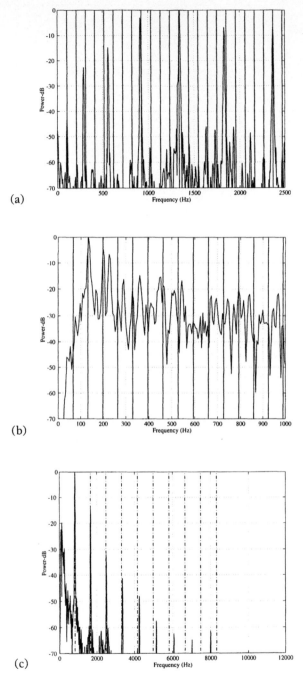

(a)

(b)

(c)

Figure 8.9 Inharmonicity: a. Spectrum of a bell sound. The series of vertical thin lines represent theoretical locations of a harmonic series of fundamental frequency 103 Hz. b. Spectrum of a tympani sound. The series of vertical thin lines represent theoretical locations of a harmonic series of fundamental frequency 66 Hz. c. Spectrum of a piano sound. The series of vertical dashed lines represents theoretical locations of a harmonic series of a fundamental frequency of 831 Hz.

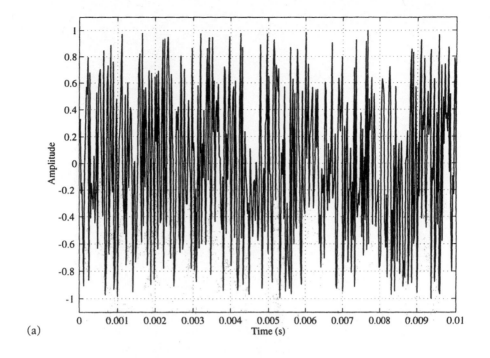

(a)

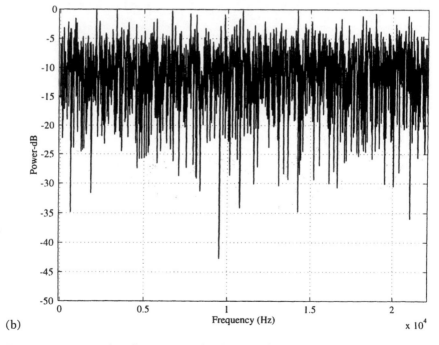

(b)

Figure 8.10 Examples of a noisy sound (white noise) a. Temporal representation.
b. Spectral representation. Notice that the spectrum of white noise is random and more
or less flat on average.

171

ing how the spectrum changes over time. This is exactly what the spectrogram does, as illustrated in the introduction of this chapter—and this, again, is something to which we will return.

Acoustical Analysis of Sounds

A waveform display allows a user to analyze a sound quite intuitively by simply looking at its temporal representation. The representation can be created at different time scales, from the "microscopic" or short-term scale, to the "macroscopic" or long-term scale. A "microscopic" time scale, which in practice is usually on the order of a few periods, preserves the waveform shape, and allows a qualitative evaluation of the presence or absence of noise and its level, as well as the presence of strong, high-order harmonic components. Figures 8.5a, 8.6a, 8.7a, 8.8a1, and 8.8b1 are temporal representations of signals at a "microscopic" time scale: this also allows one to evaluate precisely the synchronization between acoustic events. By contrast, a "macroscopic" time scale makes visible long-term tendencies such as the global evolution of the sound level, amplitude changes in the course of a melodic line, or the way notes follow one another; an example is Figure 8.4 in which the temporal envelope of a flute sound can be discerned.

Sound signals are usually displayed on computer screens using sound editor programs; some examples are *ProTools*, *AudioSculpt*, *Peak*, *SpectroGramViewer*, and *Audacity*. However there is a problem when the number of samples to be represented on the screen becomes larger than the number of available pixels: as sounds are usually sampled at 44,100 Hz (the compact disc standard), and as the highest number of pixels on each line of current screens is usually less than 2000, a complete display is possible only for durations shorter than 50 milliseconds (ms). Beyond that, several sample values have to be averaged into one pixel value (in other words, the signal has to be smoothed), and this prevents precise investigation of long-term sound characteristics, limiting the direct use of "macroscopic" sound signal displays to the analysis of global temporal evolutions. Even in the case of these global evolutions, though, there is a perceptually more meaningful means of analysis: *temporal envelope estimation*.

As an example, Figure 8.11 displays the dynamic evolution of an excerpt from Ligeti's orchestral piece *Atmosphères*, starting with a slow crescendo/decrescendo over the first 20 seconds, followed by a fast crescendo to a median level, and a slow crescendo for the next 30 seconds, and so on. Such a temporal envelope, which is calculated automatically by most sound editing programs, is again based on a series of temporal windows or frames, the duration of which is normally between 10 and 200 ms, with the window sliding along the time axis to provide an estimate of the temporal envelope at set intervals. The only setting that you need to adjust in order to get a temporal envelope is the size of the window. The chosen size will inevitably be a compromise: it has to be large enough to smooth over the fine-grained oscillations of the signal, but at the same time small enough to preserve the shape of the attack, or of the other transient parts of the sound. The problem can be seen by comparing

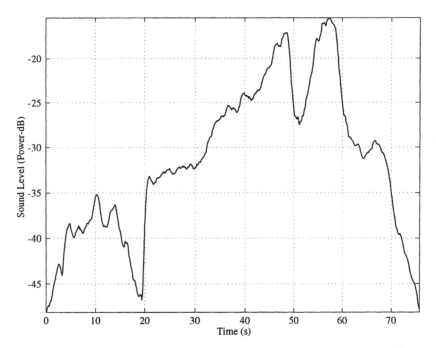

Figure 8.11.   Temporal envelope estimation for an excerpt from Ligeti's *Atmosphères*.

three different temporal envelope estimations for the temporal representation shown in Figure 8.12a, the spectrogram of which was shown in Figure 8.2. In Figure 8.12b, too small a window (5.8 ms) has been chosen, and the profile exhibits spurious oscillations that are not perceived as changes in level; Figure 8.12c represents an appropriate value (23.2 ms), whereas in Figure 8.12d the window is too large (92.8 ms) and fast changes of level (particularly between 1.5 and 2 seconds) are smoothed out. The rule of thumb is to use more than the duration of the largest period contained in the original sound; in this way, musicologists who want to use a temporal envelope analysis need to set the window size in accordance with the particular music they are studying, as well as the particular aspects of the sound in which they are interested.

For many musicological purposes a spectral representation will be the best choice for sound signal analysis. There are, however, some practical problems associated with it: one is how to estimate the spectrum of nonperiodic sounds, while another is the relationship between the sampling rate, the sampling window, and the frequency of the sounds being studied. To be completely known, a nonperiodic signal has to be observed over its entire duration, unlike a periodic signal (where observation over one period is sufficient). This means that a Fourier series representation of a nonperiodic sound is not possible: the appropriate representation is instead a *Fourier transform*. A simple way to understand the extension of the Fourier series to the Fourier transform is to think of a nonperiodic signal as a periodic signal whose

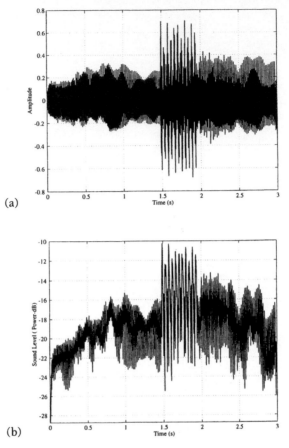

(a)

(b)

Figure 8.12 a. Temporal representation of the first three seconds of *Die Roboten* by Kraftwerk. b. Temporal envelope estimation of the sound signal displayed in (a) using a window size of 5.8 ms.

period is infinite. An example of a nonperiodic signal and its Fourier transform is given in Figure 8.13. The sound signal is a damped sinusoid, that is a sinusoid whose amplitude decreases over time. The treatment of this kind of signal is significant, since many percussion instruments (including bells, timpani, pianos, and xylophones) produce a superposition of damped sinusoids.

The Fourier transform (Figure 8.13b) exhibits a maximum close to the oscillating frequency, but there is some power at other frequencies, particularly those close to the central frequency. The sharpness of the maximum, sometimes called a *formant*, varies in inverse proportion to the degree of damping. The damping makes the oscillating sinusoid nonperiodic and spreads its power out to other frequencies; the spectrum is therefore no longer a peak (as it is for a pure sinusoid) but a smoothed curve, whose *bandwidth* (the width of the curve) increases with the damping value.

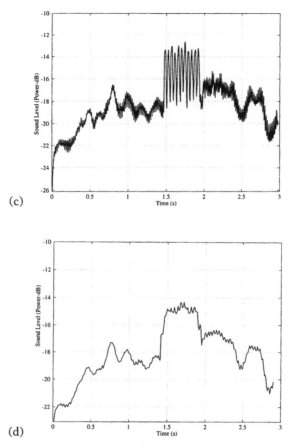

Figure 8.12 (cont'd.) Temporal envelope estimation of the sound signal displayed in (a) using: c. A window size of 23.2 ms. d. A window size of 92.8 ms.

As in the case of temporal envelope estimation, choosing the right duration as the basis for calculating the Fourier transform is a compromise: the duration needs to be small enough to maintain sufficient resolution between closely adjacent sinusoids, and yet not so large as to average out all of the temporal evolution of the sound's spectral characteristics. A good compromise is usually a duration of four to five times the period of the lowest frequency difference between the sinusoidal components of the sound. Figure 8.14 revisits the spectral analysis of the A major chord, made up of three sinusoidal sounds, that was shown in Figure 8.7: since the frequencies are 440, 550, and 660 Hz, the lowest frequency difference is 110 Hz, which (at a 44,100 Hz sampling rate) corresponds to approximately 400 samples. Figure 8.14 shows that a window size of 2,048 samples i.e., approximately 5 times 400 samples) successfully separates out the three components.

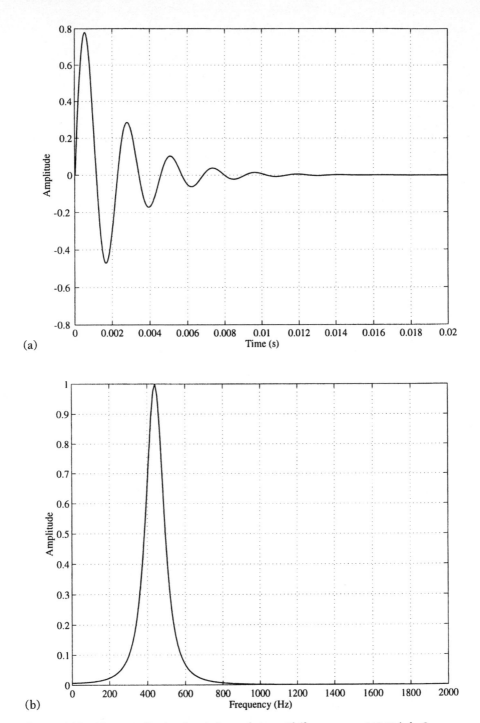

(a)

(b)

Figure 8.13   Nonperiodic signal a. A damped sinusoid (frequency = 440 Hz). b. Spectrum of a damped sinusoid (frequency = 440 Hz). Notice the continuous aspect of the spectrum.

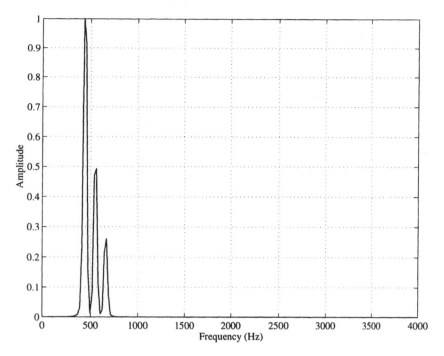

Figure 8.14.   Time-limited Fourier analysis: spectrum of the major chord from Figure 8.7 estimated with a window size of 2,048 samples.

We are now ready to come full circle, establishing the link between all the concepts developed in this section and the spectrographic representation at the very beginning of the chapter. A spectrum, resulting from a Fourier transform performed over a finite duration, provides useful information about a sound signal only when the sound is known to be stable in time. However, as already mentioned, the characteristics of natural sounds always vary in time. A spectrum taken from a window located at the beginning of a sound (Figure 8.15a) is usually different from a spectrum taken from a window located in the middle of the sound (Figure 8.15b). In order to describe the temporal variations of the spectral properties of a sound, a simple idea is to compute a series of evenly spaced *local spectra*. This is achieved by computing a Fourier transform for each of a series of sliding windows taken from the signal. The time-step increment of the sliding window is usually a proportion of the window size, and a time-shift of an eighth of the window size or less ensures perfect tracking of the temporal evolution. Each Fourier transform represents an estimate of the spectral content of the signal at the time on which the window is centered, and a simple and efficient way to display this series of spectra is to create a time/frequency representation, with the darkness of the trace representing the amplitude of each frequency (Figure 8.16). This representation, which we have already encountered, is called a *spectrogram* (or sometimes a *sonogram*).

In summary, we have seen two different kinds of two-dimensional representation of sound, and a three dimensional representation. The two-dimensional repre-

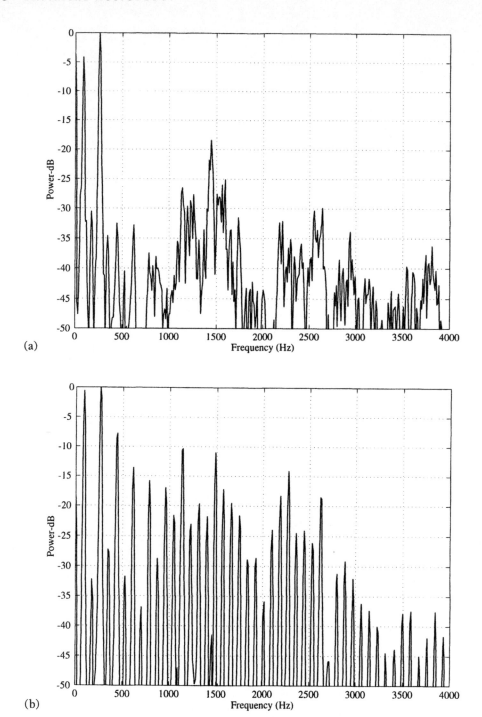

Figure 8.15   a. Spectrum of a bass clarinet tone during the attack (window centered on 0.12 second, window size of 4,096 samples). b. Spectrum of a bass clarinet tone during the sustained part (window centered on 1 second, window size of 4,096 samples).

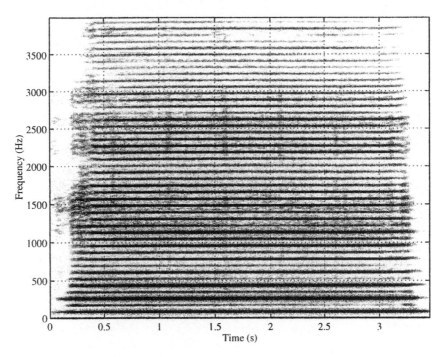

Figure 8.16.   Spectrogram of a bass clarinet sound (window size of 4,096 samples, time-step increment of 512 samples).

sentations are temporal representations (amplitude against time), and spectral representations (amplitude against frequency); the three-dimensional representation—the spectrogram—shows frequency against time on the two axes, and intensity against time in the blackness of the trace.

Analytical Applications

The most sustained example of applying acoustical principles to musical analysis, and one which makes considerable use of spectrograms, is Robert Cogan's book *New Images of Musical Sound* (Cogan 1984). The central part of the book consists of a discussion and analysis of 17 "spectrum photos" (the equivalent of spectrograms) of music from a wide variety of traditions, including Gregorian chant, jazz, a movement of a Beethoven piano sonata, electroacoustic music, and Tibetan tantric chant; the examples range from half a minute to over 11 minutes in duration, with the majority around two to four minutes long. The spectrum photos show duration on the horizontal axis and frequency on the vertical axis, with intensity represented as the brightness of the trace (while intensity is represented by blackness against a white background in the spectrograms presented in this chapter, it is shown as whiteness against a black background in Cogan's photos). The spectrum photos were created using analog signal analysis equipment, with a camera used to take photographs of the cathode ray tube for successive sections of music; these were then literally pasted together to create the resulting composite photos that appear in the book. Digital technology has made it possible to produce more flexible and finely graded representations of this kind far more easily, as the figures in this chapter demonstrate.

Cogan uses the spectrum photos to analyze and demonstrate a variety of different features of the music, the diversity of which is intended to show how many different features can be addressed through these means. His discussion of Billie Holiday's recording of "Strange Fruit," for example, focuses on the ways in which Holiday uses continuous pitch changes and the timbral effects of different vowel sounds to articulate semantic relationships in the text, and to expose its savage ironies: "Note bending is a motif that recurs with ever-increasing intensity. 'The gallant South' is immediately echoed with growing irony at 'sweet and fresh,' again bending to the voice's lowest depth. Then a string of increasingly bent phrases. . . . leads with gathering intensity to the explicit recall of the first stanza . . . " (Cogan 1984: 35)

By comparison, the discussion of Elliott Carter's *Etude III for Wind Quartet* focuses on the timbral changes that result both from instrumental entries and exits, and from continuous dynamic changes, rhythmic augmentation, and diminution. This analysis is unusual in using spectral representations (rather than temporal representations) to give more detail about the relative balance of different spectral components in the sound than is possible in the spectrograms used elsewhere in the book: because time is eliminated from the representation, Cogan presents a sequence of 18 spectral "snapshots" to demonstrate how the timbre evolves over the piece. Without getting involved in the detail of Cogan's analysis, a sense of what he claims such an analysis can achieve can be gathered from the following (Cogan 1984: 71–72):

> Spectrum analysis provides a tool whereby the important similarity of these passages—the initial one characterized by instrumental change and rhythmic diminution, the climactic one by dynamic change and rhythmic augmentation—can be discovered and shown. Remove the spectral features and the most critical formal links of the entire étude . . . disappear. Without spectral understanding, the link between the successive transformations—instrumental, rhythmic, and dynamic . . . would evaporate. . . . We noted at the beginning of this commentary that, in the light of earlier analytic methods, this étude could emerge only as incomprehensible, static, or both. It now, however, reveals itself to be a set of succinct, precise spectral formations whose roles and relationships, whether of identity or opposition, are clear at every instant.

Two further examples of the way in which spectral analysis can be used for musicological purposes are provided by Peter Johnson's (1999) discussion of two performances of the aria "Erbarme Dich" from Bach's *St. Matthew Passion*, and David Brackett's (2000) analysis of a track by Elvis Costello. The subject of Johnson's paper is a wide-ranging discussion of the relationship between performance and listening, with Bach's aria as a focal example viewed from aesthetic and more concretely analytical perspectives. Central to Johnson's argument is his insistence that the impact of the *sound* of a performance on listeners' experience is consistently underestimated by commentators and analysts, and an important part of the paper is thus devoted to a detailed consideration of the acoustical characteristics of two performances of the aria. Johnson focuses primarily on differences in the frequency domain, highlighting distinctions in the use of vibrato, timbre, and intonation in the first eight bars of the aria as taken from recordings directed by John Eliot Gardiner and Karl Richter. On the basis of both spectral and temporal representations of the sound characteristics of the first few bars of the instrumental opening, obtained using the signal processing and plotting software in the Matlab program, Johnson demonstrates how Gardiner's recording features a more transparent timbre, much less vibrato in the solo violin part, and a more fluctuating amplitude profile, with a consistent tendency for the amplitude to drop away at group and phrase endings; Richter's recording, by contrast, demonstrates a more constant vibrato and amplitude level, a thicker timbre, and the use of expressive intonation (a flattening of the mediant note).

Johnson acknowledges that

> much of what is shown by spectrographic analysis is little more than a visual analogue of what we have already recognized and perceived through listening. Nonetheless, acoustic analysis reinforces the experiential claims of the listening musician, namely that (1) performance can significantly determine the properties of the experience itself, and (2) the listening experience is not wholly private: hearing is not entirely "subjective" in the sense of a strictly unverifiable or purely solipsistic mode of perception. . . . Finally, acoustic analysis is a powerful medium for the education of the ear and as a diagnostic tool for the conscientious performer, the didactic possibilities of which have barely begun to be exploited. (Johnson 1999: 83–84)

In fact Johnson uses the acoustic characteristics of the two recordings to argue that the two interpretations offer distinctly different musical and theological perspectives. Richter's recording, he claims, conveys a sense of reverence and authority (in relation both to Bach and the biblical narrative) in its even lines, thick textures, constant amplitude, tempo and vibrato, and solemnly "depressed" expressive intonation. Gardiner's, by contrast, is more enigmatic, using a faster and more flexible tempo and a more transparent sound to conjoin the secular connotations of dance with the seriousness of the biblical text; Johnson describes it as a "rediscovery in later 20th century Bach performance practice of the physical, the kinesthetic, not (here) as licentiousness but as a medium through which even a Passion can find new (or old) meanings." (Johnson 1999: 99)

Brackett's (2000) use of spectrum photos is more cursory and restricted, but worth considering because of the comparative rarity of this approach in the study of popular music—perhaps surprisingly, given that it is a non-score-based tradition in which acoustic characteristics (such as timbre, texture and space) are acknowledged to be of particular importance. Brackett's aim in his chapter on Elvis Costello's song "Pills and Soap" is to demonstrate various ways in which Costello maintains an elusive relationship with different musical traditions—particularly in his negotiations with art music. Brackett uses spectrum photos similar to Cogan's to make points about both the overall timbral shape of "Pills and Soap," and more detailed aspects of word setting. An example of the latter is Brackett's demonstration (p. 187) that successive repetitions of the word "needle" in the song become increasingly timbrally bright and accented, as a way of drawing attention to the word and its narrative/semantic function. At a "middleground" level, he points out that vocal timbre (as well as pitch height) is used to give a sense of teleology to each verse, pushing the song forward. Finally (and this is where the connection with art music becomes more explicit), Brackett uses spectral information to support his claim that the song represents a particular kind of skirmish with Western art music. He shows how an increasingly oppositional relationship between high- and low-frequency timbral components characterizes the large-scale shape of the song, and argues that this

> is much more typical of pieces of Western art music than it is of almost any other form of music in the world, be it popular, "traditional," or non-Western "art" music. Examination of the photos in Robert Cogan's *New Images of Musical Sound* reveals a greater similarity between the spectrum photo of "Pills and Soap" and the photos of a Gregorian chant, a Beethoven piano sonata, the "Confutatis" from Mozart's *Requiem*, Debussy's "Nuages," and Varèse's *Hyperprism*, than between "Pills and Soap" and the Tibetan Tantric chant or Balinese shadow-play music. For that matter, the photo of "Pills and Soap" more closely resembles these pieces of art music than it does the photo for "Hey Good Lookin'," the photo of which may reveal timbral contrast on a local level without that contrast contributing to a larger sense of teleological form. (Brackett 2000: 195)

Whether the argument that Brackett advances here stands up to scrutiny or not (there might be all kinds of reasons why "Pills and Soap" doesn't have a spectral shape that looks anything like Tibetan chant, Balinese shadow-play music, or another arbitrarily chosen popular song), the point that it makes is that the empirical evidence provided by spectral and temporal representations can furnish an important tool in a musicological enterprise—and that is what this chapter is intended to demonstrate.

The examples presented here, however, also illustrate some of the problems and pitfalls of using such information; it is very hard to find representational methods and analytical approaches that successfully reconcile detailed investigation with some sense of overall shape. Johnson's analysis, in focusing on the details of vibrato, timing, and intonation, doesn't go beyond bar 8 of the Bach aria; by contrast, Brackett's analysis of Costello, and many of Cogan's analyses, present spectrum photos at such a global level and with such inadequate resolution that some of the features and distinctions they discuss are all but invisible—and have to be taken on trust to more or less the same degree as if the authors were simply to tell the reader that the timbre gets brighter, or that there's a tiny articulation between phrases, or that there is an increasing accent on a word. In other words, there is a question about whether all the visual apparatus can really convince a reader of very much at all.

In part this is a purely technological matter, and the technology has certainly improved dramatically since the time of Cogan's book. But as shown by the much more sophisticated representations that Johnson uses, and as argued in this chapter, the problem is by no means solved by technological progress: there is still a real problem in extracting the salient features from a data representation that contains a potentially overwhelming amount of information, only a tiny fraction of which may be relevant at any moment. The problem is testimony to the extraordinary analytical powers of the human auditory system: in the mass of detail that is presented in a "close-up" view of the sound, the auditory system finds structure and distinctiveness. Some of the principles that account for this human capacity, and the ways in which they may contribute to musicological considerations, are the subject of the final section of this chapter.

Perceptual Analysis of Sounds

Music presents a challenge to the human auditory system, because it often contains several sources of sound (instruments, voices, electronics) whose behavior is coordinated in time. In order to make sense of this kind of musical material, the characteristics of the individual sounds, of concurrent combinations of them, and of sequences of them, must be identified by the auditory system. But to do this, the brain has to "decide" which bits of sound belong together, and which bits do not. As we will see, the grouping of sounds into perceptual units (events, streams, and textures) determines the perceived properties or attributes of these units. Thus, in considering the perceptual impact of the sounds represented in a score or a spectrogram, it is necessary to keep in mind a certain number of basic principles of perceptual processing.

Music played by several instruments presents a complex sound field to the human auditory system. The vibrations created by each instrument are propagated through the air to the listeners' ears, and combine with those of the other instruments as well as with the echoes and reverberations that result from reflections off walls, ceiling, furniture, and so on. What arrives at the ears is a very complex waveform indeed. To make matters worse, this composite signal is initially analyzed as a whole. The vibrations transmitted through the ear canal to the eardrum and then through the ossicles of the middle ear are finally processed biomechanically in the inner ear (the cochlea), such that different frequency regions of the incoming signal stimulate different sets of auditory nerve fibers. This is the aural equivalent of the spectral analysis described in the first main section of this chapter; one might consider the activity in the auditory nerve fibers over time as a kind of neural spectrogram. So if several instruments have closely related frequencies of vibration in their waveforms, they will collectively stimulate the same fibers: that is, they will be mixed together in the sequence of neural spikes that travel along that fiber to the brain. As we shall see, this would be the case for the different instruments playing the *Boléro* melody in parallel in a close approximation to a harmonic series.

It should be noted, however, that the different frequencies are still represented in the time intervals between successive nerve spikes, since the time structure of the spike train is closely related to the acoustic waveform. Furthermore, a sound from a single musical instrument is composed of several different frequencies (see the bass clarinet example in Figure 8.16) and thus stimulates many different sets of fibers; that is, it is analyzed into separate components distributed across the array of auditory nerve fibers. The problem that this presents to the brain is to aggregate the separate bits that come from the same source, and to segregate the information that comes from distinct sources. Furthermore, the sequence of events coming from the same sound source must be linked together over time, in order to follow a melody played by a given instrument. Let us consider a few examples of the kinds of problem this poses.

In some polyphonic music (such as Bach's orchestral suites or Ligeti's *Wind Quintet*), the intention of the composer is to create counterpoint, the success of which clearly depends on achieving segregation of the different instruments (Wright and Bregman 1987): what must be done to ensure that the instruments do not fuse together? In other polyphonic music, however (Ravel's *Boléro*, Ligeti's *Atmosphères*), the composer may seek a blending of different instruments and this would depend on achieving fusion or textural integration of the instruments: what must the musicians do to maximize the fusion and how can this be evaluated objectively? Finally, in some instrumental music an impression of two or more "voices" can be created from a monophonic source (such as in Telemann's recorder music or Bach's cello suites), or a single melodic line may be composed across several timbrally distinct instruments (as in Webern's *Six Pieces for Large Orchestra*, op. 6): what determines melodic continuity over time, and how might the integration or fragmentation be predicted from the score or for a given performance? For all these questions, the most important issue is how the perceptual result can be characterized from representations of the music (scores for notated music, acoustic representations for recorded or synthesized music). Obviously one can simply listen and use an aurally based analytical approach, but this restricts the account to the analyst's own (perhaps idiosyncratic) perceptions; if the aim is to provide a more generalized interpretation, the solution is to use basic principles of auditory perception as tools for understanding the musical process.

Grouping processes determine the perception of unified musical events (notes or aggregates of notes forming a vertical sonority), of coherent streams of events (having the connectedness necessary to perceive melody and rhythm), and of more or less dense regions of events that give rise to a homogeneous texture. *Perceptual fusion* is a grouping of concurrent acoustic components into a single auditory event (a perceptual unit having a beginning and an end); the perception of musical attributes such as pitch, timbre, loudness, and spatial position depends on which acoustic components are grouped together. *Auditory stream integration* is a grouping of sequences of events into a coherent, connected form, and determines what is heard as melody and rhythm. Texture is a more difficult notion to define, and has been the object of very little perceptual research, but intuitively the perception of a homogeneous musical texture requires a grouping of many events across pitch, timbre, and time into a kind of unitary structure, the textural quality of which depends on the relations among the events that are grouped together (certain works by Ligeti, Xenakis, and Penderecki come to mind, as do any number of electroacoustic works). Note that the main notion behind the word "grouping" is a kind of perceptual connectedness or association, called "binding" by neuroscientists. It seems clear that many levels of grouping can operate simultaneously, and that what is perceived depends to some extent on the kind of structure upon which a listener focuses. Since a large amount of scientific research has been conducted on concurrent and sequential sound organization processes, we will consider these in more detail, before moving on to discuss the perception of the musical properties (spatial location, loudness, pitch, timbre) that emerge from the auditory images formed by the primary grouping process.

There are two main factors that determine the perceptual fusion of acoustic components into unified auditory events, or their segregation into separate events: *onset synchrony* and *harmonicity*. A number of other factors were originally thought by perception researchers to be involved in grouping, but are probably more implicated either in increasing the perceptual salience of an event (vibrato and tremolo), or in allowing a listener to focus on a given sound source in the presence of several others (spatial position; for reviews see McAdams 1984, Bregman 1990, 1993, Darwin and Carlyon 1995, Deutsch 1999). We will focus here on the grouping factors.

Acoustic components that start at the same time are unlikely to arise from different sound sources and so tend to be grouped together into a single event. Onset asynchronies between components on the order of as little as 30 ms are sufficient to give the impression of two sources and to allow listeners in some cases to identify the sounds as separate; to get a perspective on the accuracy necessary to produce synchrony within this very small time window, one might note that skilled professional musicians playing in trios (strings, winds, or recorders) have asynchronies in the range of 30 to 50 ms, giving a sense of playing together while allowing perceptual segregation of the instruments (Rasch 1988). If musicians play in perfect synchrony, by contrast, there is a greater tendency for their sounds to fuse together and for the identity of each instrument or voice to be lost. These phenomena can also be manipulated compositionally: Huron (1993) has shown by statistical analyses that the voice asynchronies used by Bach in his two-part inventions were greater than those used in his work as a whole, suggesting an intention on the part of the composer to maximize the separation of the voices in these works. If, on the other hand, voices in a polyphony are synchronous, what may result is a global timbre that comes from the fusion of the composite—though considerable precision is needed to achieve such a result.

The other main grouping principle is that sound components tend to be perceived as a single entity when they are related by a common fundamental period. This is particularly the case if, when the fundamental period changes, all of the components change in similar fashion, as would be the case in playing vibrato, or in a single instrument playing a legato melody. Forced vibrating systems, such as blown air columns (wind instruments) and bowed strings, create nearly perfect harmonic sounds, with a strongly fused quality and an unambiguous pitch—in contrast to the several audible pitches of some inharmonic, free-vibrating systems such as a struck gong or church bell. This harmonicity-based fusion principle has again been used intuitively by composers of polyphonic music: a statistical analysis of Bach's keyboard music by Huron (1991) showed that the composer avoided harmonic intervals in proportion to the degree to which they promote tonal fusion, thus helping to ensure voice independence.

An important perceptual principle is demonstrated through such fusion: if sounds are grouped together, the perceptual attributes that arise—such as a new composite timbre—may be different from those of the individual constituent sounds, and may be difficult to imagine merely from looking at the score or even at a spectrogram. The principle that the perceived qualities of simultaneities depend on grouping led Wright and Bregman (1987) to examine the role of nonsimultaneous voice entries in the control of musical dissonance: they argued that the dissonant effect of an interval such as a major seventh is much reduced if the voices composing the interval do not enter synchronously, and similar results also apply to fusion based on harmonicity (see McAdams 1999). All this demonstrates the need to consider issues of sonority in the perceptual analysis of pitch structures.

As a concrete example, Ravel's *Boléro* arguably represents an example of intended fusion. Up to bar 148, the main melody is played in succession by different instrumental soloists. But at this point it is played simultaneously by five voices on three types of instrument: French horn, celesta, and piccolos (Figure 8.1b); the basic melody is played by the French horn, and is transposed to the octave, 12th, double octave, and double octave plus a major third for the celesta (LH), piccolo (2), celesta (RH), and piccolo (1), respectively. Note that this forms a harmonic series and that these harmonic intervals are maintained since the transpositions are exact (so that the fundamental, octave, and double octave melodies are played in C major, the 12th melody in G major, and the double octave plus a third melody in E major). Ravel thus respects the harmonicity principle to the letter, and since all the melodies are also presented in strict synchrony, the resulting fusion—with the individual instrument identities subsumed into a single new composite timbre—depends only on accurate tuning and timing being maintained by the performers. This procedure is repeated by Ravel for various other instrumental combinations in the course of the piece, the consequent timbral evolution contributing to the global crescendo.

An inverse example can be found in the mixed instrumental and electroacoustic work *Archipelago* by Roger Reynolds, for ensemble and four-channel computer-generated tape. In the tape part, recordings of the musical materials used elsewhere in the work by different instruments were analyzed by computer and resynthesized with modifications. In particular, the even and odd harmonics were either processed together as in the original sound, giving a temporally extended resynthesis of the same instrument timbre, or processed separately with independent vibratos and spatial trajectories, resulting in a perceptual fission into two new sounds. Selecting only the odd harmonics of an instrument sound leaves the pitch the same, but makes the timbre more "hollow" sounding, moving in the direction of a clarinet sound (which has weak even-numbered harmonics in the lower part of its frequency spectrum); selecting only the even harmonics produces an octave jump in pitch, since a series of even harmonics is the same as a harmonic series an octave higher. The perceptual result is therefore two new sounds with pitches an octave apart and timbres that are also different compared to the original sound. An example from *Archipelago* is the split of an oboe sound (Figure 8.17), which results in a clarinetlike sound at the original pitch and a soprano-like sound an octave higher. When the vibrato patterns are made coherent again, the sound fuses back into the original oboe.

Sequential sound organization concerns the integration of successive events into auditory streams and the segregation of streams that appear to come from different sources. In real-world settings, a stream generally constitutes a series of events

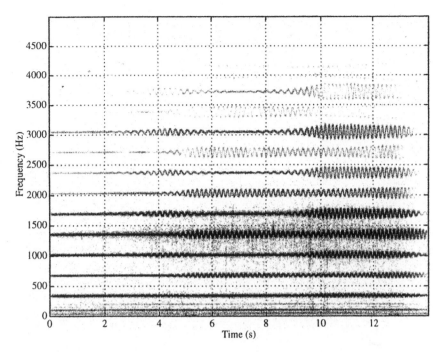

Figure 8.17.   Splitting of an oboe sound in Roger Reynolds's *Archipelago*.
At around 3 seconds the odd-numbered harmonics start to have an independent
vibrato which grows and then decays in strength. A similar pattern occurs on the
even-numbered harmonics from about 5 seconds. Finally, each group swells in
vibrato, but with independent vibration patterns at around 9 seconds.

emitted over time by a single source. As we will see, however, there are limits to what
a listener can hear as an auditory stream, which does not always correspond to what
real physical sources can actually do. So we can say that an auditory stream is a coherent "mental" representation of a succession of events. The main principle that affects this mental coherence is a trade-off between the temporal proximity of successive sound events and their relative similarity: the brain seems to prefer to connect
a succession of sounds of similar quality which together create a perceptual continuity. Continuity, however, is relative since a given difference between successive
events may be perceived as continuous at slow tempi, but will be split into different
streams at fast tempi. The main parameters affecting continuity include spectrotemporal properties, sound level, and spatial position; continuous variation in all of
these parameters gives a single stream, whereas rapid variation (particularly in all
three together, as would often be the case for two independent sound sources playing at the same time) can induce the fission of a physical sequence of notes into two
streams, one corresponding to the sequence emitted by each individual instrument.

In order to illustrate the basic principles, let us examine spectrotemporal continuity, which is affected by pitch and timbre change between successive notes.
Melodies played by a single instrument with steps and small skips tend to be heard
as unified, with easily detectable pitch and rhythmic intervals, while rapid jumps

across registers or between instruments may give rise to the perception of two or more melodies being played simultaneously, as illustrated in Figure 8.18 (an excerpt from a recorder piece by Telemann). In this case the perceived "melody" (i.e., the specific pattern of pitch and rhythmic intervals) corresponds to the relationships among the notes that have been grouped into a single stream or into multiple streams. Over the first six seconds of the excerpt shown, a listener will hear (and the spectrogram shows) a relatively slow ascending melody, a static pedal note, and a sequence of more rapid three-note descending motifs. Because listeners often have great difficulty perceiving relationships across streams, such as rhythmic intervals and even relative temporal order of events, there can be some surprising rhythmic results from apparently simple materials. The example in Figure 8.19 illustrates how two interleaved, isochronous rhythms played by separate xylophone players can produce a complex rhythmic pattern (note the irregular spacing of the sound events in the 250 to 1,000 Hz range in the spectrogram) due to the way the notes from the two players are combined perceptually into a single stream with unpredictable discontinuities in the melodic contour.

Once the acoustic waveform has been analyzed into separate source-related events, the auditory features of the events can be extracted. These musical qualities depend on various acoustic properties of the events, of which the most important are spatial location, loudness, pitch, and timbre. Each of these will be considered separately.

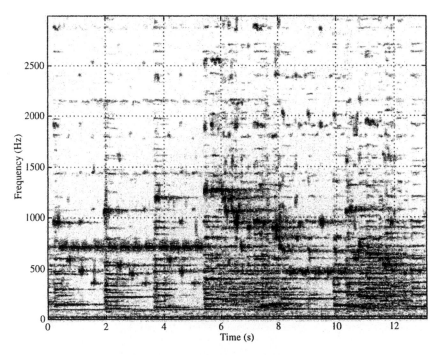

Figure 8.18.   Spectrogram of an excerpt of a recorder piece by Telemann. The fundamental frequencies of the recorder notes lie in the range 400 to 1,500 Hz.

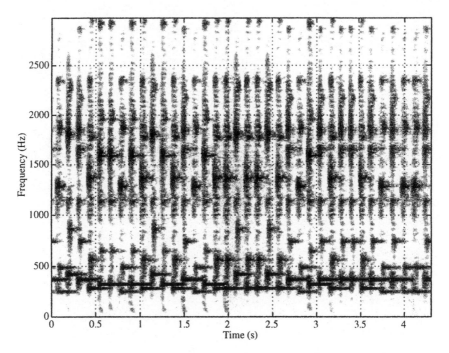

Figure 8.19.   Spectrogram of a rhythm played by separate players on an African xylophone.

The *spatial location* of an event depends on several kinds of cues in the sound. In the first place, since we have two ears that are separated in space, the sound that arrives at the two ear drums depends on the position of the sound source relative to the listener's head, and is different for each ear: a sound coming from one side is both more intense and arrives earlier at the closer ear. Also the convoluted, irregular shape of the outer part of the ear (the pinna) creates position-dependent modifications of the sound entering the ear canal, and these are interpreted by the brain as cues for localization. Second, and more difficult to research, are the cues that allow us to infer the distance of the source (Grantham 1995). There are several possible acoustic cues for distance: one is the relative level, since level decreases as a function of distance, while another is the relative amount of reverberated sound in the environment as compared with the direct sound from the source (the ratio of reverberated to direct sound increases with distance). Finally, since higher frequencies are more easily absorbed and/or dispersed in the atmosphere than are lower frequencies, the spectral shape of the received signal can also contribute to the impression of distance. Such binaural, pinna, and distance cues are useful in virtual reality displays and in creating spatial effects in electroacoustic music.

For simple sounds, *loudness* corresponds fairly directly to sound level; but for complex sounds, the global loudness results from a kind of summation of power across the whole frequency range. It is as if the brain adds together the activity in all of the auditory nerve fibers that are being stimulated by a musical sound to calculate the total loudness. When several sounds are present at the same time and their frequency spectra overlap, a louder sound can cover up a softer sound either partially, making it even softer, or totally, making it inaudible: this process is called masking, and seems to be related to the neural activity of one sound swamping that of another. Masking may be partially responsible for the difficulty in hearing out inner voices when listening to polyphonies with three or more voices. Again, loudness is affected by duration: a very short staccato note (say around 50 ms) with the same physical intensity as a longer note (say around 500 ms) will sound softer. This seems to be because loudness accumulates over time, and the accumulation process takes time: for a long steady note, the perceived loudness stabilizes after about 200 ms. This principle is useful in instruments that produce sustained notes over whose intensity no control is possible, but whose duration can be controlled. For example, the production of agogic accents on the organ is obtained by playing certain notes slightly longer than their neighboring notes.

For any harmonic or periodic sound, the main *pitch* heard corresponds to the fundamental frequency, though this perceived pitch is the result of a perceptual synthesis of the acoustic information, rather than the analytic perception of the frequency component corresponding to the fundamental. (One can listen to a low-register instrument playing in the bottom of its tessitura over a small transistor radio and still hear the melody being played at the correct pitch, even though the spectrum of the signal shows that all of the lower-order harmonics are missing due to the very small size of the loudspeaker in the radio.) But many musical sound sources that are not purely harmonic (including carillon bells, tubular bells, and various percussion instruments) still give at least a vague impression of pitchedness; it seems that pitch perception is not an all-or-none affair, so that perceived pitch can be more or less strong or salient. For example, try singing a tune just by whispering and not using your vocal chords: you will find that you change the vowel you are singing to produce the pitch, which suggests that a noise sound with a prominent resonance peak can produce enough of a pitch percept to specify recognizable pitch relations between adjacent sound events. Similarly, the sound processing techniques used in electroacoustic and pop music can create spectral modifications of broadband noise (such as crowd or ocean sounds) with a regular series of peaks and dips in the spectrum: if the spacing between the centers of the noise peaks corresponds to a harmonic series, a weak pitch is heard, allowing musicians to "tune" noise sounds to more clearly pitched harmonic sounds.

Finally, *timbre* is a vague term that is used differently by different people and even according to the context. The "official" scientific definition is a nondefinition: the attribute of auditory sensation that distinguishes two sounds that are otherwise equal in terms of pitch, duration, and loudness, and that are presented under similar conditions (presumably taking into account room effects and so on). That leaves a lot of room for variation! Over the last 30 years, however, a new approach to timbre perception has developed, which allows psychoacousticians to characterize more systematically what timbre is, rather than what it is not. Using special data analysis techniques, called multidimensional scaling (Plomp 1970, Grey 1977, McAdams et al. 1995), researchers have been able to identify a number of perceptual dimensions that constitute timbre, allowing a kind of deconstruction of this global category into more precise elements. Attributes in terms of which timbres may be distinguished include the following:

- Spectral centroid (visible in a spectral representation: the relative weight of high and low-frequency parts of the spectrum, a higher centroid giving a "brighter" sound).
- Attack quality (visible in a temporal representation, and including the attack time and the presence of attack transients at the beginning of a sound).
- Smoothness of the spectral envelope (visible in a spectral representation: the clarinet has strong odd-numbered harmonics and weak even-numbered harmonics, giving a ragged spectral envelope).
- Degree of evolution of the spectral envelope over the course of a note (visible in a time-frequency representation: some instruments, like the clarinet, have a fairly steady envelope, whereas others have an envelope that opens up toward the high frequencies as the intensity of the note increases, as in the case of brass instruments).
- Roughness (visible in a temporal representation: smooth sounds have very little beating and fluctuation, whereas rough sounds are more grating and inherently dissonant).
- Noisiness/inharmonicity (visible in a spectral representation: nearly pure harmonic sounds, like blown and bowed instruments, can be distinguished from inharmonic sounds like tubular bells and steel drums, or from clearly noisy sounds such as those of crash cymbals and snare drums).

A greater understanding of the relative importance of these different "dimensions" of timbre may help musicologists develop systematic classification systems for musical instruments and even sound effects or electroacoustic sounds.

Analytical Application

As an example of the way in which psychoacoustical principles can be empirically applied to the analysis of pitch and timbre, Tsang (2002) uses a number of perceptually based approaches to analyze the structure of *Farben*—the third of Schoenberg's *Five Orchestral Pieces, Op. 16*, which is celebrated for its innovative use of orchestral timbre. Taking principles developed by Parncutt (1989) for estimating the salience of individual pitches, and by Huron (2001) for explaining voice-leading in perceptual terms, Tsang discusses the perceptibility of the canonic structure of the opening section of *Farben*. By applying Parncutt's pitch salience algorithm (a formula used to calculate how noticeable any given pitch is in the context of other simultaneous pitches), Tsang concludes that "Schoenberg's choice of pitches ensures that relatively strong harmonic components often draw the listener's attention to the canonic voices that are moving or are about to move" (Tsang 2002: 29). Huron's perceptual principles relating to voice-leading, which take into account a wider variety of psychoacoustical considerations than pitch alone, partially support this conclusion, suggesting that Schoenberg tailored his choices of orchestration so as to bring out the canonic movement, but that other factors serve to disguise the canon.

At the end of his study, Tsang notes that the different attentional strategies listeners bring to bear on the music will inevitably result in different perceptual experiences, as will comparatively slight differences of interpretation on the part of conductors and orchestras—particularly in a piece that seems to place itself deliberately at the threshold of perceptual discriminability. These considerations suggest a high level of indeterminacy between what a perceptually informed analysis might suggest and what any particular listener may experience—an indeterminacy that would be damaging to a narrowly descriptive (let alone rigidly prescriptive) notion of the relationship between analysis and experience. But as many authors have pointed out (e.g., McAdams 1984, Cook 1990), to propose such a tight linkage is neither necessary nor even desirable.

A further example of an attempt to relate perceptual principles to musicological concerns is provided by Huron (2001). The goals of this ambitious paper are "to explain voice-leading practice by using perceptual principles, predominantly principles associated with the theory of auditory stream segregation . . .", and "to identify the goals of voice-leading, to show how following traditional voice-leading rules contributes to the achievement of these goals, and to propose a cognitive explanation for why the goals might be deemed worthwhile in the first place" (Huron 2001: 2–3). As this makes clear, perceptual principles are being used here to address not only matters of compositional practice, but also aesthetic issues. The form of the paper is first to present a review of accepted rules of voice-leading for Western art music; second to identify a number of pertinent perceptual principles; third to see whether the rules of voice-leading can be derived from the perceptual principles; fourth to introduce a number of auxiliary perceptual principles which provide a perspective on different musical genres; and finally to consider the possible aesthetic motivations for the compositional practices that are commonly found in Western music and which do not always simply adhere to the perceptual principles that Huron identifies.

Huron makes use of six perceptual principles in the central part of the paper, each of which is supported with extensive empirical evidence from auditory and music perception research, and is shown to correspond to compositional practice often sampled over quite substantial bodies of musical repertoire (using Huron's *Humdrum* software—see chapter 6, this volume). To give some idea of what the perceptual principles are like, and how they are used to derive voice-leading rules, consider as an example the third perceptual principle, which Huron calls the "minimum masking principle": "In order to minimize auditory masking within some vertical sonority, approximately equivalent amounts of spectral energy should fall in each critical band. For typical complex harmonic tones, this generally means that simultaneously sounding notes should be more widely spaced as the register descends." (Huron 2001: 18)

In support of this principle, Huron assembles a considerable amount of evidence from well-established psychoacoustical research dating back to the 1960s showing that pitches falling within a certain range of one another (i.e., the "critical band," which roughly corresponds to the bandwidth of the auditory filters in the cochlea) both tend to obscure ("mask") one another, and interact to create a sense of instability or roughness (often referred to as "sensory dissonance"). When Huron goes on to derive perceptually-based voice-leading rules, the "minimum masking principle" is used to motivate two rules, one traditional, and one which Huron calls "nontraditional"; "nontraditional" rules are those that seem to follow from perceptual principles, but are not acknowledged as explicit voice-leading rules in standard texts. The traditional rule is stated as follows (Huron 2001: 33): "Chord Spacing Rule. *In general, chordal tones should be spaced with wider intervals between the lower voices.*" The nontraditional rule (ibid.) is: "Tessitura-Sensitive Spacing Rule. *It is more important to have large intervals separating the lower voices in the case of sonorities that are lower in overall pitch.*" Huron refers to work showing that this rule, although not explicitly recognized in standard texts on voice-leading, is adhered to in musical practice. The five other perceptual principles work in a similar fashion, generating individually, and in combination with one another, a total of 22 voice-leading rules, of which nine are traditional. All of the 13 nontraditional rules are found to be supported by compositional practice, demonstrating rather convincingly how a perceptually-based approach can reveal implicit, but previously unrecognized, compositional principles.

Having derived the voice-leading principles, Huron introduces four additional perceptual principles which are used to address questions of musical genre. Again, to get a flavor of what is involved, consider just one of the four (Huron, 2001: 49): "Timbral Differentiation Principle. *If a composer intends to write music in which the parts have a high degree of perceptual independence, then each part should maintain a unique timbral character.*" The striking thing about this principle, as Huron points out, is the extent to which it is ignored in compositional practice. Although wind quintets and other small mixed chamber ensembles show significant differentiation, string quartets, brass ensembles, madrigal groups, and keyboards all make use of timbrally undifferentiated textures for polyphonic purposes. Why is this? Huron suggests that there may be a number of factors. One is pragmatic: it may simply have been more difficult for composers to assemble heterogeneous instrumental groups, and so the goal of distinguishable polyphony was bracketed or abandoned in favor of practical possibility. A second reason may be the operation of a contrary aesthetic goal: Huron suggests that composers tend to prefer instrumental ensembles that show a high degree of "blend," and homogeneous instrumentation may be one way to achieve this. And a third reason may be balance: it is much harder to achieve an acceptable balance between voices in a very diverse instrumental group, and composers may have decided that this was a more important goal.

It is interesting in this regard that Schoenberg's practice, from the middle period of his atonal style, of indicating instrumental parts as "Hauptstimme" and "Nebenstimme" (main voice and subsidiary voice) was motivated by a concern that the correct balance between instrumental parts in his chamber and orchestral works might not be attained; given the dramatic explosion of writing for mixed chamber ensembles in the twentieth century, influenced strongly by the ensemble that Schoenberg used in *Pierrot Lunaire*, this does seem to be a recognition of the balance problem that Huron identifies. Equally, the striking way in which Webern uses timbral differentiation to cut across the serial structure in the first movement of the *Symphony*, Op. 21, provides support (through counterevidence) for the timbral differentiation principle: timbral identity and differentiation disguise the serial structure, instead superimposing a different structure that is articulated by timbre itself—a timbral palindrome.

The Webern example already demonstrates the complex interaction between compositional and aesthetic goals on the one hand, and perceptual principles on the other—and it is this subject that the final part of Huron's paper addresses. Huron proposes that achieving perceptual clarity in perceptually challenging contexts (e.g., finding hidden objects in visual arrays, as exploited in many children's puzzles) is an intrinsically pleasurable and rewarding process, and that this is one way to understand why voice-leading rules and compositional practice both conform to, and flout, perceptual principles. If all music simply adhered to perceptual imperatives, then there would be little motivation to move beyond the most straightforward monophony. But social considerations (the need, or desire, to develop musical styles in which groups of singers or instrumentalists with different pitch ranges, timbral qualities or dynamic characteristics can sing and play together), aesthetic goals and a whole range of other factors have resulted in the historical development of an enormous variety of textures and styles. One strand within this, Huron suggests, is the possibility that some multipart music is organized deliberately to challenge the listener's perceptual capacities—precisely because of the pleasure that can be gained from successfully resolving these complex textures.

> Early Renaissance polyphonists discovered [that] . . . by challenging the listener's auditory parsing abilities, the potential for a pleasing effect could be heightened. However, this heightened pleasure would be possible only if listeners could indeed successfully parse the more complex auditory scenes. Having increased the perceptual challenge, composers would need to take care in providing adequate streaming cues. Following the rules of voice-leading and limiting the density of parts . . . might be essential aids for listeners. (Huron 2001: 57)

What is striking about this discussion is that it brings together perceptual principles based on extensive empirical support, aesthetic considerations, and a rather different perspective on music history in a way that manages to avoid the potential pitfalls of a perceptual determinism. Huron's final paragraph is significant for the care with which it recognizes that perceptual principles act neither as the arbiters of musical value, nor as constraints on future creativity. Noting that his interpretation of the aesthetic origins of voice-leading "should in no way be construed as evidence for the superiority of polyphonic music over other types of music," he continues (Huron 2001: 58):

> In the first instance, different genres might manifest different perceptual goals that evoke aesthetic pleasure in other ways. Nor should we expect pleasure to be limited only to perceptual phenomena. As we have already emphasized, the construction of a musical work may be influenced by innumerable goals, from social and cultural goals to financial and idiomatic goals. . . . The identification of perceptual mechanisms need not hamstring musical creativity. On the contrary, it may be that the overt identification of the operative perceptual principles may spur creative endeavors to generate unprecedented musical genres.

Conclusion

In this chapter, we have tried to show how acoustical and perceptual analyses can supplement and "animate" an analytical understanding drawn from scores and recordings in important ways. The representations and analytical methods considered here can be a significant key to a more *sound*-based understanding of music than the score-reading approach has traditionally encouraged, and in this way attributes of musical structure and process that remain hidden from view in the score, and that often pass by too rapidly and with too much complexity in performance or recording, can be brought to light and given appropriate consideration. But as we have seen, there are still problems to be overcome: as the figures in this chapter demonstrate, representations of sound often contain large amounts of information, with the result that it can be difficult to strike an effective balance between analyzing musically appropriate stretches of material and risking information overload on the one hand, and focusing on a frustratingly tiny fragment of music on the other. Although the analysis of musical sound is still in early stages of development, and more powerful summarizing tools will no doubt be developed in the future, in the long run there may be no easy solution to a problem which is a testimony to the exceptional power of human perception.

As the example from Tsang (2002) has already made clear, the kind of approach discussed in this chapter is necessarily generic, and unable to *explain* individual listening experiences—even if it brings new tools with which to *illustrate* those experiences. It is, after all, based on a "culture-free" approach in which the salience and impact of events, for example, is based solely on their acoustical and perceptual properties and not on their cultural resonances or semiotic significance. A well-established finding in the psychology of perception, sometimes referred to as the "cocktail party phenomenon," demonstrates that when people are attending to multiple sound sources, a source that has special significance for them (such as their name, or an emotionally charged word) will catch their attention even when it competes with other sound sources that may be considerably more salient (louder, nearer, timbrally more prominent). Thus the analyst is in no measure freed by this wealth of empirical data from either the responsibility or the opportunity to explore, and try to explain, why music might be heard or understood in particular ways. Nonetheless, acoustical and perceptual analyses can usefully complement more culturally oriented approaches by providing a rich source of information on which the latter might be based, and in terms of which they are certainly grounded. As with any empirical approach, the value of such an outlook is not in the data that it may accumulate but in the way in which data rub up against theory—formal or informal—in ways that may be supportive and confirmatory, or uncomfortable and mind changing.

References

Brackett, D. (2000). *Interpreting Popular Music*. Berkeley: University of California Press.

Bregman, A. S. (1990). *Auditory Scene Analysis: The Perceptual Organization of Sound*. Cambridge, Mass.: MIT Press.

Bregman, A. S. (1993). "Auditory scene analysis: Hearing in complex environments," in
    S. McAdams and E. Bigand (eds.), *Thinking in Sound: The Cognitive Psychology of
    Human Audition*. Oxford: Oxford University Press, 10–36.
Cogan, R. (1984). *New Images of Musical Sound.* Cambridge, Mass.: Harvard University
    Press.
Cook, N. (1990). *Music, Imagination, and Culture*. Oxford: Clarendon Press.
Darwin, C. J., and Carlyon, R. P. (1995). "Auditory grouping," in B. C. J. Moore (ed.),
    Hearing. San Diego, Calif.: Academic Press, 387–424.
Deutsch, D. (1999). "Grouping mechanisms in music," in D. Deutsch (ed.), *The Psychol-
    ogy of Music,* 2nd ed. San Diego, Calif.: Academic Press, 299–348.
Grantham, D. W. (1995). "Spatial hearing and related phenomena," in B. C. J. Moore
    (ed.), *Hearing*. San Diego, Calif.: Academic Press, 297–345.
Grey, J. M. (1977). "Multidimensional perceptual scaling of musical timbres." *Journal of
    the Acoustical Society of America* 61: 1270–1277.
Huron, D. (1991). "Tonal consonance versus tonal fusion in polyphonic sonorities." *Music
    Perception* 9: 135–154.
Huron, D. (1993). "Note-onset asynchrony in J. S. Bach's two-part inventions." *Music Per-
    ception* 10: 435–444.
Huron, D. (2001). "Tone and voice: A derivation of the rules of voice-leading from per-
    ceptual principles." *Music Perception* 19: 1–64.
Johnson, P. (1999). "Performance and the listening experience: Bach's 'Erbarme Dich'," in
    N. Cook, P. Johnson, and H. Zender (eds.), *Theory into Practice: Composition, Perfor-
    mance and the Listening Experience*. Leuven (Louvain), Belgium: Leuven University
    Press, 55–101.
McAdams, S. (1984). "The auditory image: A metaphor for musical and psychological
    research on auditory organization," in W. R. Crozier and A. J. Chapman (eds.), *Cog-
    nitive Processes in the Perception of Art*. Amsterdam: North-Holland, 289–323.
McAdams, S. (1999). "Perspectives on the contribution of timbre to musical structure."
    Computer Music Journal 23: 96–113.
McAdams, S., Winsberg, S., Donnadieu, S., De Soete, G., and Krimphoff, J. (1995).
    "Perceptual scaling of synthesized musical timbres: Common dimensions, specifici-
    ties, and latent subject classes." *Psychological Research* 58: 177–192.
Parncutt, R. (1989). *Harmony: A Psychoacoustical Approach*. Berlin: Springer-Verlag.
Plomp, R. (1970). "Timbre as a multidimensional attribute of complex tones," in
    R. Plomp and G. F. Smoorenburg (eds.), *Frequency Analysis and Periodicity Detection
    in Hearing*. Leiden: Sijthoff, 397–414.
Rasch, R. A. (1988). "Timing and synchronization in ensemble performance," in
    J. A. Sloboda (ed.), *Generative Processes in Music: The Psychology of Performance, Im-
    provisation, and Composition*. Oxford: Oxford University Press, 71–90.
Tsang, L. (2002). "Towards a theory of timbre for music analysis." *Musicae Scientiae* 6:
    23–52.
Wright, J. K., and Bregman, A. S. (1987). "Auditory stream segregation and the control of
    dissonance in polyphonic music." *Contemporary Music Review* 2/1: 63–92.

CHAPTER 9

Data Collection, Experimental Design, and Statistics in Musical Research

W. Luke Windsor

Introduction

This chapter provides a brief introduction to the ways in which musical research has drawn upon the quantitative methods of the empirical social sciences. The past 25 years have seen increasing moves toward the use of such methods in musical research, especially in the domain that has become variously known as "music psychology," "psychology of music," "music cognition," "music perception," or even "psychomusicology." Although these methods can be applied directly to musical data derived from a score, this chapter focuses upon quantitative analytical techniques that can be applied to musical events that involve either listeners or performers. Research on music perception and performance can be carried out using quite standard statistical and experimental methods, but often requires novel approaches to their application.

In carrying out an empirical study, hypotheses, or at least some concrete research questions, must be generated before comparing, describing, coding, or collecting data. This is because it is only in the light of such hypotheses that you can decide precisely what data are relevant, and how irrelevant factors are to be excluded: to this extent the approach must be top-down, rather than bottom-up. Hence, although the first *practical* step in doing empirical research is observation, a prior *conceptual* step should be an informed decision about what to observe, how to quantify it, and how to analyze the resulting data. It is pointless collecting data that turn out to be inappropriate for analysis, or which fail to provide evidence that can be used to support or challenge the relevant arguments.

However, not all quantitative research need be experimental in this classical sense. It is perfectly acceptable to collect data in a more exploratory manner as long as it is recognized that it may be hard to understand the relationship between different variables. The "real world" is a complex place, and laboratory researchers often pay a price for ensuring that their experimental results are easy to interpret. This price is loss of "realism" or "ecological validity," and can result in findings that only hold under extremely unusual and constrained circumstances (such as those within a laboratory). It may be convenient for analytical purposes to take into account only certain things, such as, for example, the duration and pitch-class of events in melodic sequences, but there is a danger of finding out too late that some

197

other factor, such as melodic contour, was a relevant variable. An experimental approach tends to be reductive, in that it reduces the number of factors involved so as to show more clearly their influence on one another. There is always a danger that such a reductive approach changes the observed phenomenon so much that the findings are hard to apply to the real world.

This chapter is organized so as to mirror the different stages a piece of empirical research might involve. First, I consider issues in the collection of data: this section summarizes the different kinds of quantitative data that can be gathered from performers and listeners, and suggests appropriate methods of data collection. The second section explores various methods of organizing and transforming data. It is often the case that data are noisy, or in the wrong format for a particular kind of analysis: they may need to be systematically filtered, or encoded. The third section outlines some basic statistical techniques for describing and summarizing quantitative data, including visual and other methods for representing data in such a way as to draw general conclusions. The fourth section explores the discovery and measurement of trends in data, with examples of methods that allow the comparison of two or more sets of data. The final section returns to issues of experimental method in relation to hypothesis testing, compared to less strict and more exploratory approaches to empirical research.

Collecting Data from Listeners and Performers

It seems self-evident that a sensible way of learning about music might be to observe and measure the behavior of performers and listeners. In the classical Western tradition, for example, expert listeners (themselves often expert performers) must select the winners in prestigious competitions, and teachers of music must diagnose problems in listening and performance. Musicians of all kinds must self-diagnose their shortcomings in order to improve, and must be able to apply sophisticated perceptual and cognitive skills to succeed in coordinating their ensemble performances. Some forms of observation and measurement are judgmental, while some are rather less value-laden, but it would be quite wrong to assume that an empirical attitude to musical behavior is something alien to everyday musical life.

The direct collection of *quantitative* data, and the quantification of more qualitative observations, is familiar to any musician who works within a structured educational context. It is common for performers to be assessed by examinations that not only provide written feedback, but also a breakdown of numerical marks in different areas of performance (such as the ability to play scales and arpeggios, pieces, and to sight-read). The total number of marks acquired in such an examination is intended to express their standard of performance at a particular level: a qualitative assessment of performance becomes quantitative, and judgments are then made about the relative success of different candidates. In a more subtle sense, audition panels and competition juries regularly translate their qualitative assessments of performers into rankings, which also represents a move away from qualitative toward quantitative empiricism. Such ratings and rankings of musical skill are just one way in which quantitative data might be collected from musicians.

Before moving on to a consideration of different types of musical data, a basic distinction can be made between more or less direct methods of collection. For example, if one imagines a continuum between observing a pianist playing and asking the pianist to fill out a questionnaire about their performance, it is easy to see that the former might represent a more direct method of collecting data about the performance itself. The questionnaire might be a direct way of gathering data on the pianist's motivations, but hardly on his or her performance as such, since there are intervening effects of memory and interpretation—which may be interesting in themselves, but which represent a considerable move away from direct measurement and observation. While the relative directness of methods will change with context (measuring a performance is a very indirect way of discovering which edition of the music has been played as compared to asking the performer), the number of stages of interpretation through which information must pass before analysis should always be considered. This chain of interpretation must be taken into account when analyzing data: each stage introduces uncertainty—which may be necessary, but must be noted. If a study of performance was to be based on the judgments of listeners, it would have to take into account the possible biases and unreliability of the judges, whereas a study based on Musical Instrument Digital Interface (MIDI) data gathered from performances need not do so. Of course, the latter would say nothing about whether anything measured had any relevance to listeners: directness is no guarantee of appropriate design.

Both direct and indirect methods of measurement have been described in the preceding chapters. Many studies of performance have more or less directly measured the timing and magnitude of musicians' movements through analysis of video data (e.g., Davidson 1993). Timing and intensity data from performances have been directly gathered from either specially modified conventional instruments (e.g. Seashore 1938; Shaffer 1981), or MIDI instruments (e.g., Palmer 1989), or from analysis of audio signals (e.g., Repp 1992). Digital signal processors also make available a wealth of detailed data about the internal structure of sounds, useful in the analysis of instrumental or vocal timbre (see chapter 8, this volume). Although most of these techniques are primarily suited to the analysis of performance, perceptual issues can also be studied, as long as the indirect nature of the response is taken into account. A listener might be asked to imitate a musical sequence (Clarke 1993), or to tap along to it (Repp 1999), so providing data relevant to the study of perception. More direct methods of collecting data about performance might include the measurement or observation of changes in physiological state; for example, common measures used in studies of performance anxiety include heart rate, blood pressure and skin conductivity (Abel and Larkin 1990). Again, both perception and production studies have begun to measure the spatial location and temporal pattern of brain activity, whether measured in terms of temperature, electrical activity or blood flow (see, for example, Besson and Faïta 1995).

Rather more indirect methods may also be appropriate, however. When studying perceptual phenomena, it may be most practical to collect the responses to some form of listening test, where listeners have to make their response either on paper or via computer software. For example, a study might investigate how similar a listener thinks two musical events are (e.g., Grey 1977), or how well one event fits with another (e.g., Krumhansl and Kessler 1982): here the data might take the form of numbers corresponding to the magnitude of the perceived similarity or goodness of fit along some scale. Similarly, a task might require subjects to identify an event, or discriminate between different events (e.g., Windsor 1993), and again the data can be represented quantitatively. In a different context, more complex psychometric tests might be employed, such as those that purport to assess musical ability (for instance the Seashore Measures of Musical Talents), standard of performance (such as the Associated Board of the Royal Schools of Music examinations in the U.K.), or anxiety levels (the State-Trait Anxiety Inventory), all of which give a numerical score or set of scores. Using preexisting tests has advantages and disadvantages: such tests are often well standardized for particular populations, but just for this reason they may be misleading if applied outside this group of people. Other measures of training or ability might also be made: simply counting the number of years of musical involvement can be used as a rough measure of certain types of musical skill, for example, especially since there is now strong empirical evidence for a direct relationship between the quantity of practice and resulting musical expertise (Sloboda, Davidson, Howe, and Moore, 1996).

One approach which I will do no more than touch on (but which is discussed in chapter 4, this volume) is the questionnaire study. Although rather indirect and sometimes difficult to verify, questionnaires can be an extremely good source of certain kinds of quantitative data, such as that deriving from self-assessment of the time spent practicing (Sloboda, Davidson, Howe, and Moore 1996), or from self-coding of attitudes or states of mind. The standard text on formulating questionnaires is Oppenheim (1966); although now quite old, it contains excellent advice on how to find out about people's beliefs and attitudes through questionnaires.

Data Types and Variables

Before deciding upon a method of collecting data and investing in the equipment and software needed, it is necessary to make an informed choice about what kind of data to collect, and in which form it would most usefully be encoded. It is also important at this stage to take account of the statistical consequences of one's choices. Different types of data require and allow for different types of statistical test, and an attempt will be made here to outline some of the consequences of choosing particular types of quantitative *variable*. Sometimes the same thing can be measured in different ways, and the choice may be influenced by the kinds of intended analysis.

A primary distinction is between three types of data: *nominal*, or category data; *ordinal* data; and *continuous* data. *Nominal* data are differentiated only in name, not in magnitude, and each data point, or observation, is represented by one of a number of symbols. A simple example of this might be the categorization of listeners in a study into musicians and nonmusicians, perhaps using a questionnaire. The possibility that there might be a continuum between musicians and nonmusicians, and that their degree of musicianship might be quantifiable, is disregarded in this nominal measure— an approach that may or may not be justified according to the circumstances of the individual study. Some categorical distinctions seem more "natural" than others, such as that between male and female, and therefore more appropriate for nominal representation. However, even that might not always be appropriate: a study that assessed listeners' masculinity might need to allow for intermediate values between male and female and a way of expressing their relative magnitude.

Table 9.1 shows some imaginary data collected from 20 listeners. There are two variables, listener and training. The former is nominal, and has 20 categories, one for each listener. The latter is represented in three different ways in the table, in the first instance as two (nominal) categories. Note that although the listeners have been categorized using numerals, the magnitude of these numerals is meaningless since this variable is nominal. However, the data still lend themselves to certain kinds of quantitative analysis: for instance, measuring the number of musicians in the group, their *frequency*, and comparing this with the number (frequency) of nonmusicians. By measuring and comparing frequencies one can create quite sensitive and informative analyses: some simple examples are covered later in this chapter. Frequency data are often derived from questionnaires, where each question has a number of choices such as "yes," "no," and "not sure," or questions such as "are you male or female?," where only certain alternatives are available.

Ordinal data are differentiated from nominal data in that they include a notion of rank order. Instead of asking a group of subjects whether they are musically

Table 9.1. Imaginary data on the level of training of 20 listeners, presented in three different ways.

Listener	Training (Nominal— two categories)	Training (Ordinal— three levels)	Training (Continuous— number of years)
1	musician	professional	20
2	non-musician	untrained	2
3	musician	amateur	18
4	musician	amateur	12
5	non-musician	untrained	1
6	non-musician	untrained	3
7	musician	amateur	5
8	musician	professional	13
9	non-musician	untrained	0
10	musician	amateur	10
11	musician	amateur	12
12	non-musician	untrained	1
13	non-musician	untrained	2
14	musician	professional	40
15	musician	professional	28
16	musician	professional	25
17	musician	professional	30
18	musician	amateur	35
19	non-musician	untrained	5
20	musician	professional	32

trained or not, they might be asked to rate their expertise using three categories: "untrained," "amateur," and "professional," as shown in the second column in Table 9.1. An ordinal coding assumes that the levels of expertise among these three groups are not only different in kind, but can also be rank ordered. If it is assumed (though this assumption may be incorrect, see below) that untrained subjects have the lowest level of expertise, amateurs a moderate level, and professionals the highest, then it is straightforward enough to translate these categorical variables into the levels of an ordinal variable. Ordered from smallest to largest the three levels of this variable are "untrained," "amateur," and "professional": the variable now contains the notion of *order*, unlike a nominal variable where each level is merely qualitatively different from the others.

Nominal and ordinal data, and their associated statistical analyses, are rarely seen in empirical research applied to music. Instead, most studies collect and analyze *continuous* data. Rather than asking someone to categorize herself into one of a number of ordinally differentiated levels, or measuring gross differences in performance on some task, it is more commonplace to measure or categorize behavior along a continuum. Time, distance, and speed are common examples of continuous variables. In order to measure training or expertise along a continuous scale, subjects might be asked how long they have been playing an instrument (as in the third column of Table 9.1), or how many hours per week they spend practicing. The variable now captures not only order and magnitude, but also the relative distance between data points. A performer with eight years of professional experience has twice as much professional playing time as one with four years of experience; one with six years falls midway between the other two. Continuous variables allow for some subtle and sensitive statistical tests, which is why they are generally preferred. However, close perusal of Table 9.1 shows that continuous data can have disadvantages—it might be helpful to be able to distinguish between professional and amateur musicians who may have equivalent years of experience.

One final distinction can be made between variable types, which is vital when analyzing data. Statistical tests are generally divided into two categories: *parametric*, so called because they are designed to deal with data that come from a continuous parameter or distribution; and *nonparametric*, which make no such assumption. Parametric tests on the whole are more sensitive and give more detailed results. The simplest way of determining whether a parametric test is appropriate is to ask the following two questions: (1) are the data continuous, and (2) do the data resemble a normal distribution? The answer to question (1) is covered above, although some researchers differ on whether they regard nonstandard measurements (other than time, distance, velocity, mass, and so on) to be truly continuous. The answer to (2) is more complex and will be addressed below on p. 207.

Measurement and Observation

The most uncontroversial way of collecting data is by direct measurement of what a listener or performer does while listening or performing. Provided that that the tools for making measurements are accurate and correctly calibrated, such an approach helps avoid bias or observer-induced variability, and tends to produce data that can be analyzed using parametric statistical tests. This does not remove all doubt, however, since even the most accurately measured aspects of human performance may turn out not to bear upon the questions asked.

A clear example of such direct measurement, which I have already mentioned, is the long tradition of collecting and analyzing performance data from the mechanism of pianos. Seashore (1938) describes a large body of work from the early part of the last century, which has been continued and extended by researchers such as Shaffer (e.g., 1981) and Palmer (e.g., 1989). Such techniques normally allow researchers to collect timing and intensity data (see chapter 5, this volume).

It is also possible to collect indirect data about performance by observing or measuring listeners' responses. There are instances in which researchers observe and record their own responses, but it is generally preferable to use a qualified group of observers or listeners in order to avoid accusations of researcher bias. Repp (1997) used a listening panel's rank orderings of performances to derive a numerical index of preferences for different performances of the same piece. Similarly, Williamon (1999) used expert and novice ratings of different performances as a measure of listeners' preferences, and Clarke and Windsor (2000) asked listeners both to categorize performances by edition and to rate each performance for its aesthetic quality. Such listening panels can be thought of as a method of gaining either indirect data about performance, or direct data about listeners' responses.

The difficulty with *directly* observing or measuring listeners' activity in laboratory-style contexts is that there may be little or no overt behavior to capture. One way round this is to use physiological measures (e.g., Krumhansl 1997). In social situations, however, there may be many actions to observe and record: North and Hargreaves (1996), for example, recorded the number of times an advice desk was visited while different music was played, and even the country of origin of the wine that was purchased when music with different national associations was played in a supermarket (North, Hargreaves, and McKendrick 1999).

In summary, by observing and measuring the actions people make when engaged in music-making or listening, it is possible to obtain accurate, and often continuous, data that allow for considerable statistical power and flexibility when analyzed. Before turning to methods of manipulating, representing, and analyzing such data, the main alternative to direct observation and measurement will be addressed.

Testing

There are many situations in which direct measurement or observation of behavior is inappropriate. Although perceptual questions may be addressed by observing subjects' performance on a related task, it is often more appropriate to access their responses by asking them to provide a written, verbal, or diagrammatic response to some stimulus material; this is particularly the case where subjects' attitudinal, affective, or qualitative responses to a situation or question are at issue. Established psychometric tests, such as those designed by Wing (1981) or Seashore (1919) to assess musical aptitude or achievement, can have a useful function in providing information against which to judge performance in more specific tasks, whether or not one believes that such tests have a role to play in applied educational contexts. Similarly, more general tests of subjects' mental states may be useful: for instance the State-Trait Anxiety Inventory (STAI) assessment of anxiety can be used to shed light on subjects' performance in a particular situation (Abel and Larkin 1990).

One of the simplest kinds of test is that in which subjects listen to a series of sounds which differ in some way and choose from a limited range or number of responses. Windsor (1993), for example, asked subjects to classify rhythms into two categories, and in a second experiment to decide whether a given rhythm is the same as the preceding one; such data can then be represented in terms of the number of responses in each category for each rhythm, or the number of correct responses in the second task. More subtle perceptual judgments can be arranged to form a continuous scale. Grey (1977) asked subjects to rate the similarity of different instrumental timbres, while Krumhansl and Kessler (1982) played subjects a set of tones and then asked them to rate how well a further (or "probe") tone fitted within this context. Both of these examples restricted subjects' responses to a scale of integers (common scales are between 1 and 5, or 1 and 7), with the higher number reflecting the greatest similarity, or degree of fit. Although strictly speaking such designs generate ordinal rather than continuous data, it is common to regard the data as continuous, the assumption being that subjects use the entire scale and do so in a reasonably continuous fashion. It is, however, possible to obtain truly continuous data; Clarke and Krumhansl (1990), for example, asked subjects to indicate their response with a pencil mark on a continuous line that could then be measured. Such responses along a continuum can be used to create multidimensional analyses, where listeners are asked to make more than one judgment for each sound they hear: Juslin (1997), for example, used responses along a number of such continua to assess listeners' emotional responses to passages of music.

Moving away from such directly perceptual tasks, but staying in the area of multidimensional studies, Sloboda, Davidson, Howe, and Moore (1996) provide an example of collecting retrospective and longitudinal data: in their many studies of the role of practice in musical development, a battery of contrasted measures was used. This allowed for comparison of the many different factors that might have some effect on instrumental success. However, such studies require careful control; it is often easier to interpret data from a smaller number of measurements, and if decisions can be made to facilitate this, the analysis can be less complex and provide much clearer results.

Coding, Organizing, and Transforming Data

Having collected data, it is often necessary to convert them from one format into another, and to organize and store them in a practical manner. Although this can be a laborious task, there are some excellent software packages that can help with this. This section explores these preliminary, pre-analysis stages in data-handling.

Recoding

It may be necessary or convenient to notate observations in a different format from that required by a particular analysis. For example, subjects might be asked to indicate which of two possible performers they are hearing on a number of occasions. The data of interest, however, might be whether the listeners are correct or incorrect in their judgments. Hence, one listener's responses to 20 performances might be recoded as shown in Table 9.2. A correct response is represented by 1, an incorrect one by 0. Although this can be achieved by hand, it is also possible to recode data automatically, using a formula in a spreadsheet program.

Another instance in which considerable recoding might be needed is where qualitative data have been recorded, but are to be analyzed quantitatively. For example, a verbal transcript from an interview could be recoded such that certain themes, phrases, or words are assigned to categories. The frequency with which each category of utterance is used can then be calculated on the basis of these labels.

A more complex problem is the recoding of data acquired by some form of instrumentation. For example, MIDI data may need to be recoded to give real times in milliseconds, rather than the sequencer values of bars, beats, and ticks: although

Table 9.2.   Imaginary data for a listener's attempts to identify the performer (1 or 2) in 20 performances.

Performance	Response	Actual Performer	Correct?
1	1	1	1
2	1	1	1
3	2	2	1
4	1	1	1
5	2	1	0
6	2	2	1
7	1	2	0
8	1	2	0
9	2	1	0
10	1	1	1
11	2	2	1
12	1	1	1
13	1	2	0
14	2	2	1
15	1	1	1
16	1	1	1
17	2	1	0
18	1	2	0
19	2	2	1
20	1	2	0

some commercial sequencer packages allow this, many do not, or do not allow easy archiving of such data. Fortunately there are some helpful tools for such purposes.

Some Helpful Tools

Since almost all statistical analyses are now carried out by computer it is helpful to store data in machine readable form at the earliest possible stage. Many researchers now have subjects input their responses directly to a computer, ensuring that no errors in transcription can occur and that the data are ready for analysis as soon as collected. This is sometimes possible even without programming expertise. The software package MEDS, for example, allows the construction of complex experiments, the presentation of audio, visual, and MIDI stimuli, and the accurate recording of subject responses.[1] Issues of compatibility are paramount here. It wastes enormous amounts of time if data need to be converted from format to format, or between computers of different kinds. It is sensible to find a combination of data collection, organizational, and analysis tools that all run on the same computer system and can read and write the same types of file. There will inevitably be circumstances when some reorganization or conversion of data may be required, but this should be kept to a minimum, both to decrease the risk of accidental loss of data and to ensure that errors are not introduced by inaccurate conversion.

For example, consider the chain of data-conversion involved in the analysis of moment-to-moment timing in piano performance. The pianist, seated at a MIDI piano such as a Yamaha Disklavier, performs an excerpt from a Chopin nocturne three times. The piano is connected to a laptop computer via MIDI cables and a MIDI interface, and MIDI data are transmitted from the mechanism of the piano to a laptop. At this point there is a choice. It would be possible to use commercial software consisting of a sequencer package, a spreadsheet, and a statistics package, but the alternative is to use a specialist application which transforms the MIDI data into a format which is directly readable by a statistics package.

The advantage of using commercial software is that flexibility is ensured at all stages of the process; the sequencer package is designed for easy recording and playback, and probably has useful features for displaying the recorded MIDI data to check for errors in performance. The sequencer files may be saved in standard MIDI format, or (depending on the package) in the form of a text table of timings and other MIDI information, which can then be imported into a spreadsheet or statistics package and manipulated to obtain the information required. However, such a solution becomes extremely unwieldy where there are large amounts of data, or where data need to be explored in anything other than the simplest fashion. The researcher might want to know the duration of each bar, rather than the durations between successive notes, or the interonset intervals between notes in the left hand only, or the durations between successive events in each chord, and might want to do this repeatedly for a number of different performances of the same piece. In such circumstances some automation of data-handling and a degree of "intelligence" may be desirable, or even essential. Many researchers have written their own software to meet such needs, some of which is available as commercial software, shareware, or freeware. POCO, a software environment designed by Desain and Honing (Honing

1990, see also p. 81 above), allows complex analyses involving the conversion of MIDI data from format to format and the extraction of different aspects of a dataset using prewritten routines. Like all specialist software tools, POCO has a steep learning curve, but it can repay the effort by reducing the chances of human error, and by enabling quite complex re-organizations and analyses of data to be carried out extremely quickly.

There are also instances where data need to be transformed in more substantial ways, for example to remove "drift" (such as steadily decreasing tempo in a performance) or "noise" (random variability). Many software packages allow such de-trending or smoothing of data, but it is always wise to consider whether the noise or drift can be removed without distorting the results.

Whenever quantitative analysis is required, a method of transforming test results, measurements, or observations into machine-readable form, and software to aid in organizing such data, can be a real boon. Whether a spreadsheet or some more sophisticated solution is chosen will depend upon the amount of data, the extent of transformation required, and whether the data need to be passed on to additional software for statistical analysis.

Descriptive Statistics

In this section some relatively simple ways of describing different kinds of data will be introduced: first, frequency representations and the notion of the normal distribution; second, ways of expressing the central tendency of sets of data and their dispersion. Rather than provide a detailed guide to these methods, which can be found in introductory texts on statistics (e.g., Robson 1983; Miller 1984), I will show how they can be applied to musical situations in an informative way.

Frequencies and Distributions

Assuming that the data in question are continuous, the first question to ask is whether they can be examined using parametric tests. As previously mentioned (p. 202), this depends on whether the data are normally distributed. The simplest way of determining this is to start by counting the number of occurrences—the frequency—of each measurement. For example, imagine that eighty musicians were asked to play the same piece of music and, using a stopwatch, the duration of each performance was measured. Hypothetical durations are shown in Table 9.3.

Since every performance in Table 9.3 has a unique duration, each one has the same frequency of occurrence (1), and no sense of their distribution can be obtained. In order to see a distribution, the data need to be reorganized into categories, showing the number of performances that fall within each of a series of equal sized durational 'bands'. Figure 9.1 shows the data as a histogram, with the number of performances within each 2.5 second band of durations (from 100 to 140 seconds) indicated by each bar. If the data are normally distributed, the most common duration category (that with the highest frequency) will be midway between the lowest and highest categories, and the frequencies of the other categories will taper off toward the extremes in a manner similar to that shown by the curve in Figure 9.1. The

Table 9.3. Imaginary data (in seconds) for the durations of 80 performances of the same piece of music

Perf No.	Duration (s)	Perf No.	Duration (s)	Perf No.	Duration (s)	Perf No.	Duration (s)
1	121.90	21	125.80	41	121.91	61	127.00
2	121.48	22	120.95	42	121.06	62	121.14
3	131.12	23	128.56	43	131.46	63	129.25
4	119.70	24	119.41	44	120.92	64	119.53
5	120.20	25	125.60	45	120.38	65	125.14
6	121.30	26	127.70	46	120.81	66	127.24
7	114.75	27	116.66	47	115.71	67	114.86
8	117.88	28	119.14	48	118.37	68	119.28
9	119.06	29	118.26	49	119.03	69	118.67
10	121.57	30	122.03	50	122.82	70	121.91
11	124.17	31	126.95	51	125.36	71	127.45
12	121.49	32	124.21	52	121.88	72	124.93
13	117.79	33	116.25	53	116.52	73	115.39
14	123.14	34	123.07	54	123.16	74	123.79
15	118.87	35	119.74	55	118.67	75	119.72
16	111.05	36	111.59	56	112.27	76	108.82
17	113.80	37	113.98	57	114.13	77	113.99
18	116.31	38	117.55	58	115.18	78	116.63
19	119.83	39	121.74	59	120.25	79	121.52
20	124.30	40	121.46	60	125.45	80	121.68

data resemble the curve quite closely, with the majority of the performances being around 120 seconds long; they are slightly "skewed" to the right, in that there are more performances that are longer than 120 seconds than shorter, but the imbalance is only marginal. Compare this with Figure 9.2, which shows some data that do not resemble a normal distribution: here the data are more evenly spread across their range, and there are very few performances between 125 and 130 seconds (where a peak would be expected in a normal distribution). These data would not be suitable for parametric analyses.

Central Tendencies

There are three accepted ways of expressing the central tendency of a set of data as a single number. The first is by finding the most frequent value, known as the *mode*. The second is by arranging the data in ascending order (also known as rank order) and seeing which value lies in the middle of this sequence: this is known as the *median*. The third involves calculating an arithmetic average (i.e., adding the values together and dividing by the number of values): this is known as the *mean*.

Calculating the mode requires at least two identical values in the data, and this

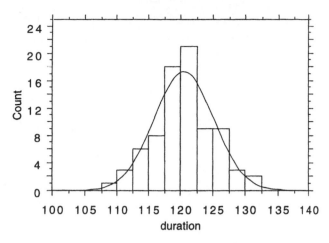

Figure 9.1.   A histogram of the data from Table 9.3 with the corresponding normal distribution (continuous line) super-imposed.

is one of its limitations as a descriptive statistic, especially if there are small amounts of data (a small "sample size"). Even with 80 samples, the data in Table 9.3 have no modal value, since no performances were of the same duration. The median (middle value) falls between 120.81 (the 40th value) and 120.92 (the 41st). In cases like this, where there is an even number of data points and thus no true middle value, the me-dian is taken as that value that lies midway between the two central data points (120.87 in this case). The most commonly used type of average, however, is the arithmetic mean, which in this case is 120.545 (see Robson 1983, on calculating both median and mean values). This captures the "central tendency" of the data

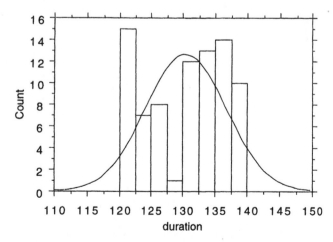

Figure 9.2.   A histogram of data that are not normally distributed, with the normal distribution superimposed.

quite well, since most of the performances were close to this duration. In other words, the mean is a useful way to describe the overall or general response to the task.

Dispersion

As well as having a central tendency, a set of continuous data will also have some spread of values, a certain *dispersion*. A very rudimentary way of expressing this would be simply to state the difference between the lowest and highest value — the *range*. In the example above, the lowest value was 108.82, the highest 131.46, giving a range of 22.64: the fastest performer played the piece 22.64 seconds faster than the slowest. This might seem worrying: if two performers can differ by this amount, how can one draw any general conclusions about the performances? The answer is not only to measure the dispersion of the data but also to compare it to the mean, and the most common way of doing this is to calculate the *standard deviation*. Each measurement will differ from the mean by a certain amount, and the standard deviation expresses the average of these differences, in units that are comparable to the individual data (see Robson 1983: 54–60); the calculation can be done automatically using a scientific calculator or spreadsheet (as can that for the mean). The standard deviation of the durations in Table 9.3 is 4.592 seconds, showing that despite the large range, most of the performances are not that different in duration: 4.6 seconds is only around 4% of the mean duration.

Useful Graphs

Musical data often consists of successive measurements of some variable over time, and in such a case the clearest way to display it is in the form of a line graph or bar chart. The upper panel of Figure 9.3 shows the durations of successive bars in a performance of a 27-bar excerpt from Chopin's Nocturne Opus 27 no. 1, and was produced using a statistical package (most spreadsheet packages will also generate simple graphs and charts); the horizontal axis represents the succession of bars, the vertical axis the duration of each bar in seconds. This type of line graph is a common way of representing changes in local timing over the course of a piece. However, it is open to misinterpretation. For instance, it is wrong to assume that the lines connecting each point represent continuous changes in tempo; the lower panel of Figure 9.3 shows the duration in seconds of each triplet quaver for the same stretch of music, illustrating that below the level of the bar the individual notes do not fall along neat lines or curves.

Another useful graph for plotting multiple sets of data is the scattergram. Figure 9.4 shows the durations of Figure 9.3 plotted alongside equivalent data for a second performance of the same piece. It can be seen from the line graph that the profiles of the two performances are similar, and the scattergram in the lower panel represents this more directly by plotting the durations of each bar in the first performance against the equivalent duration in the second. (Note, for instance, how the isolated value at the top right of the scattergram corresponds to the long duration of bar 26 in both performances.) If the performances were identical, the points would lie exactly along a diagonal line from the bottom left to top right; by contrast, if there were

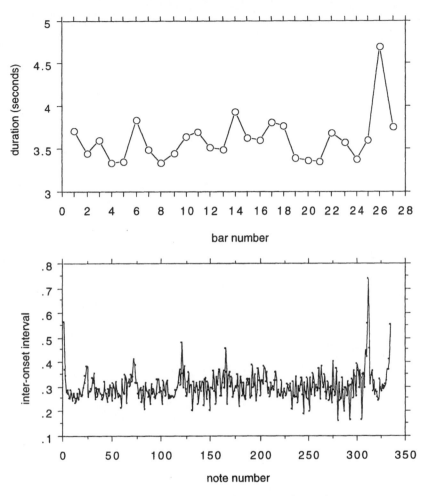

Figure 9.3.   Data from a performance of a 27-bar excerpt from Chopin's *Nocturne*, Opus 27 no. 1. The *upper panel* shows the durations of successive bars, while the the *lower panel* shows the duration in seconds of each triplet quaver for the same stretch of music.

no relationship between the performances, no overall pattern would be discernible. In the present case, the similar profiles of the two performances in the line graph result in a distribution quite close to the diagonal line. This demonstrates a close relationship between the two data sets, in other words a *correlation* between them.

Bar charts representing the means of different groups of data may also be useful, but are to be avoided where they suggest differences that are not statistically significant (see below: some form of statistical comparison of means is necessary to estimate such significance). Figure 9.5 shows the mean bar durations of the two performances discussed above, the height of the caps (which resemble Ts) on top of the bars showing the standard deviations of the two means. This chart immediately

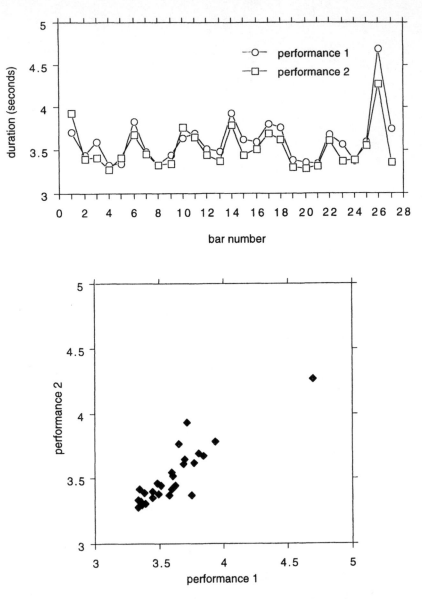

Figure 9.4.   Data from two performances of a 27-bar excerpt from Chopin's Nocturne, Op. 27, no. 1. The *upper panel* shows raw data for the durations of successive bars. The *lower panel* is a scattergram which plots the duration of each bar in the first performance against the equivalent duration in the second. The isolated value at the top right of the scattergram corresponds to the long duration of bar 26 in both performances.

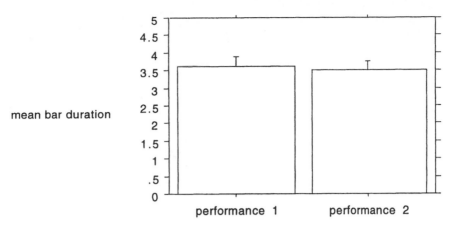

Figure 9.5.   Mean bar durations for the two performances shown in Figure 9.4. The height of the caps (which resemble Ts) on top of the bars show the standard deviations of the two means.

demonstrates the small absolute difference between the means, and between the standard deviations, just as the line graph and scattergram show the similarities at the level of individual measurements. Putting all this together, we can say on the basis of figures 9.4 and 9.5 that the two performances have not only a similar pattern of relative timing from bar to bar, but also a similar overall tempo (mean bar durations), and similar variability between individual bars (standard deviations).

Comparative Statistics

Although describing a single set of data may be useful and interesting, most empirical research proceeds by comparing two or more sets of data. A classical experiment tends to compare the same variable under different conditions, for example, by measuring the durations of performances under examination and rehearsal conditions. It may also be necessary to compare different variables: correlating supposedly related factors determines whether there is some predictable relationship between them, and how strong it is. For example, a correlation of the duration of performances with factors such as age, a measure of experience, average heart rate, or anxiety levels might uncover systematic relationships between these variables. In this section a number of different ways of carrying out such statistical comparisons will be demonstrated. The calculations will not be shown in detail, but reference will be made to standard statistical texts and software.

Comparison of Means: The *t*-Test

In addition to the 80 pianists performing a short piece in rehearsal measured above, imagine that the durations of 80 more performances under examination conditions were measured. The mean duration of the performances in the rehearsal condition was 120.545 seconds; the mean duration for the exam condition turns out to be 131.496 seconds. In other words, the exam performances are, on average, about 11 (10.951) seconds slower than the rehearsals. This seems like a large difference, but the absolute difference between the means is not a reliable indicator of a *significant* difference between the two groups. The criterion that many statistical tests use to determine this is based on the probability that such a difference is due to chance. This would clearly be the case if the exam performances were measured again on a different occasion and their mean duration this time was actually smaller than that of the rehearsal performances. Statistical tests allow one to calculate the likelihood that the differences are actually related to differences between the two conditions, and are not due to random variation.

The *t*-test is a relatively simple parametric test that can be used to determine this. Although it can be carried out using a calculator, or pen and paper, most statistical software packages calculate *t*-tests quickly and easily; however it is worthwhile calculating *t*-tests by hand to grasp how they work before using a statistical package (Robson 1983: 76–89 gives an excellent guide). In brief, the *t* statistic is essentially an arbitrary index of the size of an effect, and is based on a comparison of all the individual data in each of the two conditions being compared (in this case the 80 durations in rehearsal, and the 80 durations in examination): the larger the effect, the larger the value of *t*. In the present case, the calculation results in a value of $t = 14.924$ (larger values are more likely to be significant), and the probability of the difference in means being due to chance is less than 1 in 1000 ($p < .001$). Normally, experimental results are considered significant if this probability value is less than or equal to 5 in 100 ($p \leq 0.05$), so the result here is extremely reliable.

As a comparison, a *t*-test between the two sets of bar durations whose means are shown in Figure 9.5 gives a smaller but still significant value of t (3.395; $p = 0.0022$). Hence, the timing of the two performances was reliably different, but only by a tiny amount (85 milliseconds).

Correlation

I introduced the concept of correlation when discussing the use of graphs, particularly the scattergram. The relationship between two variables (or the same variable measured on different occasions) can be evaluated in a number of different ways. The most common parametric method is the product-moment correlation, or *Pearson's r*. A number of nonparametric alternatives are also available, and Robson (1983) discusses both these and parametric correlations in some detail.

The two panels of Figure 9.4 show a strong correlation between the bar by bar timings of the two performances. However, it is necessary to check whether any correlation is strong enough to be statistically significant—that is, not due to chance. A correlation coefficient indicates the magnitude of the relationship between two variables and its direction: a value of 1 represents a perfect correlation, a value of −1 is a perfect *negative* correlation, and 0 implies a completely random relationship between the two variables. In the case of Figure 9.4 the correlation is 0.884, confirming the strong positive relationship. However, there may be more complex circumstances where both positive and negative correlations are involved. For example, Figure 9.6

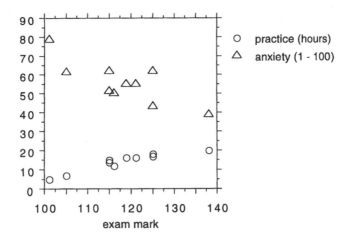

Figure 9.6.   Imaginary scores (out of 150) for 10 violin students taking a performance exam, plotted against the amount of practice (in hours).

shows imaginary scores (out of 150) for 10 violin students taking a performance exam, plotted against the amount of practice (in hours) in the preceding 2 weeks, and their level of anxiety (on a self-assessed scale between 0 and 100) just prior to the exam.

There seems to be a negative relationship between anxiety and performance in the exam; low values of anxiety correlate with high exam scores. Also, it is easy to see that there is a positive correlation between practice and performance: high exam marks correlate with more hours spent practicing. In each case we can quantify the correlation, and the chances of it being a random effect: in the case of anxiety, $r = -0.789$ ($p = 0.0046$), whereas in the case of practice $r = 0.94$ ($p < 0.0001$). Both anxiety and practice, in other words, are strong predictors of examination performance. But it is impossible to determine from this analysis which of the two variables is influencing performance directly. The most obvious interpretation is that practice enhances performance, and so decreases anxiety. However, it might be that practice has no direct effect on performance: instead it decreases anxiety, which in turn enhances performance. It could even be that better musicians are simply less anxious but practice more. In other words, performance increases at the same time and rate as practice, and decreases with anxiety, but it is not clear what the relationship is between these three variables. The issue may seem merely academic, but consider the following: if one claims that better performance is directly related to practice and anxiety, it would follow that both encouraging students who performed worse to practice more, and treating their anxiety, should improve their performance. On the other hand, if it is actually the case that better musicians perform well for other reasons, and that their success leads them to practice more and to have lower anxiety levels, then no amount of treatment or increased practice will improve the scores of the poorer performers. There are methods for making such causal connections clearer, especially where there are more than two variables, some of which will be introduced below.

More Complex Techniques

Most experimental work uses statistical tests which are rather more complex than correlations and t-tests. It is impossible to deal with them in detail here, but it is worth mentioning the problems they can be used to solve, and the situations to which they have been applied in musical research. We have just seen that correlations are not necessarily a good way of discovering causal relationships. A set of related techniques, including *regression* and *partial correlation*, can be used effectively in situations where causality or multiple variables are to be analyzed. Applied to the example above, it would be possible not only to investigate whether practice has a causal relationship with performance, but also to show how strong this relationship is when the effects of anxiety have been taken into account.

Linear regression analysis tests whether two variables are related in a linear fashion; more exactly, it attempts to fit the data points to a line which has a certain slope. When plotted on a scattergram (see Figure 9.4, above) a close correlation appears as a diagonal relationship between the two variables, and regression is a means of quantifying the fit between line and data. Figure 9.7 shows the examination data in the same format; the regression is expressed as the square of a simple correlation (R^2). In this case the fit is very close: $R^2 = 0.884$. It should be noted that regressions, unlike simple correlations, are always positive, so care has to be taken to check the direction of the relationship.

It is possible to test whether the fit of the data to this line is significantly better than its fit to a horizontal line drawn at the mean of the predicted variable (in this case the performance score) on the vertical axis. This will indicate whether the data points are better fitted to the sloped regression line, as against the unsloped mean. In this case they are, and at a high level of significance ($p < 0.0001$).

It is also possible to fit more than one predictor variable (practice and anxiety) to the predicted variable (performance), to see what their combined and individual predictive power is. This is done by *stepwise regression*: variables are added one at a time to see whether they improve the fit, and by how much. It is even possible to use *multiple regression* to fit the variables at the same time—though such complex techniques are not required in the present case. It is, however, always sensible to compute *partial correlations* between the variables, in order to see whether each one is significant when the influence of the other variables has been taken into account. The partial correlation between practice and performance, subtracting the influence of anxiety, is still significant at well below the 0.05 criterion ($r = 0.876$, $p < 0.01$), but when the influence of practice is taken into account, anxiety is no longer significantly correlated with either performance ($r = -0.497$), or practice ($r = 0.136$); neither of these partial correlations is below the 0.05 probability level. In other words, the data do not support the notion that anxiety, in itself, had any significant effect on performance in the exam, nor that practice reduced anxiety.

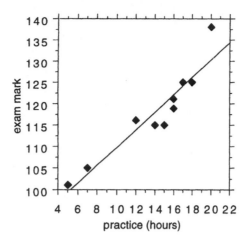

Figure 9.7. The correlation between hours of practice and anxiety level (taken from the data shown in Figure 9.6), showing the corresponding regression line.

The only supportable claim is that the amount of practice is related to an increase in the exam mark.

Just as regression analysis extends the notion of correlation, so the pairwise comparison of means afforded by the *t*-test can be extended using *analysis of variance* (ANOVA). Whereas a *t*-test can only measure the relationship between one pair of variables at a time, ANOVA can be used to show differences where there are more variables and more than one level within each variable. For example, to extend the *t*-test example above, consider a situation in which student performers were playing under three different conditions: one week before an exam, one day before, and during the exam itself. Each performance is timed as before. Now a second variable is added: the performers are split into two equal groups of girls and boys and we have two variables—gender and time of performance. An ANOVA could be used to determine whether there were any significant changes in the duration of the piece as the exam approached, and whether these changes were the same for both girls and boys.

Even more complex analyses are available where there are many possible relationships between variables. For example, *factor analysis* allows the researcher to see which of a large number of continuous variables are most closely related, and to categorize these relationships according to their salience. Repp (1992), for example, used factor analysis to analyze the commonalities in timing between different performances of the same piece of music. One result of factor analysis can be the extraction of a number of principal components from a large dataset. In Repp's analysis, three principal components were extracted, which could be seen as representing three clearly distinguishable ways in which the pianists timed their performances. This achieves a large reduction of complexity, with many potential dimensions becoming just a few.

A related technique is *multidimensional scaling* which has been used to represent correlations, or judgments of similarity, between many variables as distances within a two- or three-dimensional space. Grey (1977) has used such techniques to represent the perceptual distances between instrumental timbres along a number of dimensions, while Kendall and Carterette (1991) have shown how such spaces can be used to make subtle predictions about instrumental "blend," and Krumhansl and Kessler (1982) have used them to represent distance between keys.

Most of these more complex techniques are carried out with the help of computer software, but some understanding of how they are calculated is essential to making sense of their results. There are many guides to particular analyses, such as Sage Books' guides to ANOVA (Iversen and Norpoth 1976) and linear regression (Dunterman 1984); these are excellent starting points for the more mathematically minded. It is also helpful to use the sample data and tutorials that come with most statistical packages: there is no substitute for seeing how the techniques work on actual data.

Analyzing Frequency Data

Thus far the examples have all used continuous data. Where frequency data are involved, *cross-tabulation* (crosstabs) and the *chi-square* statistic are essential tools. Imagine a situation in which the question is whether students are satisfied with different aspects of a keyboard harmony course. Each student is asked two questions: (1) was the practical teaching satisfactory? and (2) was the theoretical teaching successful? Their responses can be displayed in a two-by-two table as shown in Table 9.4.

The 10 students answered a total of 20 questions, and if they were responding randomly, or were undecided as a group, we would expect on average to see ten "yes" responses and ten "no" responses. However, we can see from the table that a clear majority were satisfied with the practical teaching, but not with the theoretical teaching. The chi-square statistic tests whether the distribution of the frequencies across the four cells is nonrandom. In other words it tests to see whether there is a significant difference between the observed frequencies and an assumed even distribution, which in the case of Table 9.4 would mean five responses in each cell of the matrix. In this case chi-square = 5.3, which is statistically significant below the 0.05 level ($p = .0213$), so we can say that the students were responding differently to the two questions. Such cross-tabulation can also work where there are more than two response categories (such as "yes," "no," and "maybe," or "agree," "disagree," and "not sure") and conditions (a number of different question types), although the results can become more difficult to interpret as the matrix gets larger.

Table 9.4.   Imaginary data for 10 students' assessments of whether the practical and theoretical components of keyboard harmony tuition were satisfactory.

count	no	yes	row total
practical	3	7	10
theoretical	8	2	10
column total	11	9	20

Experiments and the "Real World"

At the outset of this chapter, I made some preliminary comments regarding the relationship between strict experimentation and empirical approaches of a more flexible and exploratory nature. In conclusion I address this relationship in more detail.

In the natural sciences, and in experimental psychology, the most common method of proceeding is to carry out experiments that test hypotheses. Imagine studying the factors that influence musicians' success in a dictation task. Perhaps there is a suspicion that musicians who play a keyboard instrument as their principal study are better at dictation than those who specialize on another instrument. This then, is a clear hypothesis: keyboard players will be better at dictation than other instrumentalists. More technically, the experiment is designed around the *null hypothesis* that there is no correlation between keyboard playing and being good at dictation. The experiment can disprove the null hypothesis by showing that there is such a correlation, but it can never prove the null hypothesis; if no correlation is found, that might just be because the experiment was badly designed or executed, perhaps because there was some complicating factor that was not allowed for. One simple way of setting up an experiment to study this would be to select a number of musicians and divide them into two groups, one containing first-study keyboard players, the other all the remaining musicians. This division into groups produces an *independent* variable. A *dependent* variable is also required: for example, a score on a standard dictation task. The hypothesis would be tested by comparing the mean scores of the two groups using a *t*-test.

Simple as the experimental design is, and familiar as the task is, this example illustrates some of the difficulties in doing controlled research in music. Dividing the subjects into two groups assumes that any differences in their performance must be explained by whether or not they are keyboard players. But there are all sorts of ways in which this assumption might be confounded. It might be the case, for instance, that the keyboard players are of a higher overall standard than the other musicians, because these others have been drawn from a music school that needs to maintain its orchestras and therefore applies less exacting entry standards for orchestral musicians; if this were the case, then grouping the students into keyboard and non-keyboard players would not be independent of their level of skill, so that the experiment might end up finding out about differing overall skill or aptitude levels rather than differences based on keyboard skills alone. Then again, there will be differences between the different subjects, some of which may affect their performance on the task: a particular subject may be more easily distracted, or may have received more training in dictation than another. These *subject* variables cannot be removed entirely, though their effect can be reduced (it may be possible to establish, for example, that neither group is better trained overall). Finally, it is important to ensure that *situational* variables do not distort the results. Imagine that while one group was being tested a noisy plane flew overhead, impairing the performance of that group as against the other. If the group in question was the keyboard one, such a situational variable might obscure their better performance.

What this means is that not all aspects of musical behavior are best investigated through such highly constrained methods. There are many virtues to collecting and analyzing data that are relatively uncontrolled by the researcher; doing an experiment may artificially constrain the very behavior at issue. While something like dictation is a task that can easily be transformed into an experimental design, not all things one might wish to study are structured in this way. Consider, for example, trying to study emotional responses to music by asking subjects to decide whether a particular piece was "happy" or "sad." Leaving aside the fact that more choices might be helpful, such a task is extremely different from how we normally experience and respond to the emotional character of music. This is not to say that emotion cannot be studied experimentally, but it serves to illustrate the fact that an experiment may be so different from our normal way of listening to, or playing, music that the data may have little useful to say about real musical experiences. Experimental control reduces the ecological validity of the research: the real world is highly variable and complex, and any control you exert runs the risk of reducing this complexity to such an extent that the behavior you observe has little connection with that world.

Another reason to question whether experimental data are always the most useful is the problem of underlying, unmeasured variables. Returning to our experimental example above, it is possible that there is a relationship between keyboard skill and a musical skill that was not measured in the experiment. Keyboard players might start playing earlier than other musicians, so that the real reason that they perform better is that they have simply been playing for longer. To discover whether this is true requires the collection of data from the real world, through a questionnaire, for example.

The official name for a study that simply measures and compares existing variables is a correlation (which can be tested using a test of association such as Pearson's r), and it allows one to make claims about whether two variables are related. As we saw above, correlating two or more types of observation is a powerful way of determining whether one has some predictable relationship with the other. Robson's (1993) excellent textbook on so-called "real-world" research shows how techniques more commonly used in the laboratory can be applied to more realistic situations.

Such non-experimental data has limitations: it is difficult, for example, to tell whether there is any causal relationship between two variables collected in this way. An experiment can show whether something the experimenter does (like giving different instructions to two groups) causes a change in their behavior; she or he controls the cause, and can be reasonably clear that it precedes its effect. In the end it comes down to a matter of combining less formal and more experimental approaches. A common way of doing this is to start by collecting some real-world data in a relatively informal manner, thus identifying related variables before attempting to show clear causation with a more controlled study. Alternatively, a process of *triangulation*, in which data and methods of different kinds are simultaneously brought to bear on the same set of questions, can be effective.

Concluding Remarks

Whether the aim is to study performance, perception, memory or the distribution of particular events in scores or recordings, a repertoire of methodological skills allows the researcher to tackle projects in both a flexible and a systematic manner. The use of established procedures and tests is an integral part of this approach, not only because it ensures that data are not misinterpreted, but also because it means that results will be accessible to, and understood by, a wide body of potential readers. However, one should not be hidebound by a small number of techniques; although methods should correctly fit the type of data and the questions asked, it would be a shame if research were held back for want of an appropriate ready-made method. Although this chapter has done no more than introduce some of the most common techniques, I hope to have shown that data analysis is worth knowing about, and that such knowledge can be directly applied to the search for answers to musical questions.

Note

1. Information about the MEDS software, and a downloadable version of the program, can be found at http://www.ethnomusic.ucla.edu/systematic/Faculty/Kendall/meds.htm.

References

Abel, J. L., and Larkin, K. T. (1990). "Anticipation of performance among musicians: Physiological arousal, confidence, and state-anxiety." *Psychology of Music* 18: 171–182.

Besson, M., and Faïta, F. (1995). "An event-related potential (ERP) study of musical expectancy: Comparison of musicians with nonmusicians." *Journal of Experimental Psychology: Human Perception and Performance* 21: 1278–1296.

Clarke, E. F. (1993). "Imitating and evaluating real and transformed musical performances." *Music Perception* 10: 317–341.

Clarke, E. F., and Krumhansl, C. L. (1990). "Perceiving musical time." *Music Perception* 7: 213–252.

Clarke, E. F., and Windsor, W. L. (2000). "Real and simulated expression: A listening study." *Music Perception* 17: 1–37.

Davidson, J. W. (1993). "Visual perception of performance manner in the movements of solo musicians." *Psychology of Music* 21: 103–113.

Dunterman, G. H. (1984). *Introduction to linear models.* Beverly Hills, Calif.: Sage.

Grey, J. M. (1977) "Multidimensional perceptual scaling of musical timbres." *Journal of the Acoustical Society of America* 61: 1270–1277.

Honing, H. (1990). "POCO: An environment for analysing, modifying, and generating expression in music." *Proceedings of the 1990 International Computer Music Conference.* San Francisco: Computer Music Association, 364–368.

Iversen, G. R., and Norpoth, H. (1976). *Analysis of Variance.* Beverly Hills, Calif.: Sage.

Juslin, P. N. (1997). "Emotional communication in music performance: A functionalist perspective and some data." *Music Perception* 14: 383–418.

Kendall, R. A., and Carterette, E. C. (1991). "Perceptual scaling of simultaneous wind instrument timbres." *Music Perception* 8: 369–404.

Krumhansl, C. L. (1997) "An exploratory study of musical emotions and psychophysiology." *Canadian Journal of Experimental Psychology* 51: 336–353.

Krumhansl, C. L., and Kessler, E. J. (1982). "Tracing the dynamic changes in perceived tonal organization in a spatial representation of musical keys." *Psychological Review* 89: 334–368.

Miller, S. (1984). *Experimental Design and Statistics*. London: Methuen.

North, A. C., and Hargreaves, D. J. (1996). "The effects of music on responses to a dining area." *Journal of Environmental Psychology* 16: 55–64.

North, A. C., Hargreaves, D. J., and McKendrick, J. (1999). "The influence of in-store music on wine selections." *Journal of Applied Psychology* 84: 271–276.

Oppenheim, A. N. (1966). *Questionnaire Design and Attitude Measurement*. London: Heinemann.

Palmer, C. (1989). "Mapping musical thought to musical performance." *Journal of Experimental Psychology: Human Perception and Performance* 15: 331–346.

Repp, B. H. (1992). "Diversity and commonality in music performance: An analysis of timing microstructure in Schumann's *Träumerei*." *Journal of the Acoustical Society of America* 92: 2546–2568.

Repp, B. H. (1997). "The aesthetic quality of a quantitatively average music performance: Two preliminary experiments." *Music Perception* 14: 419–444.

Repp, B. H. (1999). "Detecting deviations from metronomic timing in music: Effects of perceptual structure on the mental timekeeper." *Perception and Psychophysics* 61: 529–548.

Robson, C. (1983). *Experiment, Design and Statistics in Psychology*. Harmondsworth: Penguin.

Robson, C. (1993). *Real World Research*. Oxford: Blackwell.

Seashore, C. E. (1919) *Seashore Measures of Musical Talent*. New York: Columbia Phonograph Co.

Seashore, C. [1967 (1938)]. *Psychology of Music*. McGraw-Hill. (Republished by Dover Books, New York, 1967.).

Shaffer, L. H. (1981). "Performances of Chopin, Bach and Bartók: Studies in motor programming." *Cognitive Psychology* 13: 326–376.

Sloboda, J. A., Davidson, J. W., Howe, M. J. A. and Moore, D. G. (1996). "The role of practice in the development of expert musical performance." *British Journal of Psychology* 87: 287–309.

Williamon, A. (1999). "The value of performing from memory." *Psychology of Music* 27: 84–95.

Windsor, W. L. (1993). "Dynamic accents and the categorical perception of metre." *Psychology of Music* 21: 127–140.

Wing, H.D. (1918). *Standardised Tests of Musical Intelligence*. Windsor: NFER-Nelson.